Video Shooter
Mastering Storytelling Techniques

Barry Braverman

Focal Press
Taylor & Francis Group

NEW YORK AND LONDON

First published 2014 by Focal Press
70 Blanchard Road, Suite 402, Burlington, MA 01803

Simultaneously published in the UK by Focal Press
2 Park Square, Milton Park, Abingdon, Oxon OX14 4RN

Focal Press is an imprint of the Taylor & Francis Group, an informa business

Notices
Knowledge and best practice in this field are constantly changing. As new research and experience broaden our understanding, changes in research methods, professional practices, or medical treatment may become necessary.

Practitioners and researchers must always rely on their own experience and knowledge in evaluating and using any information, methods, compounds, or experiments described herein. In using such information or methods they should be mindful of their own safety and the safety of others, including parties for whom they have a professional responsibility.

Product or corporate names may be trademarks or registered trademarks, and are used only for identification and explanation without intent to infringe.

Library of Congress Cataloging in Publication Data
Braverman, Barry.
  Video shooter: mastering storytelling techniques / Barry Braverman. — [Third edition]
    pages cm
  1. Video recordings—Production and direction. 2. Digital cinematography. I. Title.
    PN1992.94.B75 2013
    384.55'8—dc23
    2013006522

ISBN: 978-0-240-82517-5 (pbk)
ISBN: 978-0-240-82522-9 (ebk)

Typeset in Times
By Apex CoVantage, LLC

Printed in the United States of America by Courier, Kendallville, Indiana

Bound to Create

You are a creator.

Whatever your form of expression — photography, filmmaking, animation, games, audio, media communication, web design, or theatre — you simply want to create without limitation. Bound by nothing except your own creativity and determination.

Focal Press can help.

For over 75 years Focal has published books that support your creative goals. Our founder, Andor Kraszna-Krausz, established Focal in 1938 so you could have access to leading-edge expert knowledge, techniques, and tools that allow you to create without constraint. We strive to create exceptional, engaging, and practical content that helps you master your passion.

Focal Press and you.

Bound to create.

We'd love to hear how we've helped you create. Share your experience:
www.focalpress.com/boundtocreate

Focal Press
Taylor & Francis Group

To my father, who taught me to see the beauty in technical things

Contents

Getting a Leg Up 274

Place Anywhere 278

You Shoot; Therefore, You Are 278

CHAPTER 12 Listening to Your Story **281**

An Unsound Proposition?...282

Sound Advice 282

Bad Connections = Bad Sound 283

Keep Balance in Your Life 284

Mixing It Up 285

Setting Audio Level 286

For the Love of Mic 287

Riding (Short) Shotgun..287

Going Wireless 288

Going Boom 289

Noise Reduction for the Video Shooter.....................................290

Shooting Double System: Is It Necessary? 291

You are Surrounded 292

To Improvise Is Good 293

CHAPTER 13 Going with the Flow **295**

Not One Workflow...296

The Promise of MXF...297

The Beauty of Metadata 298

We Should Be Less Fearful Now...299

The Advent of SSD 300

Proxy Video and the iPhone 301

Outputting Your Story 302

The Decline of DVD..303

Eye on the Encoded Image 304

Encoders Have Personalities 305

Scenes That Spell Trouble 306

The Noise-Reduction Imperative..306

Know Your Encoding Mode 307

Blu-Ray, Anyone? 308

Reaching for the Clouds 309

The Archiving Challenge..310

AFTERWORD There Is No Best Button **313**

Beware the Hype 314

Resist Complexity 315

Future of Viewing..316

Rapid Change Is Upon Us 317

Dog-Eat-Dog World 318

Index 321

Acknowledgements

My many students over the years around the world, who have been and continue to be the source of great inspiration and motivation; my friend Wes Anderson, who taught me how to let go of my stodgy old ways; Mira Nair, who encouraged me to mentor a new generation of East African filmmakers and offer camera craft workshops in far flung places; Carlin Reagan and Dennis McGonagle, the gentle disciplinarians at Focal Press, who exercised almost godlike patience waiting for this manuscript; Donald Lampasome, Don Milano, Tim Kolb, Jason Osder, and Jack James, who offered thoughtful suggestions and advice during the review process; Doug Leighton from Panasonic in the United States and the amazing and charming Janet Lam from Panasonic Singapore, who put up with me through thick and thin and provided me with endless favors; Tom Di Nome at Sony, who supported me more than was perhaps wise or prudent; Wayne Schulman from Manfrotto, who bent over backwards to fulfill my oddest requests; Fujinon's Dave Waddell, who never tired of my questions about lenses; the inimitable Karla Berry, my BFF and the finest film instructor and laugher in the Western World; Driss Benyaklef and Anadil Hossain, my partners in crime who know more about how the movie business really works than anyone; Simone Sultana, my indefatigable collaborator and source of boundless energy in London, Bangladesh, and elsewhere; Lee Bobker at Vision Associates, who gave me my first professional assignment 35 years ago shooting soybean fields; Ira Tiffen, whose vast knowledge, enthusiasm, and love for photography I try to emulate; Sid Platt, my friend and mentor at National Geographic who placed his faith in me as a young inexperienced shooter and sent me to Poland, the Amazon, the North Pole, and other weird places; Ben and Zoe, my fabulous son and daughter, who so graciously posed for dozens of pictures and illustrations; and Debbie, Karen, and my many friends, who've had to put up with me and my difficult ways, and who in their own fashions and expressions of love encouraged me to write this book.

The Shooter's Point of View

Dear Video Shooter:

This is your task. This is your struggle to uniquely and eloquently express your point of view. Whatever it is. Wherever it takes you. For the shooter-storyteller, this exploration can be exhilarating and personal. It's what makes your point of view different and enables you to tell visually compelling stories like no other video shooter in the world.

In May 1988 while on assignment for National Geographic in Poland, I learned a profound lesson about the power of personal video and point of view. The aging Communist regime had amassed a thousand soldiers with tanks in front of the Gdansk Shipyard to crush a strike by workers belonging to the banned Solidarity union. I happened to be shooting in Gdansk, and despite it not being part of my assignment I ventured over to the shipyard anyway in light of the world's attention being focused there and the compelling human drama unfolding inside.

Out of sight of my government minder, I understood I could've been beaten or been rendered persona non grata, but I took the chance anyway as I was convinced that history was in the making. The night before, the military had stormed a coalmine in southern Poland and had brutally beaten many strikers as they slept. Not a single photo or frame of video emerged to tell the tale, but news of the carnage spread anyway through unofficial channels. The shipyard workers figured they were in for the same fate, and I wanted to record it.

Considering the regime's total control over the press and TV, it was no surprise that the Polish InterPress Office would deny my 16mm Arriflex and me access to the shipyard. But that didn't stop my two Polish friends with less obvious video gear from slipping inside the complex in the back of a delivery van.

Throughout the previous fall and winter, Piotr Bikont and Leszek Dziumovicz had been secretly shooting and editing half-hour newsreels out of a Gdansk church loft. Circumventing the regime's chokehold on the media, the two men distributed the programs through a makeshift network of church schools, recruiting young school kids to ferry the videocassettes home in their backpacks.

As this latest shipyard drama unfolded, Piotr and Leszek vowed to stay with the strikers to capture the assault and almost certain bloodbath. Piotr's physical well-being didn't matter, he kept telling me. In fact, he looked forward to being beaten, provided he could get the footage out of the shipyard to me, and to the watchful world.

But for days and weeks the attack didn't come, and Piotr and Leszek held their ground, capturing in riveting detail the exhaustion of the strikers as the siege dragged on. In scenes reminiscent of the Alamo, 75 men and women facing almost certain annihilation held firm against a growing phalanx of tanks, troops, and feckless provocateurs who occasionally feigned an assault to probe the strikers' defenses.

In the course of the siege, Piotr and Leszek made a startling discovery that their little Sony camcorder could be a potent weapon against the amassed military force. On the night of what was surely to be the final assault, the strikers broadcast a desperate plea over the shipyard loudspeakers: "Camera to the gate! Camera to the gate!" The strikers were pleading for Piotr and Leszek to come with their camera and point it at the soldiers. It was pitch dark at 2 a.m., and the camera couldn't see much. But it didn't matter. When the soldiers saw the camera pointed at them, they retreated. They understood the inevitability of a postcommunist Poland and were terrified of having their faces recorded!

FIGURE 1.1

Solidarity activists Piotr Bikont and Leszek Dziumowicz with the Sony camcorder that helped transform the face of Eastern Europe in the 1980s.

As the weeks rolled by, the strikers' camera became a growing irritant to the authorities. Finally, in desperation, a government agent posing as a striker ripped the camera from Piotr's arms. After a frantic chase, the agent ducked into a building housing several other agents, not realizing, incredibly, the camera was still running!

Inside a manager's office, we see what the camera sees: a drab blank wall as the camcorder pointing nowhere in particular dutifully records the gaggle of agents plotting to smuggle the camera back *out* of the shipyard. The camera is then placed inside a paper bag, and the story continues from this point of view: The screen is completely dark as the camera inside the bag passes from one set of agents' arms to another. Alas, the image wasn't much—a black screen with no video at all—conveying a story to the world and a point of view that would in short order devastate the totalitarian regime.

FIGURE 1.2

When an undercover agent suddenly grabbed Piotr's camera, no one thought about turning the camera off!

FIGURE 1.3

What's this? A dark screen? If the context is right, you don't need much to tell a compelling story!

FIGURE 1.4

In this pivotal scene from Orson Welles' *Citizen Kane* (1941), we listen to mostly unseen characters in a dark projection room. Suppressing visual content in this way forces an audience to listen, this strategy being very effective to communicate critical dialogue or exposition

(a)

FIGURE 1.5 a,b

Conversely, we can force the viewer to focus more on the visual story by attenuating or eliminating the audio entirely. Managing the interplay of picture and sound is the essence of a filmmaker's craft. (b) The muted audio in this scene from *Saving Private Ryan* (1998) reinforces the horror of the D-Day beach landing at Normandy.

(b)

FIGURE 1.6

Ninety percent of a video story is communicated visually. Given a choice, viewers always prefer to watch than to listen. They cannot do both at the same time!

FIGURE 1.7

Show me; don't tell me! Great storytelling requires compelling visuals!

YOUR STORY'S POINT OF VIEW

I'm often asked, "Which camera should I buy?" and "Which camera is best?" These questions are loaded and often laced with fear. My answer is always the same: It's the camera that best supports the *point of view* of the story you've chosen to tell.

There are always trade-offs in whatever camera you choose, and you should be leery of selecting a make or model based on a single feature such as imager size or resolution. High-resolution cameras may have associated drawbacks like inferior low-light response, constrained dynamic range, and a bevy of shuttering artifacts owing to their large CMOS[1] sensors. These compromises along with a data-intensive workflow can have a negative impact on your filmmaking efforts, so is the highest resolution camera really what you want or need to convey your visual story and the desired point of view?

If a close-focus capability is crucial for your documentary work, then a small compact camcorder with servo focus may be preferable to a full-size model with manual optics. Pricey broadcast lenses will almost always produce sharper, more professional images, but they cannot usually focus continuously to the front element owing to the limitations of their mechanical design.

There is no perfect camera for every application. Every model has its strengths and weaknesses, the compromises in each camera being more apparent at lower price points. If you *really* know your story and the intended point of view, you can select the right camera, which need not be the most expensive or sophisticated. Similar to a carpenter, a plumber, or an auto mechanic, the smart shooter understands his or her tools and how they may advance (or hinder) his or her goals as a craftsperson.[2]

FIGURE 1.8

Shooting on a public pier without a permit? A consumer Canon HF-S100 or DSLR may be ideal. Shooting a documentary for The Discovery Channel about the mating habits of the banded mongoose? The full-size camcorder with variable frame rates and a smallish 2/3-inch sensor is perfect. Secretly capturing passenger confessions in the back of a Las Vegas taxi? The lipstick camera or even the Go Pro fits the bill. When it comes to gear, your story and intended point of view trump all other considerations!

NO MORE CHASING RAINBOWS

The notion of a shooter as a dedicated professional has been eroding for some time. For several hundred dollars and little or no training, almost anyone with a low-end Canon, Panasonic, or late-model iPhone can produce reasonably decent video, which makes for ugly competition among shooters no matter how talented or inspired we think we are.

For the shooter-storyteller to prosper in the current environment he or she must become a 21st-century Leonardo DaVinci. Classical painting, printing presses, and helicopter designs may not be our areas of expertise, but the trend is clearly toward craftspeople who can do it all: shoot, write, edit, produce, and design websites. These days, increasingly, we're talking about the same person.

---

[1] **Complementary metal–oxide semiconductor,** a digital sensor as compared to analog CCD sensors. See Chapter 4 *The Storyteller's Box.*
[2] See Chapter 4 for in-depth discussion of how to evaluate camera operation and performance.

Just as strands of DNA compose the building blocks of life and heredity, so too do zeros and ones constitute the essence of every digital device and application. Today's shooter, whether inclined to or not, must embrace the new hyper-converged reality. Whether you're a shooter, a sound recordist, a special effects artist, or a music arranger, it doesn't matter. Fundamentally, we're all manipulating the same zeros and ones.

Thirty years ago on the Hawaiian island of Maui, I spent an entire afternoon chasing a rainbow from one end of the island to the other, looking for just the right combination of background and foreground elements to frame the elusive burst of color. It was, in many ways, a typical assignment for me circa 1985.

Today, I don't think many producers for National Geographic or anyone else would care to pay my day rate for a Wild Rainbow Chase. Why? Because producers versed in the digital tools are far more likely to buy a stock shot of the Hawaiian landscape (or create one in Bryce 3D) and then add the rainbow in Adobe After Effects!

These folks like the rest of us are learning to harness the digital beast, and whereas past shooters were responsible for creating complete *finished* frames, today's shooters are more apt to furnish only the *frame elements* for rearranging and compositing later by a multitude of downstream creative types. After completion of principal photography for *The Phantom Menace* (1999),[3] George Lucas is said to have removed unwanted eye blinks from his stars' performances. Alas! No one is safe in this digital run-amok world! Not even actors!

In my camera and lighting classes, I recognize that my students are receiving training at a feverish pace. And what are they learning? To composite, reposition, and alter the color and mood of scenes; to crop, diffuse, and manipulate objects in three-dimensional (3D) space; to align, mix, and dub audio tracks—in other words, to do the combined jobs of an entire production and postproduction staff!

WEARING MANY HATS NOW

In August 2006, director Wes Anderson (*Moonrise Kingdom*, *Rushmore*, *The Royal Tenenbaums*) asked me to shoot behind the scenes for *The Darjeeling Limited*,[4] a story of three brothers aboard an Indian Railways train chattering across the Rajasthan desert. Wes didn't want just an ordinary behind the scenes (BTS) show. Instead he suggested a more engaged approach, one in which my presence as a shooter and an *interlocateur* would figure prominently.

To fund the project and my five months in India, Fox Searchlight drew on the resources of multiple studio divisions: Publicity, Home Video, Marketing, and the Web. That's how I came to wear several hats: shooting second unit for the movie and editing and producing a 1-hour HBO special, a 30-minute featurette for DVD, 16 podcasts for the website, and 6 EPK (electronic press kit) interviews of the director and cast for distribution to entertainment news outlets. So you see I was no longer just a shooter but an ersatz producer/editor/DVD author and a Web content specialist!

---

[3]Lucas, G. (Producer & Director) & McCallum, R. (Producer). (1999). *Star Wars Episode 1: The Phantom Menace* [Motion picture]. USA: LucasFilm. Note that source information for films is provided on first mention only.

[4]Ferozeuddin Alameer, S. M. (Producer), Anderson, W. (Producer & Director), Bamford, A. (Producer), Cooper, M. (Producer), Coppola, R. (Producer), Dawson, J. (Producer), . . . Rudin, S. (Producer). (2007). *The Darjeeling Limited* [Motion picture]. USA: Fox Searchlight Pictures.

FIGURE 1.9

Prowling the streets of Jodhpur, India. A full-size camcorder is ideal for shooting high-detail city scenes and landscapes.

FIGURE 1.10

A versatile go-anywhere camera greatly expands the shooter's storytelling palette.

FIGURE 1.11

The Darjeeling Limited (2007). Here I double for Bill Murray inside a taxi racing to the Jodhpur train station. The camera beside me offers audiences a unique point of view for the behind the scenes show.

LEARNING THE DISCIPLINE

During the last 10 years, advances in technology have transformed the capabilities of the camera, so much so that today even the most inexpensive camcorder is able to produce excellent images. Given this context for a shooter to be successful, it's no longer a matter of who owns the *tools*; it's who owns the *craft*.

Becoming proficient in the craft was simpler for shooters a few decades ago. We lived in a mechanical world then, which meant when our machines failed, we could look inside and figure out how they worked. We could remedy a problem and gain confidence and ability without having a theoretical understanding of bit theory or the inside track to someone at MakeItWork.com.

In past years the aspiring shooter dutifully pawed over Joseph Mascelli's masterwork *The Five C's of Cinematography,*[5] which described in exhaustive detail the rudiments of effective visual storytelling. The mastery of the Five *C*s—camera angles, continuity, cutting, close-ups, and composition—was imperative as shooters had to consider the implications of every creative and technical decision before rolling the camera, or face severe, even crippling, financial pain.

I remember my struggle to raise money for a PBS documentary in the 1970s. After months of frustration and finally landing a grant for a few thousand dollars, I can still recall the anxiety of running film through the camera. Every foot (about a second and a half) meant 42 cents out of my pocket—a figure forever etched into my consciousness. And as if to reinforce the sound of my dissipating wealth, the spring-wound Bolex would sound a mindful chime every second on its maximum 16.5-foot run.

The technology (or lack thereof) imposed its own discipline, and so by necessity, every shot had to tell a story with a beginning, middle and an end. Every frame, composition, lens choice, and background, had to be duly considered. A skilled cameraperson able to manage all this was somebody to be revered and remunerated. It is still this way for the multidimensional shooter of today, albeit the discipline of the craft must now be mostly self-imposed.

FIGURE 1.12

My '66. When it didn't start, you pushed it. No understanding of MXF, USB, or eSATA required.

FIGURE 1.13

The San Francisco cable car is the ultimate expression of the mechanical world we once knew and loved.

[5]Mascelli, J. (1998). *The five C's of cinematography: Motion picture filming techniques.* Los Angeles, CA: Silman-James Press. (Original work published in 1965)

FIGURE 1.14

The spring-wound camera propelled a perforated band of photosensitized acetate around a series of sprockets and gears. The mechanism was easy to see, study, and troubleshoot.

FIGURE 1.15

The manual nature of film cameras imposed a discipline not as readily gleaned from auto-everything digital camcorders.

NEW POINTS OF VIEW

The DV revolution transformed the medium by empowering ordinary people to engage their passions and express their points of view in venues such as Facebook and YouTube. Out of this, we are seeing the incarnation of a new breed of shooters to whom we can now credit a litany of work including

FIGURE 1.16

The DSLR as a serious imaging tool came of age with *Act of Valor* (2012). The sprawling action film grossed more than $200 million worldwide.

feature films captured in whole or in part with inexpensive camcorders and digital single-lens reflex (DSLR) cameras: *Super Size Me* (2004),[6] *Once* (2006),[7] and *Act of Valor* (2012),[8] shot almost entirely on the Canon 5D Mark II.

LOOK WHO'S SHOOTING NOW

The Five *C*s hallowed cinematographic principles may be more relevant than ever, but look who is applying them! It's not just shooters. It's anyone with a hand in the creative process: editors, directors, 3D artists, DVD menu designers—anyone with a Macintosh, a PC, or even an iPad, and that covers just about everyone.

Currently major U.S. news shows are moving rapidly to a one-person-does-it-all model, as show runners and correspondents are being increasingly asked to shoot, record sound, and in some cases even edit their own segments.

In smaller markets and for cable TV, the solo shooter-storyteller is already commonplace. Several years ago, I was asked to shoot several episodes for The History Channel's *Sworn to Secrecy* series. My first assignment required that I fly with the crew to Spokane, Washington, to interview air force pilots undergoing wilderness survival training.

Of course, in shooting such a series, I naturally assumed that audio would be a priority. So on the plane out of Los Angeles, I couldn't help but notice that my "crew" was rather small, consisting in fact of only the 22-year-old director and myself. I expressed astonishment to my boyish colleague, who thought for a moment, then smiled. I looked at him like he was nuts.

"I don't know why you're so happy," I said. "We're doing hours of interviews and we've got no soundman."

[6]Morley, J. (Producer), Pederson, D. (Producer), Pederson, D. (Producer), Winters, H. (Producer), & Spurlock, M. (Producer & Director). (2004). *Super Size Me* [Motion picture]. USA: Kathbar Pictures.

[7]Collins, D. (Producer), Niland, M. (Producer), & Carney, J. (Producer). (2006). *Once* [Motion picture]. Ireland: Bórd Scannán na hÉireann.

[8]Clark, J. (Producer), Haggart, G. (Producer), Leitman, M. (Producer), Mailis, M. J. (Producer), McCoy, M. (Producer), Pollak, J. (Producer), . . . Waugh, S. (Director). (2012). *Act of Valor* [Motion picture]. USA: Bandito Brothers.

"Yes," he said, his eyes shining brightly. "But I've got a *cameraman*!"

It was then I finally understood the digital revolution. This newbie director had been hired to write, direct, shoot, and edit a 1-hour show for an award-winning TV series. It was a fantastic opportunity for the budding director; the project drawing hugely on his extraordinary skill set, but it did make me wonder about the shooter's role in the future, and whether that role would ever really stop expanding into other disciplines such as sound.

FIGURE 1.17

Thinking about the future and the role of the video shooter? Me too.

HIRE YOUR CLIENTS!

Gaining the requisite camera skills takes lots of practice and ample work opportunities. For many folks, the latter point is the bugaboo that may require a new and more radical point of view. First, we must realize that the shooter-craftsperson cannot compete on price. Whatever rate you quote no matter how low, someone will always offer to do the job for less. If you say you'll shoot a project for $100 per day, someone with the same DSLR will bid $50. And if you bid $50, someone will offer to do it for $25, and so forth. Working cheap is never in your interest, unless of course that is what you want to be known for working cheaply. But working for *free—that can be such a beautiful thing!*

It may seem counterintuitive or even insane, but consider this: Working for free is not the same as working cheaply. Working at less or much less than the prevailing rate lowers the value of your services and diminishes your stature in the eyes of a client. It exposes you to a range of abuses, long hours, and lack of respect. But working for free is a totally different matter. Now *you* hold the power, not your employer, because you've hired *him*. You've selected *him or her* above all others, so this person owes you, and *that* shifts the relationship dynamic in your favor.

So this is it. First, you identify your dream job and you go after it. You cajole. You charm. And most of all you persevere. Once you land it, you work for free yes, but you also work hard until you are indispensable. You then write what amounts to a ransom note and threaten to leave, at which point your client/employer will likely offer you a paid position, and you say . . . what? *You say no.*

That's right. Instead you say, "Gee, I would really like to work for you and am so excited about this opportunity, but you can't afford me." So you turn your boss down. Whatever he or she offers, you're not interested. Folks, this is psychological warfare. The moment your boss lets you become indispensable, you've already won. There's no point in compromise. You can dictate your own terms.

This is how Hollywood and probably many other industries work. More important than the money, executives are mostly fearful of hiring the wrong person. Such a faux pas can be costly, embarrassing, or even calamitous, for risk-averse execs. On the other hand, if you've demonstrated with passion and confidence that you are the right person for the job, that all they have to do is hire you and their worries are over, you have eliminated their fears, which can only lead to good things, including financial rewards. If you choose your employer carefully, the days you work for free can be among the most lucrative of your career.

YOU HAVE THE POWER

Thanks to the latest low-cost cameras and the ability to reach hundreds of millions via the Internet, the shooter today wields more power than ever. You can use this power for nefarious or unsavory ends as some shooter-storytellers do, or you can use it to transform the world and create works of lasting beauty for the betterment of humankind. It all depends on your point of view and the stories you choose to tell.

EDUCATOR'S CORNER: REVIEW TOPICS

1. Consider a recent news event in which the presence of a camera played a vital role. Did the camera offer a point of view that wouldn't have been available otherwise? Is the camera's point of view more valid than, say, a witness's direct testimony?

2. Is a point of view necessary to create a compelling work? Is a documentary devoid of a point of view possible, given the inevitable shot selection, framing, and editorial choices?

3. Explore the advantages and disadvantages of a shooter wearing multiple hats. Do you feel that this compromises the effectiveness of the cameraperson?

4. Identify three (3) scenes from favorite movies that expertly manipulate picture and sound to maximize the story's impact. Is the handling of sound more critical to a movie's success than managing the picture? Please explain.

5. The proficient shooter often manipulates point of view for maximum storytelling impact. Cite three (3) examples from recent films in which the point of view was deliberately obscured to increase suspense or to add humor.

6. The video shooter has the capability to influence the world in profound ways. Cite three (3) feature films or documentaries that singularly transformed the political or social landscape.

Let Me Tell You a Story

Pressing a camera to your eye and framing a good story is no different from relating a tale around a campfire or writing the great American novel. Fundamentally, we are embarking on the same journey that begins with a single sentence: *Let me tell you a story . . .*

The great director Sidney Lumet once famously observed that *story is the conduit through which all creative [and technical] decisions flow.*[1] This includes the choice of camera, lens, recording format, resolution, and a thousand other technical and nontechnical things.

Searching for the right camera? It depends on the story you intend to tell. Selecting the right focal length lens? It depends on the story you intend to tell. Determining the correct camera placement and point of view? It all depends on the story you intend to tell.

Truth is audiences can't care less if you shoot your story on DV, 35mm Cinemascope, or Fisher-Price Pixelvision.[2] No one walks out of a movie theater and says, "Gee, that was a great movie, but it was shot 4:2:0." So as you read this book and glean something useful from it, let's keep all the tech talk in perspective. Stories work for different reasons, and can often be quite successful despite a lousy script, poor lighting, or, even I shudder to say, bad camerawork.

The latest and greatest cameras, lenses, and support systems can be fun and consuming, but the successful shooter understands it's really just about telling a compelling *visual* story. As a high school sophomore competing in the 1970 New York City Science Fair, I constructed a picturesque Rube Goldberg device that attracted considerable attention. Cobbled together from an old tube radio, recycled coffee tin, and a hodgepodge of home-ground lenses and prisms, the motley assemblage dubbed "The Sound of Color" aimed to associate wavelengths of visible light with the squeals, whines, and whistles, of an antique radio's oscillator. In an era of Apollo and men walking, driving, and playing golf on the moon, my crackpot creation purporting to *hear* color did not seem *that* out of this world. Still the concept made more than a few eyes roll among the judges, physicists, and engineers that heard my pitch, but despite this, The Sound of Color was a huge success, eventually taking top honors and a commendation from the U.S. Army.

As I think back, the army must have surely realized that one could not *really* hear color. But it didn't matter. The *storytelling* was so engaging that the army brass and everyone else it seemed couldn't look away, and isn't that what great filmmaking and winning science fair projects are all about? Telling a compelling, seductive, *visual* story?

---

[1] Lumet, S. (1996). *Making movies*. New York, NY: Vintage Press. I added the word *technical* to Sidney's quote to help make my point. Sorry, Sidney.

[2] In the late 1980s, the toy company Fisher-Price manufactured a 2-bit monochrome camera that recorded to a standard audiocassette. Pixelvision's cryptic images continue to attract a following today, as evidenced by the annual PXL THIS Film Festival in Venice, California.

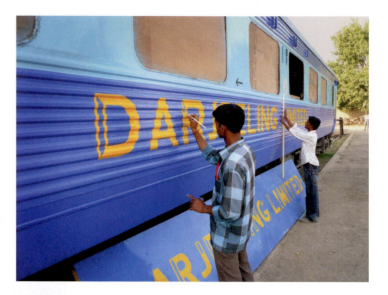

FIGURE 2.1

Every movie, campfire tale, or corporate puff-piece, begins with a single sentence: *Let me tell you a story . . .*

FIGURE 2.2

The successful shooter understands how to translate the words from a script into images that serve the story. Shooting a close-up? How close is close? Should the camera be above or below eyeline? Does a hand-held camera make sense? Should the lighting be sharply angled and dramatic or flat and neutral in color?

FIGURE 2.3

The melding of art and science. Your audience members just want to be told a good story. And they're willing to work hard to help you do it!

WHAT MAKES A GOOD STORY?

Just as in any good book or tale recounted around a campfire, our film stories must boast a compelling premise. My science fair project purporting to hear color was intriguing, but interesting *characters* also played a central role. In The Sound of Color, the "characters" were the olio of colorful junk splayed across the table: the Chase & Sanborn coffee can turned makeshift heat sink, the 1950s-era Zenith radio outputting screeches and squeals as if from an alien spaceship, the darting splashes of color across the surface of a photocell. To the public and army brass, The Sound of Color seemed somehow plausible and relatable—the two criteria that happen to lie at the heart of every good screenplay, movie, or television show.

FIGURE 2.4

Every great story has a compelling premise, interesting characters, and memorable set pieces or moments that an audience recalls later to friends. *Wasn't it great when . . .* For the shooter, it is critical to recognize a project's potential set pieces, because it allows the proper effort and resources to be applied where it matters most.

FIGURE 2.5

This celebrated moment from Rob Reiner's *When Harry Met Sally* (1989)[3] provided powerful word of mouth long after audiences left the theater. Shooters reviewing a prospective script should look for such set pieces and consider the most effective way *to have what she's having.*

KNOW YOUR GENRE AND MAKE SURE YOUR AUDIENCE KNOWS

You're reviewing the title offerings at your local video store or Redbox. On what *shelf* is your latest epic? Is it in Comedy? Horror? Suspense? Correctly identifying a story's genre is the first step toward being an effective shooter, and ultimately reaching your intended audience.

---

[3]Ephron, N. (Producer), Nicolaides, S. (Producer), Scheinman, A. (Producer), Stott, J. (Producer), & Reiner, R. (Producer & Director). *When Harry Met Sally* [Motion picture]. USA: Castle Rock Entertainment.

My philosophy regarding genre is simple: If your story is a comedy, your audience should be laughing most of the time. If your story is a drama about starving children in Africa, your audience probably shouldn't be rolling in the aisles. Of course, your comedy may have serious moments, and your drama may be quite funny at times, but the *genre* of the story should be clear from your show's first moments in the *look and feel* of the images and how they're framed, lit, and presented.

(a)   (b)

FIGURE 2.6 a,b

Thinking about your story and genre: How close should a close up be?

FIGURE 2.7

FIGURE 2.8

To prepare an audience to laugh or cry we establish the story's genre from the first frame. In *Barry Lyndon* (1975),[4] the character and placement of the lighting and candles communicate the desired genre. Stylized titles and music can also help establish the proper tone.

[4]Kubrick, S. (Producer & Director), Harlan, J. (Producer), & Williams, B. (Producer). (1995). *Barry Lyndon* [Motion picture]. United Kingdom: Peregrine.

The savvy shooter understands that the genre and story inform every creative and technical decision from camera, format, and lens choice to framing and placement of a key light. The effective shooter provides a stream of cues to properly predispose the audience. A looser close-up may be right for a romantic comedy, while a tighter close-up is more appropriate for drama or horror. Story and genre are one of the same.

FIGURE 2.9

Create a poster for your next production. Is the log line compelling? Do the characters grab you? Would you plunk down your dollars, euros, and yen, to see the movie suggested in the poster?

WHAT DOES YOUR POSTER LOOK LIKE?

Hollywood executives often pose this question in story meetings to better evaluate a filmmaker's pitch. And here's the reason: The poster is a shorthand distillation of the story. No matter if the project is a movie, commercial, music video, or corporate puff piece, the requirement of a well-tuned story idea is the same: to capture its appeal and uniqueness in a single image.

REVIEWING LOG LINES

FIGURE 2.10

Understanding the power of the log line . . .

Bottle Rocket (1996)[5]

1. THEY'RE NOT REALLY CRIMINALS. THEY ONLY THINK THEY ARE.
2. BAD AT LIFE. WORSE AT CRIME.
3. ALL THEY WANTED WAS TO BE CRIMINALS. IN THE WORST WAY.
4. CRIME. EVERYONE HAS TO BE BAD AT SOMETHING.
5. UNNATURALLY BORN CRIMINALS.
6. LOUSY IN CRIME. NO HARD FEELINGS.

Understanding the power of the log line, studio marketing departments consider and reconsider a movie's tag phrase ad infinitum. For *Bottle Rocket*, Columbia Pictures considered a long list of possibilities before making its choice.

---

[5]Boyle, B. (Producer), Brookes, J. L. (Producer), Carson, L. M. K. (Producer), Hargrave, C. (Producer), Lang, M. (Producer), Platt, P. (Producer), . . . Anderson, W. (Director). (1996). *Bottle Rocket* [Motion picture]. USA: Columbia Pictures Corporation.

KNOW YOUR LOG LINE

In the same way a poster coalesces the story into a single image so does the *log line* help communicate the story's premise in a single phrase or sentence. Ideally the few words convey the genre and tone, so the shooter and production team can work together from the same frame of reference.

EMBRACE YOUR LIMITATIONS

Whether bound by a tiny budget, lack of equipment, or too few crew, the limitations imposed on a project can be a positive force. Consider the eloquence and simplicity of Vittorio DeSica's *The Bicycle Thief*[6] produced in 1948. In the aftermath of the Second World War, the filmmaker had barely scraps of film to capture his story in the streets of Rome. There were no studios or no support teams, nor was there a budget to hire professional actors. The desperate story of an unemployed father and loving son after the theft of their bicycle was reduced to its essence, to a mere few setups focusing on the characters' survival and relationship, which is what audiences really care about anyway.

With today's digital cameras and DSLRs, you don't need much to create a compelling story. In fact, I bet you have everything you need right now to shoot your dream project: If you don't have a camera, borrow one. If you don't have a computer, use one at your local public library. And if you *still* don't think you have the resources to pull it off then, then focus more on your story! You'll be better off for it!

Story, story, story. It's what it's all about. It's all it's ever been about.[7]

FIGURE 2.11

DeSica's *The Bicycle Thief* (1948). Storytelling stripped to its essence.

---

[6]DeSica, Vittorio. (1948). *The Bicycle Thief* [Motion picture]. Italy: Independent non-studio production.
[7]This is a pretty good log line for this section!

FOR DIFFERENT REASONS

In 1997, my wife and I attended the premiere of *Titanic*[8] at Mann's Chinese Theatre. The studio executives in attendance were understandably nervous as the $200 million epic unspooled in front of hundreds of clearly less-than-enthusiastic industry insiders, including comedian Bill Maher, whose protracted moans of agony I can still vividly recall.

And who could blame him? The movie's trite dialog and banal love subplot were hardly the makings of great movie. Indeed, the polite applause at the film's end only served to underscore the inescapable fact that this movie was going to sink—and sink fast.

Of course, things didn't work out that way, and with the release of a 3D version in 2012, the movie continues to be one of the most popular films of all time. This only confirms William Goldman's often-cited observation about Hollywood that no one knows anything. For me, however, I learned a critical lesson: *Movies work for different reasons.*

In the end, *Titanic* captivated audiences who responded overwhelmingly to the movie's cinematic elements, the impressive set pieces, epic scope, and sweeping score, all serving to captivate the mostly teenage viewers who never questioned the plausibility of Kate Winslet emoting in a sleeveless dress on the ship's bow in the frigid North Atlantic. Audiences worldwide clearly accepted the story and film—hook, line, and sinker.

For the modest shooter the same lesson applies: your stories, whether shot on high-definition video (HDV), 35mm, or an iPhone, can be hugely successful if audiences are able to connect on some level. Of course, it would be foolish to tell a story with the scope of *Titanic* on DV. On the other hand, a more intimate tale such as *Beasts of the Southern Wild* (2012)[9] might work just as well or better. So when it comes to shooting a project effectively with whatever camera, it is really a matter of recognizing the entertainment value in the screen story and then focusing the bulk of your energy and resources there.

YOUR COMPARATIVE ADVANTAGE

Every shooter-storyteller needs to recognize his comparative advantage. That advantage may be personal in the types of stories you choose to tell. When you speak with passion, insight, and authenticity, your audiences listen and respond. Only you see the world in the way that you do. Only you have the stories and point of view that you do.

Today's inexpensive digital cameras offer great flexibility and economy. The trick is to recognize the strengths afforded by these devices—and then exploit the hell out of them.

Such was the case for two street musicians in Ireland whose personal experiences formed the basis of a low-budget HDV movie that was later acquired by Fox Searchlight. The scrappy heart-on-its-sleeve love story *Once* (2007) was hardly well shot; indeed, much of it was dark and out of focus! Still, the movie connected with a large and appreciative international audience, who flocked to theaters and to record stores to buy the soundtrack album.

---

[8]Cameron, J. (Producer & Director), Easley, P. (Producer), Giddings, A. (Producer), Hill, G. (Producer), Landau, J. (Producer), Mann, S. (Producer), & Sanchini, Rae (Producer). (2007). *Titanic* [Motion picture]. USA: 20th Century Fox Film Corporation.

[9]Carroll, C. (Producer), Coleman, C. (Producer), Engelhorn, P. (Producer), Evelyn, A. (Producer), Gottwald, M. (Producer), Harrison, N. (Producer), . . . Zeitlin, B. (Director). (2012). *Beasts of the Southern Wild* [Motion picture]. USA: Cinereach.

We may never compete directly with the Hollywood titans who produce *Spider-Man*[10] or *Batman Returns*,[11] but that doesn't mean we can't produce engaging well-crafted stories. We certainly can!

LIMIT YOUR CANVAS

For shooters of modest means the limiting of one's canvas is critical. Low-cost cameras, especially DSLRs, exhibit very dark shadows with little subtlety in the highlights. For this reason, shooters may wish to limit the visual scope of their projects by avoiding expansive landscapes, for example, that reveal a camera's relative inability to capture good contrast and detail. In general, character pieces work well with low-cost video, the camera and the lenses, particularly in the case of DSLRs, performing optimally when a wide dynamic range is not required.

FIGURE 2.12

Shooters with consumer camcorders must be mindful of scenes exhibiting high detail. DSLRs are especially susceptible to objectionable artifacts under such conditions.

FIGURE 2.13

The images from consumer camcorders were never intended for big-screen projection. This is changing with the advent of higher performance compact camcorders from Sony, Panasonic, and others.

[10]Arad, A. (Producer), Bryce, I. (Producer), Curtis, G. (Producer), Fugeman, H. (Producer), Lee, S. (Producer), Saeta, S. P. (Producer), . . . Raimi, S. (Director). (2002). *Spider-Man* [Motion picture]. USA: Columbia Pictures Corporation.

[11]Bryce, I. (Producer), Di Novi, D. (Producer), Franco, L. J. (Producer), Guber, P. (Producer), Melniker, B. (Producer), Peters, J. (Producer), . . . Burton, T. (Producer & Director). (1992). *Batman Returns* [Motion picture]. USA: Warner Bros.

FIGURE 2.14

The loss of detail in the highlights is the main reason why amateur video looks "amateur." Deep, impenetrable shadows can likewise communicate an amateur feel to your audience.

RESPECT YOUR CAMERA'S DYNAMIC RANGE

The DSLR revolution has taught us even the most modest camera is capable of producing superb images if you don't push it too far. The *dynamic range* of a camera is defined as its ability to capture a range of tones from light to dark. In the DSLR, the number of steps may be fewer than seven stops, with the brightest areas of scenes appearing blown out and the darkest areas appearing as a solid black mass. Respecting its dynamic range is the best thing you can do to improve the perceived performance of a modest HD camcorder.

(a)   (b)

FIGURE 2.15 a,b

The Old Masters took advantage of the Magic Hour and so should you. (a) Pictured here is *Les Glaneuses* by Millet. (b) Venice California beach at dusk.

SHOOT THE MAGIC HOUR

The challenge of a camera's limited dynamic range may be addressed simply by shooting before dawn or after sunset at so-called Magic Hour. For centuries this has been a favorite strategy of fine artists and photographers who take advantage of the time of day when the landscape is illuminated exclusively by skylight. HD shooters, like the great Old Master painters, can relish this exquisite light. With the iris wide open and error correction off high alert, even the lowliest camera can really shine at Magic Hour!

AUTHENTICITY MATTERS

Never mind the endless discussion of formats, resolutions, and pixels, the real question is what do audiences want? Most of all they want a story that is *authentic*. From actors' performances and wardrobe, to the plausibility of the script and the look and feel of your images, the production must ring true. The technical representation of a scene is not nearly as important as is the scene's perceived authenticity. It is this feeling of genuineness that resonates most profoundly with audiences.

This is why documentaries that purport to be true but are later revealed to be works of fiction are such failures. Authenticity in the cinema and the arts is highly valued; audiences, like pretty much anyone else, do not appreciate being manipulated or lied to.

FIGURE 2.16

This man's eyes are shifting and avoiding eye contact. He may be well lit and look great, but do you believe a word he says?

FIGURE 2.17

Your visual story must support the emotional stakes. Audiences sense the connection. When it's missing, viewers perceive a lack of authenticity.

The perception of authenticity trumps all other considerations. This is because audiences are constantly scanning the frame to assess the credibility of the storytelling. Your audience scrutinizes among other things the brand of cereal on a shelf in the background, the make and model of car in the driveway, the light or absence of light in a subject's eyes. In later chapters, I discuss the critical role of backgrounds, selective focus, and lighting choices, because these aspects of craft may support or undermine the perceived authenticity of your story.

THE STORY NEVER STOPS

It's a simple truth: *When the story stops, your audience stops watching.* For this reason, we typically do all we can to stay ahead of the audience. If the audience knows how a scene will end, we don't

need the scene, so we cut it. If the viewer knows how any particular shot will end, we don't need the complete shot, so we trim it. Panning too slowly or zooming in or out instead of simply cutting slows the story and allows the viewer to catch up to the story, which must be avoided at all costs! Remember excessive slowing is responsible for the death of more good stories than any other factor.

In some cases, this slowing is helpful to milk a climactic scene such as an ax murderer's confession. In this case, the change in tempo is a strategic maneuver to keep the audience engaged and hanging on every frame. But even here, the visual story like the overall story *never* stops completely as doing so will lose the audience's attention in short order.

FIGURE 2.18

The visual story never stops. Ever.

FIGURE 2.19

The shooter never pans, tilts, zooms, or hangs on a shot any longer than is necessary to maintain the story's forward thrust. Shooting a landscape? Be mindful of your panning speed! Excessively slow camera moves will bore your audience and motivate them to check their e-mail.

ETHICS MATTER

Filmmaker ethics is a topic kicked around a lot in film schools these days as *documentarians* will often resort to misrepresentation or even outright lies to support a favorite ideology or point of view.

Ethics and authenticity are one of the same. If you misrepresent the truth by clever editing, juxtaposition, or pay for testimony in what is purported to be a documentary, you are sacrificing the authenticity of the work and your power of persuasion. Audiences without a dog in the fight or already converted to your cause can smell the manipulation and lack of veracity—and will run, not walk, the other way. There is tremendous power in authenticity. You'll do well to respect this power, and be authentic in everything you do.

FIGURE 2.20 a,b,c

Documentary filmmakers have long resorted to propaganda to advance a favorite cause. Such blatant attempts to manipulate an audience can seriously undermine a filmmaker's credibility. As storytellers, we have a point of view and (hopefully) something insightful to say. But the respect we show the viewer and our commitment to authenticity must never be compromised. In *Triumph of the Will* (1934),[12] director Leni Riefenstahl adeptly manipulated the cinematic tools to glorify the Nazi regime.

[12]Riefenstahl, L. (Producer & Director). (1934). *Triump des Willens* [Triumph of the will] [Motion picture]. Germany: Leni Riefenstahl-Produktion.

EDUCATOR'S CORNER: REVIEW TOPICS

1. Think about your next project in whatever genre. Is the premise compelling? Are the characters engaging? Can you list three (3) memorable set pieces that your audience will vividly recall days after the screening?

2. How does the *look* of a show inform the viewer of the story's theme and genre?

3. Identify three (3) strategies the shooter might use to speed up or slow down the tempo of the story. Consider how each might be appropriate in a story you are contemplating.

4. Create a poster and a log line for your next production. Is the genre clear? Would you pay $12 at a local multiplex to see the movie represented in your poster?

5. Movies work for different reasons. Cite a recent film that you enjoyed. Which elements of story—premise, character, or set pieces—worked especially well for you?

6. Consider the matter of ethics: You are producing a documentary about the homeless. Is it ethical to pay a homeless person to relate his or her story? How might payment impact his or her testimony and the perceived authenticity of your program? Does it matter?

   Here are some responses from the Film & TV Professional Forum LinkedIn Group February 2012:

   • It is unethical to pay for interviews since it breaks the code of true investigative reporting. As a viewer, I would be skeptical if I knew the people interviewed were paid.

   • Yeah go for it. Budget what you can and help them out. It's no different than paid actors. *Documentary* is a pretty loose term these days anyway.

   • You shouldn't pay the homeless since they may use the money to buy alcohol or drugs.

   • Refusing to pay sources for news and documentaries is simply a cost-cutting tactic. When journalists and documentarians start working for free I will agree that sources should not be paid. Until then the strategy of filmmakers to keep all the money for themselves is transparent.

   • Of course it's not unethical to pay the homeless. There is nothing unscrupulous about it! In fact it is rather humane.

   • Pay up! As long as the homeless aren't receiving money to say something specific I think it's okay.

   • Those who would not pay the homeless haven't a clue about ethics or journalism!

   • Ethically why would you *not* pay them?

   • What I observe here is a lack of compassion for human suffering. Frankly I find it disgusting.

   • I make documentaries for public television and have never paid anyone for an interview. PBS has strict rules regarding this matter, which is why it is considered the most trusted network.

   • If you want to be a social worker that's fine, but don't confuse it with being a documentarian.

   • Where do people come up with the idea that it is unethical to pay interviewees, particularly the homeless? Journalism school? Who says *documentarians* are journalists?

The Video Storyteller

Owing to the proliferation of broadcast, cable, and Web outlets, and an emerging global media *cloud* supporting 2D and 3D content, the demand for skilled craftspeople has never been greater, with resourceful shooters regularly pursuing an array of interesting and worthwhile projects. Of course, given today's fragmented marketplace, the shooter must learn to do a lot with relatively little—and that's the focus of this chapter.

FIGURE 3.1

Along every path and byway, the world is rife with compelling stories waiting to be told.

STILL LOFTY EXPECTATIONS

In today's media environment, achieving a professional look can be a challenge, for all the scrimping and cutting of corners in budget and schedules, viewers still demand a high level of craft whether watching *American Idol*, *The Situation Room with Wolf Blitzer*, or a high school play. No doubt as a shooter, you want to meet your audience's expectations despite the monetary or time limitations imposed upon you.

Craft—not which manufacturer's camera you use, what flavor of flash media you prefer, or whose recording format you ultimately employ—will always be the principal factor in your success. Craft is the most intangible of all commodities, the elusive quality that places you head and tripod above the next guy who just happens to have the same mass-produced camera with all the bells and whistles and useless digital effects.

FIGURE 3.2

The antithesis of small-format video. American photographer and filmmaker Willard Van Dyke prepares to shoot with an 8 × 10 view camera in 1979. To the great shooters of the past, every shot had to count. Composition, lighting, and point of view all had to work and work well in service to the story. Once upon a time, the economics of the medium demanded clear uncluttered storytelling.

PUT A FRAME AROUND THE WORLD

Go ahead. What do you see? In the 1970s, in lieu of a social life, I strolled the Dartmouth College campus flaunting a yellow index card with a rectangle cut out of it. Holding the card to my eye, I'd frame the world: Oh, there's a maple tree; there's an overflowing dumpster; there's my friends streaking naked through the dining hall. It sounds silly in retrospect, but this simple exercise forced me to think about what makes a visually compelling story, and oddly it has little to do with the subject itself.

Indeed I discovered that almost *any* subject could be engaging given the proper framing and

FIGURE 3.3

Put a frame around the world. What do you see? The world is a chaotic place.

FIGURE 3.4

These old masters from Hoboken, New Jersey, rigorously control the frame boundary, excluding everything not helpful to the visual story.

FIGURE 3.5

You can help contain the world's chaos by placing a frame inside the frame by shooting through a doorway or window.

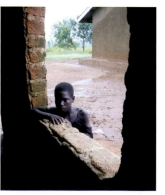

point of view. Paradoxically what mattered most was not what I included inside the frame but what I *left out*. To a young shooter developing awareness in the art of seeing and framing the world, this was a major revelation!

If you like my card idea, you can go further by placing a *second* card behind the first. Holding the cutout cards to your eye and altering the distance between them simulates the variable field of view of a zoom lens. Expensive gear manufacturers might not appreciate this (almost) no-cost gimmick, but it can be invaluable to the new shooter developing his eye and visual storytelling skills.

EXCLUDE, EXCLUDE, EXCLUDE!

This is your mantra! Your raison d'être! It's what guides and empowers you as a shooter and story-teller. You understand that every object, every frame element is included for a reason. Every light, prop, and shadow has a function. Every movement of the camera or change in field of view is deliberate and supports the story in a clear and identifiable way.

As we go about our daily lives, we don't notice the irrelevant details in the story around us; the processor[1] in our brains being adept at framing the world and effectively isolating only what is relevant. In our minds, we frame an establishing scene when we enter a new location. We walk into a coffee shop and our eye is drawn to a friend at a table, and as we move closer, our focus narrows on the story details in her face—maybe a tear, a runny nose, or a bloody lip. We see these details and try to decipher their meaning, and ignore the nonpertinent elements behind, around, and in front of her. Our brains work to reframe the world, creating a virtual movie in our mind, composing, cropping, and placing into sharp focus only those elements deemed essential to the "story."

For some folks, the brain's ability to exclude is subject to overload. Feel blessed you're not the great comic book artist Robert Crumb, who was reportedly so tormented by the visual clutter around him that it eventually drove him mad. Indeed, most of us living in large cities are only able to do so because we've learned to exclude the aural and visual noise that constantly bombard us. Just as we don't notice over time the roar of a nearby freeway, so too do we come to ignore the morass of ugly utility lines crisscrossing the urban sky. The camera however placed in front of our eye interrupts the brain's natural filtering process; the latest cameras from Sony, Panasonic, or JVC, having no ability (yet) to *exclude, exclude, exclude*!

FIGURE 3.6

The movie in our mind. Without giving it a thought, the eye frames the scene at right, excluding what is not relevant to the story. Your nifty new camcorder or DSLR has no such capability.

---

[1] See Chapter 4 for a discussion of the brain as a digital signal processor.

(a)

FIGURE 3.7

Visual noise can be just as oppressive as aural noise. In framing a scene, the shooter must consciously exclude the clutter that undermines clear visual storytelling.

(b)

MAKE 'EM SUFFER

Just as in any intimate relationship, it's a good idea to consider your loved one's needs. What do viewers *really* want when entering a theater and seeing your images flicker across the screen? Above all, they want to be shown the world in a way they haven't seen before, and they are willing to work hard, even *suffer*, to make it happen.

FIGURE 3.8

Show me a world I haven't seen before! This is your goal, your mission, and your main responsibility as a shooter!

FIGURE 3.9

"Curves Ahead" (Photo of Gypsy Rose Lee by Ralph Steiner).

I recall interviewing the great curmudgeon photographer Ralph Steiner at his Vermont home in 1973. Ralph was one of the 20th century's most gifted storytellers, and his photographs, like his manner of speaking, were anything but boring. One afternoon he clued me in to his secret:

> If you're going to just photograph a tree and do nothing more than walk outside, raise the camera to your eye, and press the shutter, what's the point of photographing the tree? You'd be better off just telling me to go out and look at the tree!

"Constantly searching for a unique perspective is not easy. *It's painful!*" Ralph bellowed, his voice shaking with passion. "You have to *suffer*! Running around with a camera can be fun once in a while, but mostly it's just a lot of suffering!"

This suffering notion is worth exploring because I truly believe the viewer wants to share our suffering. It's a noble reassuring thought. It also happens to be true.

FIGURE 3.10

Interesting angles are an adventure in seeing. They challenge the viewer and increase the perceived value of your story.

(a)

(b)

FIGURE 3.11

No medium shots at eye level! *Not now! Not ever!* Such shots are boring. It's what we see every day when we stroll past the 7-Eleven or DMV office.

(a)

(b)

FIGURE 3.12

Hey! What's in focus here? What am I supposed to look at? Make your audience *work*. Make 'em suffer and they will appreciate you more for it.

FIGURE 3.13a

Shoot far.

FIGURE 3.13b

Shoot close.

FIGURE 3.13c

Shoot high.

FIGURE 3.13d

Shoot low.

FIGURE 3.13f

Shoot down.

(a)

(b)

(c)

FIGURE 3.14

(a) The wide angle lends grandeur to a scene and communicates expanse and scope. (b) This close-up says, "Look at this! This man is important!" (c) Sometimes a close-up may inflict actual pain in an audience, as in the slitting of the eyeball from Salvador Dali's *Chien Andalou* (1929). Most viewers do not appreciate this much suffering!

A UNIQUE PERSPECTIVE

We gain this primarily through close-ups and by (a) placing less important objects out of focus, (b) cropping distracting elements out of frame, (c) attenuating the light falling on an object, or (d) de-emphasizing the offending object compositionally.

FIGURE 3.15

Go close. Get personal. Get in the face of your subject and bear her wrath!

FIGURE 3.16

A shooter searching for a unique perspective will inevitably soil the pant knees. Make sure yours are plenty dirty at the end of the day!

FIGURE 3.17

Selective focus helps isolate elements inside the frame and assigns them a relative value to the story.

FIGURE 3.18

Prudent cropping excludes what isn't helpful to the visual story.

FIGURE 3.19

The adept use of color and contrast helps direct the viewer's eye inside the frame.

FIGURE 3.20

Strong compositions de-emphasize the less essential elements. Here, my son's pointing finger gains weight in the frame while his mom (partially obscured) is compositionally reduced in importance.

OBSCURE, HIDE, AND CONCEAL

The principle of exclusion must be applied with skill and good taste. If you look at great cinematographers' work, you'll notice that many like to shoot through and around foreground objects. This helps direct the viewer's eye inside the frame and strengthen the (usually) desirable 3D illusion.

But what are we really doing by obscuring or completely concealing our subject at times, then revealing it, then hiding it again? We're making the viewer *suffer*. We're skillfully, deliciously, *teasing* the viewer, defying him to figure out what the heck we're up to. Yes, point your viewer in the right direction. Give him or her a clue or two. But make it a point to obscure what you have in mind. Smoke, shadow, and clever placement of foreground objects can all work. The key is *not* to make the visual story too easy to decipher. Make your viewers wonder what you're up to, make them squint, squirm, and *suffer*—and they'll love you and your story for it.

FIGURE 3.21

"What comes lightly is valued lightly," noted America's first postmaster, inventor, and adorner of the $100 bill. No doubt Ben Franklin would've made a great video shooter. Now if I can just see around those damn cumulus clouds!

(a)

(b)

FIGURE 3.22 a,b

The strategic placement of foreground objects imparts mystery in a scene and increases the audience's desire to see around the obstruction. When your audience must make this effort, it is more likely to appreciate the story and your images.

FIGURE 3.23

The 19th-century Impressionists didn't make it easy for viewers and neither should you! Viewing a Van Gogh is an adventure! Your images and compositions should be just as challenging.

MATTERS OF PERSPECTIVE

A shooter's primary responsibility is to represent the 3D world in a 2D medium. Communi third dimension is usually desirable because it helps to promote the illusion of real life, that players operating at a real time in a real place.

For the artist, there are two principal ways to foster the illusion of a third dimension: skillful use of *perspective* and *texture*. Usually we want to maximize both.

FIGURE 3.19

The adept use of color and contrast helps direct the viewer's eye inside the frame.

FIGURE 3.20

Strong compositions de-emphasize the less essential elements. Here, my son's pointing finger gains weight in the frame while his mom (partially obscured) is compositionally reduced in importance.

OBSCURE, HIDE, AND CONCEAL

The principle of exclusion must be applied with skill and good taste. If you look at great cinematographers' work, you'll notice that many like to shoot through and around foreground objects. This helps direct the viewer's eye inside the frame and strengthen the (usually) desirable 3D illusion.

But what are we really doing by obscuring or completely concealing our subject at times, then revealing it, then hiding it again? We're making the viewer *suffer*. We're skillfully, deliciously, *teasing* the viewer, defying him to figure out what the heck we're up to. Yes, point your viewer in the right direction. Give him or her a clue or two. But make it a point to obscure what you have in mind. Smoke, shadow, and clever placement of foreground objects can all work. The key is *not* to make the visual story too easy to decipher. Make your viewers wonder what you're up to, make them squint, squirm, and *suffer*—and they'll love you and your story for it.

FIGURE 3.21

"What comes lightly is valued lightly," noted America's first postmaster, inventor, and adorner of the $100 bill. No doubt Ben Franklin would've made a great video shooter. Now if I can just see around those damn cumulus clouds!

(a)

(b)

FIGURE 3.22 a,b

The strategic placement of foreground objects imparts mystery in a scene and increases the audience's desire to see around the obstruction. When your audience must make this effort, it is more likely to appreciate the story and your images.

FIGURE 3.23

The 19th-century Impressionists didn't make it easy for viewers and neither should you! Viewing a Van Gogh is an adventure! Your images and compositions should be just as challenging.

MATTERS OF PERSPECTIVE

A shooter's primary responsibility is to represent the 3D world in a 2D medium. Communicating a third dimension is usually desirable because it helps to promote the illusion of real life, that is, real players operating at a real time in a real place.

For the artist, there are two principal ways to foster the illusion of a third dimension: through skillful use of *perspective* and *texture*. Usually we want to maximize both.

The lonely highway converging on the horizon is a classic example of *linear perspective.* Linear perspective offers a powerful *monoscopic*[2] depth cue, conveying a strong 3D sense without resorting to *stereographic* depth cues that would require special glasses and complex stereo capture (see Chapter 7). Linear perspective often has a strong storytelling component as well, helping to guide the viewer's attention appropriately inside the frame.

Aerial perspective is gained from looking through multiple layers of atmosphere over expansive landscapes. Owing to the usual high contrast and fine detail in such scenes, aerial perspective is seldom used effectively by shooters with lower-end cameras and equipment.

Besides linear and aerial perspectives, the shooter usually strives to maximize the texture apparent in scenes. This can be achieved through lighting by producing a *raking* effect as in Figure 3.26, or by exploiting the natural quality and direction of the sun as in Figure 3.27.

FIGURE 3.24

Linear Perspective Highway, Kansas. In most cases, the shooter seeks to maximize the 3D illusion. This scene, photographed by the author while bicycling across the United States in 1971, conveys the story of a journey and highway that seem to have no end.

FIGURE 3.25

Aerial perspective seen through increasing layers of atmosphere is common in classical art and photography but is seldom used to advantage in small-format video.

FIGURE 3.26

The texture and shadow in this boy's face suggests that he is real, that he exists. A story in which he appears will also therefore seem more real.

[2] See "3D Shooter" in Chapter 7 for an in-depth discussion of "monoscopic" versus "stereoscopic" depth cues.

FIGURE 3.27

The shadows in this backlit scene strongly suggest a three-dimensional world.

FIGURE 3.28

Reduced texture in the skin is usually desirable when shooting close-ups of your favorite starlet. It can be best achieved via soft frontal lighting, application of a diffusion filter, or enabling the reduced skin detail feature in the camera.

BOX-GIRDER BRIDGES, ANYONE?

Composition plays a vital role in communicating the desired visual message. Consider the most memorable shots from movies, the great pyramids of Giza, and box-girder bridges, and it is easy to see how the triangle can be the source of great strength, lying at the heart of our most engaging and seductive creations.

FIGURE 3.29

The triangle as a source of compositional strength was widely exploited by the Old Masters, as in *The Geographer* (1668) by Vermeer.

FIGURE 3.30

The key points of interest in this travel poster form a triangular pattern.

The essence of developing a shooter's eye is learning to see the triangles around us. These triangles serve our storytelling needs by appropriately directing the viewer's eye inside the frame. In tiny-sensor cameras with great *depth of field*,[3] the relative inability to focus in clearly defined planes means we must rely more on composition and less on selective focus to highlight key picture elements. The video shooter, like a builder of steel-girder bridges, can derive great strength and storytelling prowess from compositions built on the power of the triangle.

(a)

(b)

(c)

FIGURE 3.31

Like steel girder bridges, strong compositions rely on the power of a triangle for strength. Whether realized or not, seeing the world as a series of triangles is a core capability of every competent shooter.

FIGURE 3.32

Is this the beginning of a beautiful friendship? The ensemble cast obligingly forms a triangle in the climactic scene from *Casablanca* (1942).[4]

---

[3]*Depth of field (DOF)* may be defined as the range of objects in a scene from near to far that appear in sharp focus.
[4]Warner, J. L. (Producer), Wallis, H. B. (Producer), & Curtiz, M. (Director). (1942). *Casablanca* [Motion picture]. USA: Warner Bros.

THE RULE OF THIRDS

For centuries, the strength of the triangle has been recognized by artists and engineers. The Rule of Thirds divides the frame into roughly three horizontal and vertical sections, the artist typically placing the center of interest at one of the intersecting panes. A composition built on the Rule of Thirds is the de facto approach for many shooters. Keep in mind this "rule" is in fact only a *tool*, a starting point for further exploration.

FIGURE 3.33

The Great Masters seldom placed the center of interest in the middle of their canvases. As an artist you can apply the Rule of Thirds to achieve powerful compositions. This is Turner's *Dutch Boats in a Gale* painted in 1801.

FIGURE 3.34a

The columns of the Pantheon dwarf the figures at the lower third of frame. Television's horizontal perspective generally precludes such compositions, although this may change with the streaming of content to vertically held mobile devices.

FIGURE 3.34b

The eye is drawn naturally to the laundry lines and couple trisecting this Venice alley.

FIGURE 3.34c

This trio of Bangladeshi women stakes out favorable positions inside the frame.

FIGURE 3.34d

Three pelicans in a triangle are observing the Rule of Thirds. Thanks pelicans.

THE GOLDEN RECTANGLE

Centuries ago, the School of Athens recognized the power of the widescreen canvas to woo audiences. Today shooters have much the same capability, capturing images in the 16:9 format. Most camcorders today no longer shoot 4:3 in any flavor, shape, or form!

FIGURE 3.35

Raphael's *School of Athens*. The Golden Rectangle, aka 16:9, captivated the art patrons of the Renaissance. Audiences today remain no less drawn to the format.

FIGURE 3.36

The Golden Rectangle can be highly seductive! There's a reason credit card companies choose 16:9!

EVOKING PAIN

As filmmakers and storytellers, we usually want to connect with our audience and form an intimate bond. But suppose our story requires just the opposite. Tilting the camera at a *Dutch angle* connotes emotional instability or disorientation. Cropping someone's head off makes that person seem less human. Running the frame line through a subject's knees or elbows is painful and induces the same pain in the viewer. Maybe this is what you want. Maybe it isn't.

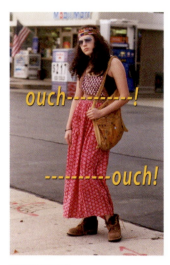

FIGURE 3.37

Ouch! Cropping through sensitive areas of the body can evoke pain in your viewer. You dig?

FIGURE 3.38

When shooting a close-up, the upper one third of frame normally passes through the subject's eyes. Most viewers accept this composition as correct.

FIGURE 3.39

Where is the president traveling today? Respecting cinematic conventions can greatly improve the efficiency of your visual storytelling. Here Air Force One is flying eastward from Los Angeles to New York.

FIGURE 3.40a

A good story has no rules! These "poorly" composed scenes for National Geographic re-created the rocking and rolling earthquake that devastated Mexico City in 1985.

FIGURE 3.40b

A wrecked building after the 1985 earthquake. The Dutch angle helps tell the story.

WHAT KIND OF PLACE?

Every location has a unique visual character. When I scout a location, I ask myself, "Is this place consistent with the story I wish to tell?" Is it a 3D or a 2D kind of place? Is it a wide-angle place or a telephoto place? Recognizing the character of a location and how it may or may not support the *desired* visual story is critical to my success as an effective shooter.

FIGURE 3.41a

Zanzibar is a 3D place. The low sun reveals exquisite texture.

FIGURE 3.41b

Sydney is a bright, pleasant day place.

FIGURE 3.41c

Provence is a 2D place, flat like a painting populated by color swatches.

FIGURE 3.41d

New York is a vertical telephoto place.

FIGURE 3.41e

Prague is a rainy/snowy night place.

FIGURE 3.41f

Los Angeles is a horizontal wide-angle place.

EMBRACE THE THEORY

Effective storytelling with a camera requires that you have a point of view and that you *assert* it. The asserted point of view may be one you're paid to represent, but it is your point of view nonetheless—and it *is* your story, at least visually. So press on. Express your view of the world. Express it with gusto. Make Jean-Paul Sartre proud!

A clear point of view demands precise camera placement, eyeline, and lens choice. After more than 100 years, the conventions of cinema are well established, and today's video shooter would be wise to understand them. Fundamentally, the shooter's craft can be reduced to only three shots:

1. We see the protagonist.
2. We see what the protagonist sees.
3. We see the protagonist react.

That's it. This triptych is then repeated over and over until our documentary, feature film, or corporate program concludes, maybe hours later.

Some filmmakers like the famed French director Jean-Luc Godard may pursue various detours along the way, but most cinema (especially *American* cinema) is constructed on this simple premise. Indeed, one reason why Hollywood stars command such huge fees is because audiences are conditioned to experience the film story though their point of view. This intimacy with the mass audience has the effect of contributing hugely to the market value of a relatively few stars.

The expression of a clear point of view is the hallmark of a great director. In *Citizen Kane*,[5] 25-year-old Orson Welles masterfully used point of view to propel the story. At a political rally, when the scene opens the camera drifts in slowly and assumes a very low angle of Kane the candidate in front of a towering campaign poster of himself. It is soon revealed that the low perspective belongs to Kane's son who (literally) looks up to his dad. As the scene progresses, however, the point of view shifts subtly until we are looking *down* on the candidate; the stature of the candidate is demeaned and reduced by the overhead perspective. This turns out to be the point of view of Kane's political rival, who then goes on to expose the extramarital affair that will ruin the man and sink his candidacy.

FIGURE 3.42

The cinema distilled to its essence: (a) the protagonist, (b) what the protagonist sees, and (c) the protagonist's reaction. Entering the protagonist's point of view quickly helps build intimacy with the viewer. Stories and characters in which the viewer feels a strong connection need not be technically flawless.

[5]Welles, O. (Producer & Director), & Schaefer, G. (Producer). (1941). *Citizen Kane* [Motion picture]. USA: RKO Radio Pictures.

(a)

(b)

FIGURE 3.43

From his son's point of view, Kane appears larger than life, but as the scene evolves the point of view shifts to the condescending down angle of Kane's political nemesis. The change in point of view propels the scene and story forward. For the shooter point of view determines where to place the camera!

CRAFT MATTERS

Given the bulk of assignments today with tiny budgets, shooters must necessarily adopt a more disciplined approach, and because digital video's perceived low cost tends to work against such discipline, the successful shooter must impose the discipline on himself—a challenge to many of us for the same reason that we tend not to eat right, get enough sleep, or go to the gym.

In the days of film cameras and pricey film stocks, the penalty for inefficiency and lack of skills was severe, so the *posers* lurking among us were quickly weeded out and returned to their day jobs. Today such weeding out seldom occurs or at least in quite the same way. Hoping to capture something, *anything*, of use the undisciplined shooter simply churns away, memory card after memory card, until fatigue or boredom sets in, which mercifully finally compels him to stop.

And does it matter if these posers are not getting anything interesting or useful? They keep rolling and rolling. Hard drive space is cheap, they'll tell you, as if that's the issue. OMG!

A better approach is having a clear shooting strategy in the first place. When shooting documentaries, I watch for moments of crossing action, objects entering and leaving the frame, and verbal cues and moments of dialogue that will make for a more easily editable show. It's really a matter of knowing what you want, which also implies knowing what you *don't* want and therefore don't have to shoot.

In the days when the recording medium (film) was expensive, shooters might barely shoot two 35mm magazines for a 30-second commercial. This happened to me on a health club spot in 1980. If I had shot more than 8 minutes of film, I'd have risked being seen as wasteful or incompetent. Now on some assignments, if I don't shoot 500GB by the end of the day, I am accused of dogging it. "What am I paying you for?" I heard one producer complain to me on a recent cable shoot.

C'mon. What are we talking? Sure, bits of data stored in whatever form are relatively cheap. But that's not the whole story. Consider the poor devil (maybe you!) who has to review, log, and capture, the endless hours of rubbish. Regardless of how cheap it may have seemed to roll the camera without any plan or forethought, the shoot-everything-in-sight approach is hardly a wise system. Not by a long shot. Better that the cameraperson edit as he or she rolls and watch *and* listen for the cut points that will make the show later.

Today, despite the advances in technology, there is *still* a severe penalty for a shooter's lack of discipline. Burning through a truckload of memory cards will not save you if you're not providing what the story and the editor needs. In most cases, this means providing adequate *coverage,* that is, the range of shots required to tell a compelling story.

In 1987, I was on assignment in Lourdes, one of the most visited tourist destinations in the world. Every year millions of devout Catholics flock to the grotto in the south of France where the young Bernadette was said to have interacted with the Virgin Mary in 1858. To the faithful legions, the water in the grotto offers the promise of a miracle, and indeed, many pilgrims in various states of failing health come seeking exactly that.

From a shooter's perspective, the intensity etched into each pilgrim's face tells the story, and if there were ever a reason for *close-ups* this would be it. I knew I needed at most two wide shots, the first to establish the grotto and streams of pilgrims and the second to reveal the crutches abandoned at the grotto exit, presumably by those who've been miraculously cured.

In practical terms, I work my subjects from the outside in, meaning I do my establishing shots first and then move in, exploring interesting angles along the way. Thus, the viewer shares in my exploration, as I uncover compelling details in tighter and tighter close-ups.

For an audience, this exploration can be exhilarating. In the grotto, I moved in steadily in back-and-forth angles, the camera riding atop my Sachtler tripod, an indispensable tool for capturing riveting close-ups. Here the close-ups were particularly emotional: the pilgrims' hands rubbing across the well-worn rock, a woman in semi-silhouette kissing the grotto wall, the believers' hands shakily clutching a crucifix or rosary.

(a)

(b)

FIGURE 3.44

This grotto scene from a 1987 Lourdes documentary illustrates good coverage. In the opening shot I establish the grotto. I reverse and work closer in shot 2. Close-up shots 3, 4, and 5 do most of the storytelling in the scene. The pilgrims crossing in shot 6 provide a transition to the tilt up to the crutches (b) abandoned presumably by miraculously cured pilgrims.

CLOSE-UPS ARE YOUR MEAT AND POTATOES

Any shooter worth his lens cap understands that close-ups do most of the heavy lifting. That close-ups should play such a major role should not be surprising as television has been traditionally a medium of close-ups. With laptop computers and mobile devices becoming increasingly popular, the viewing limitations of a small screen are not likely to change; the smart shooter knows that effective stories in the future will continue to rely primarily on close ups to help focus and engage the viewer.

FIGURE 3.45

It's not the amount of footage you shoot. It's the coverage you provide! Partake heartily.

FIGURE 3.46a

A tear running down a cheek. This is a sad story.

FIGURE 3.46b

Getting married. This is the story of a happy couple.

FIGURE 3.46c

Zoe and Theo. This is one incredible love story.

I often describe my job as analogous to a plumber. To assemble a working system I need a range of fittings—a way in, a way out—plus the runs of longer pipe, that is, the close-ups that do most of the work and ensure functionality. Similar to the plumber with boxes of useless tees or elbows, the video storyteller can do little with umpteen cases of tapes or memory cards if he isn't providing the range of shots to craft a compelling tale.

ATTACK OBLIQUELY

Just as a tiger won't attack its prey too head-on, so, too, should you not approach your subject too directly. Sometimes a lazy cameraman will simply push in with the zoom to grab a close-up. This *lazy close-up* should be avoided, because the point of view becomes unclear and the story's natural flow and shot progression are disrupted. Better that the camera come around and unmistakably enter one or the other character's perspective.

FIGURE 3.47

Don't just zoom in! Come around! The lazy close up is confusing because it has no clearly associated point of view.

SHOT PROGRESSION AND FRAME SIZE

The shooter-craftsperson understands the importance of shot progression and maintaining proper frame size. In narrative-type projects employing less professional gear, this can be a challenge because many cameras' controls for zoom and focus preclude a high degree of precision from one setup to the next.

FIGURE 3.48

The story is in the close ups so most shooters want to get in close and stay close, widening out *only* to introduce a new character or event that moves the story forward.

The usual shot progression serves up a series of alternating *singles* of each actor and his respective point of view. If the talent on screen is not consistently sized or if the eyeline is not as expected, the viewer may become disoriented, and the visual story may stall.

To ensure continuity and a smooth, visual story, note the lens focal length and the distance for each setup by referencing a tape measure or a camera readout to ensure accurate placement of talent in subsequent close-ups or reaction shots.

THE POWER OF EYELINE

In the campaign rally scene from *Citizen Kane*, the eyeline from below imparts great power and stature in the Kane character whereas the downward angle has the opposite effect. With multiple actors in a scene, the level and direction of an eyeline helps orient the audience to the geography and relative positions of the players. When shooting interviews, we generally place the camera slightly below eye level. This imparts the respect and authority we usually want without appearing heavy-handed or manipulative.

FIGURE 3.49

Who is heck is the actor at right looking at? Proper eyeline helps ensure a seamless continuity. In this case, the incorrect eyeline suggests a third character has entered the scene.

FIGURE 3.50

A documentary or news shooter must often adjust his position up or down to achieve the proper eyeline. Strong thigh muscles are a must!

FIGURE 3.51

In narrative projects, the focal length, f-stop, and subject distance from camera should be recorded for every setup. On a crowded set a cloth measure (not steel) is preferred because it is quieter, more flexible, and less likely to snap back and decapitate an actor.

SHOOTING THE LESS THAN PERFECT

Eyeline can also serve to de-emphasize shortcomings in an actor's face. A double chin or broad large nostrils are much less noticeable with the camera set slightly above eye level. Conversely, a self-conscious man with thinning hair might appreciate a *lower* eyeline that reduces the visibility of his naked pate.

Here are a few tips to handle more potentially delicate issues:

• Shooting someone with an unusually long nose? Consider a more frontal orientation. For someone with a broad, flat nose consider more of a profile.

• Shooting someone uncomfortable with a facial scar or disfigurement? Turn the imperfection away from camera. If this is not possible, reduce the camera detail, use a diffusion filter, and/or light flatly and frontally to reduce texture in the face.

FIGURE 3.52b

Facial scars and other imperfections may help support an actor's character. Use caution when mitigating, and let the story be your guide!

FIGURE 3.52a

Be careful. In the case of some actors an unusually long nose may BE the story!

FIGURE 3.53

Working with a narcissistic screen star? Be sure to study his or her facial features to determine the most flattering perspective. This is excellent career advice for the aspiring shooter!

THE STORY WITHIN THE STORY

The smart shooter is eager to exploit cues within the frame to more effectively convey the visual story. At public events, protests, and film festival screenings, a plethora of signs and placards can often be seen amid the crowd; use such native elements to give your story impetus and clearly establish the point and the point of view of a scene.

(a)

(b)

FIGURE 3.54

Signage, newspapers, and handwritten placards are great communicators of story. Look to exploit such organic elements whenever possible.

(a)

(b)

(c)

FIGURE 3.55

The "story" of this Uganda school is inscribed on the buildings' walls.

BACKGROUNDS TELL THE REAL STORY

It came as a revelation to me that backgrounds often communicate more than foregrounds or even the subject itself. This is because audiences are suspicious, continuously scanning the edges of the frame for story and credibility cues: Are they supposed to laugh or cry? Feel sympathy or antipathy? Believe what someone on screen is saying or not? The audience seeks such cues in order to determine the *truth* of a scene.

Poor control of background elements may undermine your story and may communicate the opposite of what you intend. In the 1970s, I recall a radical soundman friend who invested every dollar he earned in pro-Soviet propaganda films. His latest chef d'oeuvre sought to equate Watergate-era America with Nazi Germany and to ultimately open the minds of Westerners to the enlightened Soviet system. The world has changed since 1976, and few folks would care to make this movie today, but at the time, intellectuals ate this stuff up.

Now, you have to remember this guy was a *soundman*, so it was understandable that he would focus primarily on the audio story. Indeed, the film was little more than a series of talking heads of out-of-touch university professors and fellow radicals. I recall one scene in front of an auto plant in the Midwest. The union foreman was railing against his low wages: "Capitalism is all about f—ing the working man!" he ranted.

Not surprisingly, the message and film played well in the Soviet Union where officials were eager to broadcast the anticapitalist message on state television. When the show aired, it drew a large appreciative audience much to the delight of government apparatchiks and the filmmaker, but not for the reason they imagined.

In the scene at the car plant, the foreman came across as compelling. His remarks were well expressed, and he *sounded* sincere. But Soviet audiences were focused on something else. Something *visual.*

In the background by the entrance to the plant, viewers could glimpse a parking lot where the workers' cars were parked. This was unfathomable to the Soviet workers at the time that the employees could actually own the cars they assembled. To Russian audiences, the workers' cars in the background told the *real* story; that glimpse and the tiniest fragment of the frame completely undercut what the union foreman was articulating.

So the lesson is this: The most innocuous background, if not duly considered, can have a devastating effect on the story you're trying to tell. *When you take control of the frame, you take control of your story!*

FIGURE 3.56

Is this rickshaw driver pulled over on a busy street or stranded in the middle of nowhere? Background elements not serving the intended story must be removed or de-emphasized.

WE ARE ALL LIARS AND CHEATS

As honest and scrupulous as we try to be in our daily lives the successful shooter-storyteller is frequently required to misrepresent reality. Skateboard shooters do this all the time, relying on the extreme wide-angle lens to increase the apparent height and speed of their subjects' leaps and tail grinds.

I recall shooting (what was supposed to be) a hyperactive trading floor at a commodities exchange in Portugal years ago. I've shot such locales before, with traders clambering on their desks while shrieking quotes at the top of their lungs. This was definitely not the case in Lisbon, where I found seven very sedate traders sitting around, sipping espressos, and discussing a recent soccer match.

Yet a paid assignment is a paid assignment, and I was obligated to tell the client's story, which included capturing in all its glory the wild excitement of what was supposed to be Europe's latest and most vibrant trading floor.

So this is what I was thinking: First, I would forget the wide angle. Such a perspective would have only made the trading floor appear more deserted and devoid of activity. No, this was clearly the time for the telephoto to narrow and compress the floor space to take best advantage of the few inert bodies I had at my disposal.

By stacking one trader behind the other, I created the impression (albeit a false one) that the hall was teaming with brokers. Of course, I still had to compel my laidback cadre to wave their arms and bark a few orders, but that was easy. The main thing was framing the close-ups and filling them to the point of *busting*, suggesting an *unimaginable* frenzy of buying and selling *outside* the frame. The viewer *assumed* from the frenzy of the close-ups that the entire floor *must* be packed with riotous traders when, of course, the reverse was true. What a cheat! What a lie!

So there it is again: What is *excluded* from the frame is more critical to the story than what is included! *Exclude, exclude, exclude!*

FIGURE 3.57

The shooter-storyteller is often required to creatively interpret reality. Using tight framing, a long lens, and abundant close ups, this nearly abandoned trading floor appears full of life.

FIGURE 3.58

Psst. The "speeding" train isn't actually moving. What a lie! What a cheat!

SHOOTING THE ROTUND

Question from reader: My boss thinks he looks fat on camera. Do you have any tried and true ways to make him look and feel thinner on camera? I can't shoot him above the waist or behind a desk all the time.

 Barry B. responds:

 One suggestion: Light in limbo. The less you show, the less you know! You can use a strong sidelight to hide half his mass. Keep it soft to de-emphasize the fat rolls. You can also add a slight vertical squeeze in the NLE [nonlinear editor]. A few points in the right direction can work wonders!

FIGURE 3.59a

Shooting the rotund (before).

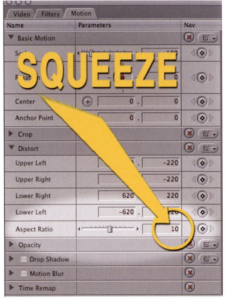

FIGURE 3.59b

Applying the squeeze. Hey, it's a lot quicker than Jenny Craig!

FIGURE 3.59a

Shooting the rotund (after).

KNOW WHAT YOU WANT

It's frustrating to work with directors who don't know what they want, and unfortunately these days, the business attracts them in droves. One reason may be simply the increased number of low- and no-budget productions as newbie directors think it's somehow OK not to do their homework when the financial stakes are low. The experienced shooter can help these shopper types choose a direction by clearly defining the visual story well before the first day of shooting.

 A director's storyboard encapsulates the visual story and helps communicate that vision to the crew.

(a)   (b)

FIGURE 3.60

No shopping allowed! If you're a director, do your homework, know what you want and communicate it to your collaborators. A shooter needs clear direction to do his or her best work!

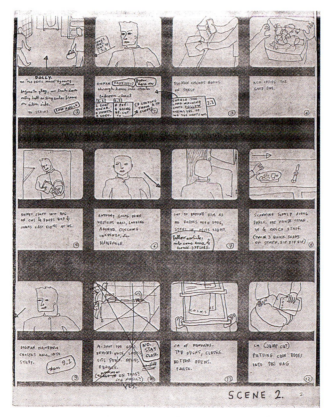

FIGURE 3.61

A director's storyboard is a blueprint of the visual story and shot progression.

WORKING WITH THE EGO-CRAZED

The ability to manage and survive difficult personalities is a skill worth developing. On any given production, you're likely to encounter these types—maybe you're one yourself—so it stands to reason that shooters should acquire the interpersonal skills necessary to collaborate most successfully.

I know a lot about this subject because I used to be one of these difficult people. I took myself way too seriously. Sure I was good at what I did and was widely recognized for it. But I was also a prick. And it cost me in my relationships, the quantity and the quality of my assignments, and the evolution of my craft. It was bad for me on all fronts.

It's no secret that strong personal and professional relationships contribute to our success as a video shooter. This is a business after all where freelancers rule the roost, and most of us work from project to project and client to client. We rely on our relationships almost entirely for our financial and creative wellbeing.

In my own career spanning more than 30 years, I've never had a staff job. As a freelancer, I know one phone call can change my life and whisk me off to some exotic land. This may sound exciting and it is much of the time, but it is also highly unpredictable. No wonder then that freelance shooters in general are such a fearful and insecure lot.

Thus, I have learned only late in life how important it is to separate who I am from what I do. Whether you're an actor, a writer, a director, or a cameraperson, rejection is inevitable. When my collaborators reject my work or ideas, it is *only* me as a cameraman and not me as person who is being repulsed. Yes, I am an artist skilled in my craft and I understand that completely, but I am also

FIGURE 3.62

Egomaniacs. Deal with them. Learn from them. Don't include yourself among them.

FIGURE 3.63

Disagreements with collaborators are part of the creative process.
How you handle these conflicts is pivotal to your success as a shooter-
storyteller, and human being.

able to listen and respond constructively to a collaborator, even when disagreeing to the core with his
or her opinions or unreasonable dictates.

Once I adopted this attitude, I was finally able to grow as an artist. In fact, many of my collaborators' suggestions that I thought asinine at the time I now consider strokes of genius and have integrated
them into my craft and into this book! I am a better shooter and a happier human being for it.

EDUCATOR'S CORNER: REVIEW TOPICS

1. Consider the video shooter's mantra to *exclude, exclude, exclude!* Explain how this principle
   might apply to other cinema crafts—direction, script, sound, acting, and editing. The shooter is
   not alone seeking to exclude elements that may interfere with a compelling story.

2. Explore the wisdom of making your viewers suffer. What strategies can you use—focus, lighting
   and composition—to pursue this noble goal?

3. Think about the critical role of close-ups to convey effective visual stories. Some directors do
   not use close-ups and are nevertheless successful. How do you explain this? What other factors
   might be in play?

4. Discuss the storytelling implications of eyeline and camera placement in the following scenes:
   an interrogation in a police station, a political rally, a mother reprimanding her child, and a day
   in the life of a dog.

5. Every video shooter is a liar. Do you agree?

6. Los Angeles is frequently used as a stand in for New York. The look and light are much different. How do different textures of light impact the visual story?

7. Identify and photograph six (6) triangles in the world around you. Are the triangles subtle or
   relatively obvious? Is there any point to this exercise?

8. Egomaniacs are some of the most successful artists and businessmen in the world. Is egomania
   the price we must pay to excel at the highest levels of our craft?

The Storyteller's Box

4

The onslaught of new cameras and technology can be daunting. If we are to survive this tumult and tell compelling stories, we must accept to some extent the steady bombardment of new formats, cameras, sensors, and all the rest. We've chosen this medium for our livelihood (or serious avocation), and so we must remember the business of video storytelling should be fun even in the face of unrelenting madness. At times, I feel like Slim Pickens in *Dr. Strangelove*[1] cackling atop the A-bomb hurtling to earth. At least we should enjoy the ride to our mutually assured destruction!

FIGURE 4.1

Go ahead! Enjoy the ride! You should relish the power of today's cameras beneath you!

TOO MANY CHOICES

There's a California restaurant chain called In-N-Out Burger. It is enormously successful despite the fact (or *due* to the fact) that its posted menu features only three options: you get a plain hamburger with a medium soda and fries, a cheeseburger with a medium soda and fries, a double hamburger with a medium soda and fries. That's it. No anguished equivocation, no soul-sapping handwringing, no paralysis at the drive-up window. When it comes to burgers, I say yes to despotism and lack of choice.[2]

Now compare the In-N-Out experience with the mayhem that is HD. At last count, there were at least 43 different types and formats of HD video at various frame rates and resolutions. Throw in a dozen or more compression types, scan modes with or without pull-down, segmented frames, MXF,

---

[1] Kubrick, S. (Producer & Director), Lyndon, V. (Producer), & Minoff, L. (Producer). (1964). *Dr. Strangelove or: How I Learned to Stop Worrying and Love the Bomb* [Motion picture]. USA: Columbia Pictures.
[2] I'm told that it's possible to order items off the menu at In-N-Out, but you need to know a secret handshake or code word or something. It's worth investigating.

FIGURE 4.2

You know it and I know it: Human beings are happiest with fewer choices.

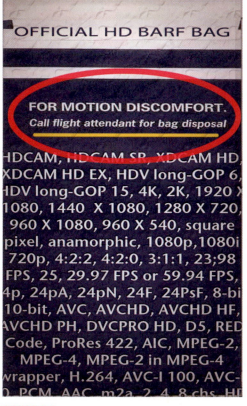

FIGURE 4.3

Nauseating. Really.

MPEG-2, MPEG-4, DNx, umpteen aspect ratios, and pretty soon we're talking about some real choices. Yikes! When I think about this book, I should have included a motion discomfort bag!

Still, one can say with regard to camera technology at least that *newer is usually better.* This means we can assume that the Sony HDCAM introduced in 1997 is not going to perform as well or as efficiently as a Panasonic AVC-Ultra model introduced in 2013. Similarly, in consumer camcorders, we see much better performance in new AVCHD models than in older HDV units grappling with the rigors of MPEG-2.[3]

CAMERAS REFLECT THE CHANGES

Tape-based cameras were inherently fragile, sensitive to moisture, and needed periodic and costly maintenance. The spinning heads and tape transport operated at a constant 60 frames (or fields) per second. The Canon XL1 in 1997 epitomized the tape reality. Recording to a single format (DV) at a single frame rate (29.97FPS), the XL1 offered ruggedness and usability but little versatility.

Zoom ahead 15 years. The solid-state Panasonic HPX370 records 24p in more than 30 different ways, at 1080i, 1080p, 720p, and a multitude of standard definition resolutions. The camera can shoot DV, DVCPRO, DVCPRO HD, and 10-bit AVC-Intra, plus single-frame animation, and various frame rates from 12fps to 60fps—a far cry from the hobbled tape-based cameras of only a few years ago. Table 4.1 provides a vague assessment of the profound discomfort we're facing.

---

[3] AVCHD utilizing H.264 compression is much more efficient than HDV (MPEG-2) at roughly the same bitrate (21–24 Mbps).

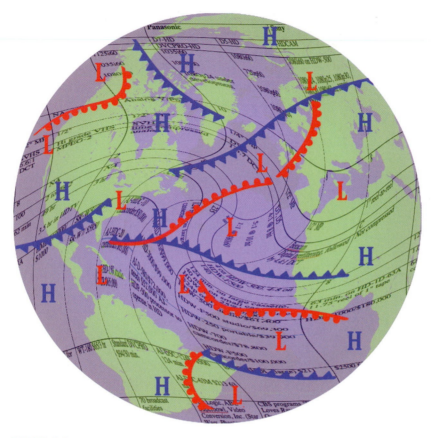

FIGURE 4.4

Don't like the weather? Just wait a minute. The world has seen more than a few video formats blow in and out over the years.

FIGURE 4.5

Go ahead. Pick one.

SONY SxS PRO CARD RECORDING TIMES

FORMATS	RESOLUTIONS / FRAME RATES	8 GB	16 GB	32 GB
HQ Mode (35 Mbps, VBR)	1920 x 1080 @ 59.94i, 29.97P, 23.98P; 1280 x 720 @ 59.94P, 29.97P, 23.98P	25 minutes	50 minutes	100 minutes
SP Mode (25 Mbps, CBR)	1440 x 1080 @ 59.94i, 23.98PsF with 2-3 pull-down	35 minutes	70 minutes	140 minutes

PANASONIC P2 CARD RECORDING TIMES

FORMATS	RESOLUTIONS / FRAME RATES	16 GB	32 GB	64 GB
AVC INTRA 100	1080/59.94i, 1080/30pN, 1080/50i, 1080/25pN, 720/59.94, 720/50p	16 minutes	32 minutes	64 minutes
	1080/23.98pN, 24pN	20 minutes	40 minutes	80 minutes
	720/23.98pN	40 minutes	80 minutes	160 minutes
	720/25pN, 720/30pN	32 minutes	64 minutes	128 minutes
AVC INTRA 50	1080/59.94i, 1080/30pN, 1080/50i, 1080/25pN, 720/59.94p, 720/50p	32 minutes	64 minutes	128 minutes
	1080/23.98pN, 1080/24pN	40 minutes	80 minutes	160 minutes
	720/23.98pN	80 minutes	160 minutes	320 minutes
	720/25pN, 720/30pN	64 minutes	128 minutes	256 minutes
DVCPRO HD	1080/59.94i, 1080/30p, 1080/23.98p, 1080/23.98pA, 1080/50i, 1080/25p, 720/59.94p, 720/50p	16 minutes	32 minutes	64 minutes
	720/23.98pN	40 minutes	80 minutes	160 minutes
	720/25pN, 720/30pN	32 minutes	64 minutes	128 minutes
DVCPRO50	480i (all)	32 minutes	64 minutes	128 minutes
DVCPRO/DV	480i (all)	64 minutes	128 minutes	256 minutes

RED CAMERA STORAGE MEDIA RECORDING TIMES

FORMATS	RESOLUTIONS / FRAME RATES	16 GB CF CARD	RED DRIVE 320 GB	RED RAM 128 GB
RED CODE 28	4K/ 23.98P	10 minutes	200 minutes	80 minutes
RED CODE 36	4K/ 23.98P	8 minutes	160 minutes	64 minutes
RED CODE 42	4K/ 23.98P	N/A	120 minutes	48 minutes

CF CARD RECORDING TIMES

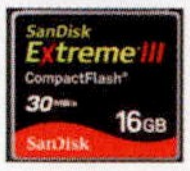

FORMATS	RESOLUTIONS / FRAME RATES	4 GB	8 GB	16 GB
MPEG-4	1920 X 1080/ 29.97P, 23.98P	12 minutes	24 minutes	48 minutes
MPEG-4	640 X 480/ 30P	24 minutes	48 minutes	96 minutes

FIGURE 4.6

The recording times indicated are approximate.

FRAMING THE ARGUMENT

Setting aside the 2K- and 4K-resolution options, the shooter faces a multitude of HD choices at 1080p, 1080i, and 720p. Reflecting industry practice we specify the frame's *vertical* dimension so 1920 × 1080 or 1440 × 1080 is referred to as *1080* whereas 1280 × 720 or 960 × 720 is referred to as *720*. Images may be captured *progressively* like film in a single scan, or in an *interlaced* manner by scanning every frame twice, the odd and even fields merging to produce a complete frame.

There are advantages to each approach. Progressive frames eliminate the temporal (1/50th or 1/60th second) *aliasing* that can occur between fields, thus contributing to the improved perceived resolution at 24p.[4] Many professionals citing The Kell Factor[5] insist that progressive images at 720 deliver higher resolution than interlaced 1080 images, owing to the absence of aliasing artifacts.

Progressive capture has many advantages including more efficient compression in-camera, the ability to shoot at various frame rates, and simpler frame-based keying and color correction in post. There is also inherent compatibility with progressive playback devices such as DVD and Blu-ray players, which owing to the demands of the entertainment industry are 24p devices.

Progressive frames don't always make for superior images, however. When shooting sports or panning rapidly an interlaced frame may provide a smoother, more faithful representation than the same scene recorded at 24p or even 30p.

ABOUT STANDARDS

The "standard" is what everyone ignores. What everyone actually observes is called "industry practice."

Table 4.1 *Format assessment*

This chart assesses the relative quality of SD and HD formats on a scale of 1to 10, uncompressed HD = 10, rough and ready VHS = 1. You may want to take these rankings with a grain of oxide or cobalt binder to go with your In N Out burger.	
Uncompressed HD	10.0
Panasonic AVC-Ultra 200 444	9.8
Sony HDCAM SR	9.4
Panasonic D-5	9.3
Panasonic AVC-Intra 100	9.2
Sony XDCAM HD 422	8.6
Panasonic DVCPRO HD	8.3
Panasonic AVC-Intra 50	8.2
Sony XDCAM EX	7.9
Sony XDCAM HD 420	7.5
Canon MPEG-2 50 Mbps	7.4
Blu-ray (H.264)	7.2
Sony DigiBeta	6.4
DVCPRO 50	5.8
Sony Betacam SP	4.6
HDV	4.3
Sony Betacam	4.0
Sony DVCAM	3.8
DV (multiple manufacturers)	3.6
DVD-Video	2.9
MPEG-1 Video	1.2
VHS	1.0
Fisher-Price Pixelvision	0.05
Hand shadows on wall	0.00001

---

[4] A progressive scan is indicated by the letter p; when referring to interlaced frame rates, we specify fields per second followed by the letter i. So 24p refers to 24 progressive frames per second whereas 60i refers to 30 *interlaced* frames per second.

[5] The Kell Factor specifies a 30% reduction in resolution for interlaced frames due to blurring between fields compared to progressive frames.

Progressive frames captured at 24 FPS are subject to *strobing*, a phenomenon whereby viewers perceive the individual frame *samples* instead of continuous motion. Although the interlaced frame contains a blurring of fields displaced slightly in time, the progressive shooter finds no such comfort so the motion blur must be added in some other way to reduce the strobing risk. For this reason, when shooting 24p it is advisable to increase the camera's shutter angle from 180° to 210°, the wider angle and longer shutter time increasing the amount of motion blur inside the progressive frame. Although this sacrifices a bit of sharpness, the slower shutter/longer exposure time produces smoother motion while also improving a camera's low-light capability by about 20%.[6]

SAFE TRACKING AND PANNING SPEEDS

At 24 FPS, *strobing* may occur in consecutive frames when the displacement of a scene is more than half its width while panning. High-contrast subjects with strong vertical elements such as a white picket fence or a spinning wagon wheel are more likely to strobe. If feasible, it is advisable to shoot at a frame rate greater than 24 FPS and to maintain the higher rate, say, 30 FPS, from image capture through postproduction and output of the edited master.

In many cases, the client or network dictates the shooting format, frame rate, and delivery requirements. If you're shooting for ESPN or ABC, you'll likely be shooting 720p, which is the standard for these networks. If you're shooting for CBS, CNN, SKY, or any number of other broadcasters, you'll probably originate in 1080i. Keep in mind that deriving 1080i from 720p is straightforward and mostly pain-free, but the reverse is not the case. In other words if you're shooting 720p you can *uprez* to 1080i with little ill effect, but *downrezzing* from 1080i to 720p is another matter with substantial risk for image degradation.

Note that 1080 contains 2.25 times more lines than 720. If you need the larger frame for output to digital cinema, then 1080 (preferably, 1080p) is the clear choice. Many cameras can shoot 1080p24, which is ideal for narrative projects destined for the big screen, DVD, or Blu-ray. If you're shooting a documentary or other nonfiction program then 720p is a good option, allowing for easy upconversion later to 1080i, if required.

In general, a camera performs best at its native resolution frame size. Thus, the Panasonic HPX2700 with a 1280 × 720 3-CCD sensor performs best at 720, whereas the Sony EX3 with a native resolution of 1920 × 1080 performs optimally at 1080. As in all matters, the story you choose dictates the right resolution and frame rate. And, oh yes, your client's requirements may play a small role as well.

FIGURE 4.7

Although 1080i has more lines and higher "resolution," the suppression of aliasing artifacts contributes to 720p's sharper look. Error correction applied to the de-interlaced frame in a progressive display may produce an inaccurate result. (Images courtesy of NASA.)

---

[6] Variable shutter is expressed in fractions of a second or in degrees of the shutter opening as in a traditional film camera. The default in most cameras is 180° or 1/48th of a second at 24 FPS.

FIGURE 4.8

When panning across an interlaced frame, the telephone pole is displaced leading to a "combing" effect when the odd and even fields are merged. Shooting in progressive mode eliminates the aliasing seen in interlaced images.

FIGURE 4.9

Interlaced frames capture fast-moving objects more effectively owing to the slight blurring between fields. Progressive frames comprised of a single field must rely on motion blur alone to capture smooth action. Cartoon speed lines are drawn intentionally to mimic the artifacts associated with interlaced images.

FIGURE 4.10

Recent camcorder models offer a range of recording options, including 1080p at 24 FPS. The setting is ideal for output to film, digital cinema, DVD and Blu-ray.

WHAT'S THIS?

1080i24p?? How can a format be both interlaced and progressive? The "1080i" *system setting* refers to the output to a monitor, that is, what a monitor "sees" when plugged into the camera. The second reference is the frame rate and scan mode of the imager, in this case, 24 frames per second progressive (24p).

2K, 4K, AND HIGHER RESOLUTION

The advent of cameras such as the Sony F55, ARRI Alexa, and the RED has raised the specter of *Higher Resolution Folly*. It's an ongoing threat, which we ought to resist, given the implications on our budget, workflow, and efficiency. Still we have to wonder: Is there any benefit to shooting at higher than HD resolution?

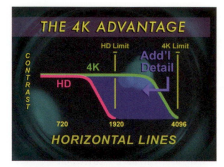

FIGURE 4.11

Two curves plot the contrast of HD and 4K-resolution images versus detail fineness. At 1920, HD's fine detail is maximized, but the lowering of contrast reduces the perceived sharpness. 4K's advantage is apparent owing to the higher contrast retained at the 1920 HD cutoff. Shooting at 2K resolution offers a similar albeit somewhat less dramatic improvement in contrast when output to HD.

(a)

(b)

FIGURE 4.12

Shooting for the cinema (a) at 2K, 4K, or higher resolution allows for greater aspect ratio flexibility, which is based on traditional film sizing. Compare to (b) HD 1.78:1.

For digital cinema applications, the answer is *yes*. Although 1920 × 1080 provides more than ample contrast and sharpness for most *nontheatrical* programming given a good camera, lighting, and the appropriate optics, there is another factor to consider: Just as originating in 35mm yielded a more professional look when outputting to VHS than shooting VHS in the first place, so, too, does shooting 2K or 4K yield a more polished look when output to HD, DVD, or Blu-ray.

The fact is 2K and 4K origination makes our HD images look better! For some shooters, this is reason enough to forego HD origination in favor of higher resolution capture. There are practical tradeoffs of course, but the additional fineness and contrast is evident in the *downrezzed* HD frame.

GRAPPLING WITH THE TECHNICAL

In stories that are otherwise riveting, the shooter needs not be overly concerned with an occasional picture anomaly as a minor defect, such as a hue shift, is not likely to threaten the integrity of the storytelling. Four decades ago, I suspect the U.S. Army recognized The Sound of Color not for its engineering marvel (which was dubious at best) but for its engaging storytelling. The judges appreciated the *feeling* and whimsy of the color and sound interplay. And if the army's humorless engineers can respond in such a way, there must be hope for the rest of us with similar unsmiling dispositions.

Engineers tell us that only 109% of a video signal can be captured before *clipping* and loss of detail occurs. But what does this mean in the context of telling a compelling story? Do we not shoot an emotional, gut-wrenching scene because the waveform is peaking at 110%? Is someone going to track us down like rabid beasts and clobber us over the head with our panhandles?

Some of us have engineer friends, and so we know they can be a fabulous lot at parties and when drinking a lot of beer. Years ago, I recall a tech who complained bitterly to the director about my *flagrant* disregard for sacred technical scripture. He claimed, and he was right, that I was exceeding 109% on his waveform! OMG! Was it true? Was I guilty of such a thing?

I admit it. I did it. But isn't that what an artist is supposed to do? Push the envelope and then push it some more? Fail most of the time but also succeed once in a while by defying convention, exceeding 109%, and pushing one's craft to the brink?

And so that is our challenge: to wed our knowledge of the technical with the demands of our creativity and the visual story. Yes, we need the tools—camera, tripod, lights, and all the rest—and we should have a decent technical understanding of them. But let's not forget our *real* goal is to connect with our audience in a unique and compelling way.

To be clear, my intent is not to transform you into a troglodyte[7] or to launch a pogrom against guileless engineers. Rather, I wish to offer you the dear inspired shooter a measure of insight into a universe that is inherently full of compromises.

WHAT YOU NEED TO KNOW

We discussed how story is the conduit through which all creative and technical decisions flow. Although *story, story, story* is our mantra, it isn't the whole story. Just as a painter needs an understanding of his brushes and paints, the video shooter needs an understanding of his tools—the camera, lenses, and the many accessories that make up his working kit. You don't have to go nuts in the technical arena. You just need to know what you need to know.

Truth is that the shooter's craft can compensate for many if not most technical shortcomings. After all, when audiences are engaged they don't care if you shot your movie with a 100-man crew on 35mm or single-handedly on your iPhone. It's your ability to tell a compelling story that matters, not which camera has a larger imager, more pixels, or better signal-to-noise ratio. The goal of this chapter is to address the technical issues but only so much as they have an impact on the quality of images and the effectiveness of your storytelling.

Consider *The Blair Witch Project*[8] shot on a hodgepodge of film and video formats. Given the movie's success, it is clear that audiences will tolerate a cornucopia of technical shortcomings in stories that captivate.

FIGURE 4.13

The success of THE BLAIR WITCH PROJECT (1999) underscores the potential of low- and no-budget filmmakers with a strong sense of craft. The movie's ragged images were a part of the story, a lesson to shooters looking to leverage low-cost video's flexibility.

[7] A troglodyte is a subspecies of Morlocks created by H. G. Wells for the novel *The Time Machine* (London, England: Heinemann, 1895). The dim-witted folks dwelt in the underground English countryside of 802,000 AD.
[8] Cowie, R. (Producer), Eick, B. (Producer), Foxe, K. J. (Producer), Hale, G. (Producer), Monello, M. (Producer), Myrick, D. (Director), & Sánches, E. (Director). (1999). The Blair Witch Project [Motion picture]. USA: Haxan Films.

But present a tale that is stagnant, boring, or uninvolving, you better watch out. Every poorly lit scene, bit of video noise, or picture defect will be duly noted and mercilessly criticized.

WHEN THE TECHNICAL MATTERS

Every shooter understands that audiences have a breaking point. Often this point is hard to recognize, because viewers are not able to articulate even the most obvious technical flaws or craft failings, such as an actor's face illogically draped in shadow beside a lit candle.

This doesn't mean that these flaws don't have an impact. They certainly do! Illogical lighting, poor framing, and unmotivated camera gyrations all take their toll because the audience *feels* every technical and craft-related defect you throw at it. The issue is whether these glitches in total are enough to propel the viewer out of the story.

FIGURE 4.14

Overexposed. Out of focus. Poor color. Maybe this *is* your story!

FIGURE 4.15

Stay in control! Illogical lighting and technical flaws can undermine your storytelling.

THE TECHNICAL NATURE OF THE WORLD

Sometimes while sitting in the endless snarl of Los Angeles' 405 freeway, I ponder the nature of the world: Is this an analog mess we live in, or a digital one?

At first glance, there is evidence to support the analog perspective. After all, as I sit idly on the 405, I can look around and see the sun rise and set, the sky brightening and darkening in a smooth continuous way. That seems pretty analog. And 99% of folks would agree that the world is an analog place.

But wait. Consider for a moment my ninth-grade science teacher in his horn-rimmed glasses explaining how the eye works. So now I'm thinking this freeway experience is flashing at me at the rate of *15* snapshots per second[9] *upside down* on the back of my retinas. Why then am I not seeing the cars and road-raging drivers like images in a flipbook, inverted, and creeping along with an obvious stutter?

THE PROCESSOR IN YOUR MIND

The brain as a *digital processor* flips the images and smooths the motion by filling in the missing snapshots (*or samples*) through a process of *interpolation.* In math, we call this phenomenon *the fusion frequency*; in science, we call it *persistence of vision*; and in video, we call it *error correction.* However, you describe it the world we know and love may only *seem* like an analog place. It could be a digital mess after all—or some combination of the two.

FIGURE 4.16

Is this an analog or digital mess?

FIGURE 4.17

Each day the sun breaks the horizon and the sky brightens in a continuous way. Yup. The world seems like an analog place.

FIGURE 4.18

Auto everything. Great in low light. Pretty slow frame rate.

LET'S HAVE AN ANALOG EXPERIENCE

Attach a dimmer to an incandescent table lamp. Over the course of 1 second, raise and lower the light's intensity from 0% to 100% to 0%. Plotting this profound experience on a graph we see:

---

[9]Although many scientists acknowledge the sample rate of the eye at 15 FPS, some engineers consider the interpolated frame rate of about 60 FPS as potentially more relevant.

(a)

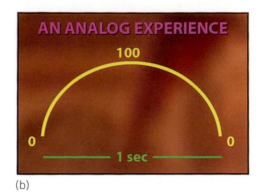

(b)

FIGURE 4.19 a,b

The output of an incandescent lamp (a) is smooth, continuous, and analog. The best digital recording closely approximates the analog curve (b), which is how through our conditioning we perceive and experience the world.

FIGURE 4.19c

Sampling the world at only fifteen 'snapshots' per second we need a LOT of error correction to get through our day!

FIGURE 4.20

Let's play Guess the Missing Sample! If you say "3" you will receive credit on a standard test and be deemed 'intelligent'. But must "3" be the correct response? The x can be any value, but "3" seems correct because we assume the world is an analog place where information flows smoothly. Thus, the brain applying error correction draws a continuous curve from 2 to 4 through the missing sample "3."

IMPROVING OUR DIGITAL RECORDINGS

Our brain's digital processor interpolates missing samples based on analog assumptions of the world. *Compressed* recordings with samples deliberately omitted to reduce file size are prone to inaccuracies when reconstructing the original media file. To reduce the *error correction* required during playback we can better approximate the original analog curve by increasing the number of sample snapshots per second.

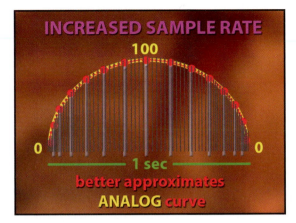

FIGURE 4.21

Increasing the sample rate produces a more accurate representation of the smooth analog curve—and a better digital recording.

A BIT OF KNOWLEDGE

Increased *bit-depth* is the second major way to improve the fidelity of digital recordings. Whereas a higher sample rate reduces the step size and produces a smoother more analog curve a greater bit-depth more faithfully *places* a sample along the curve, thus improving the color precision.

I often ask my students, "What is the most common element on Earth?" I usually receive a range of responses: Someone will suggest iron, which would be correct if we lived on Mars the Red Planet. Somebody else might say water, which isn't an element but a compound. Still other folks may volunteer carbon, hydrogen, carbon dioxide, or any number of other possibilities.

Although nitrogen comprises three quarters of the earth's atmosphere, silicon is the most abundant element in the earth's crust and is the principal component of sand. Essentially free for the taking, silicon belongs to a group of elements known as *semiconductors* because they might or might not conduct electricity depending on the presence of an electron bond.[10] If the bond is present, silicon assumes the qualities of a conductor like any metal. But if the bond is not present—that is, the electrons have gone off to do some work, say, run a Game Boy or charge a battery—the silicon that's left is essentially a nonmetal, a nonconductor.

The two states of silicon form the basis of all computers and digital devices. Engineers assign a value of one to a silicon *bit* that is conductive, or zero if it is not. Your Macbook Pro, iPad, or PlayStation executes untold complex calculations every second according to the conductive states of trillions of these silicon bits.

The CCD[11] imager in a camera is linked to an analog-to-digital converter, which samples the electron stream emanating from the sensor. If the camera processor were composed of only a single bit, it would be rather ineffective given that only two possible values—conductor or nonconductor, one or zero—could be assigned to each sample. Of course, the world is more complex and exhibits a range of grey tones that can't be adequately represented by a one-bit processor that knows only black or white.

Adding a second bit improves the digital representation as the processor may assign one of *four* possible values: 0–0, 0–1, 1–0, and 1–1. In other words, both bits could be conductive, neither bit could be conductive, one or the other could be conductive, or vice versa. In 1986, Fisher-Price introduced the Pixelvision

---

[10] Yeah, I know it's more complicated than this, and we should really be talking about N- and P-type silicon, multi-electron impurities, and covalent bonding. See www.playhookey.com/semiconductors/basic_structure.html for a more in-depth discussion of semiconductor theory.

[11] Charge-Coupled Devices (CCDs) are fundamentally analog devices. Complementary Metal-Oxide Semiconductor (CMOS) sensors perform the analog-to-digital conversion on the imager surface itself.

camera, a children's toy utilizing a 2-bit processor that recorded to an ordinary audiocassette. The camera captured crude images that inspired a cult following and an annual film festival in Venice, California.[12]

Most modern CCD cameras utilize a 14-bit analog-to-digital converter. Because greater bit-depth enables more accurate sampling, a camera employing a 14-bit analog-to-digital converter (ADC) produces markedly better more detailed images than an older-generation 8- or 10-bit model. The Panasonic HPX170 with a 14-bit A → D can select from a staggering 16,384 possible values for every sample compared to only one of 256 discrete values in a 1990s-era 8-bit Canon XL1. Given the range of values available to a 14-bit processor, it's likely that one will be a fairly accurate representation of reality!

FIGURE 4.22

The element silicon contained in sand forms the basis of every digital device. A silicon "bit" may assume one of two states: conductor or nonconductor, zero or one, black or white. You get the idea.

FIGURE 4.23

A 1-bit processor can assign only one of two possible values to each sample: pure black or pure white. A 2-bit processor increases to four the number of assignable values to each sample. The result is a dramatic improvement in grey scale in the captured image. An 8-bit processor produces near-continuous gray and color scales. NTSC, PAL, and most HD formats, including Blu-ray are 8-bit systems.

FIGURE 4.24

The 1986 Pixelvision featured a crude 2-bit processor and recorded to a common audiocassette. The camera's cryptic images have gained an artsy following.

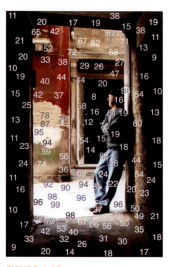

FIGURE 4.25

The world's passageways feature a delicate interplay of light and shadow. To capture the subtlety and nuance, the shooter must have an understanding of analog and digital processes. The luminance values in this Venice doorway are indicated on an analog scale from 7.5 to 100 (NTSC).

---

[12] The PXL THIS festival has been held each year in Venice CA since 1991.

THE 10-BIT WORKFLOW

The value of 10-bit recording cannot be overstated. Given the vast crop of 8-bit formats on the market, 10-bit capture to HDCAM SR, AVC-Intra, or Apple ProRes, enables four times more precise sampling of color and luminance, eliminating or greatly reducing the contour ridges and jagged edges often seen in 8-bit images. Beyond smoother gradients 10-bit capture also enables more efficient color correction and keying especially for green screen applications.

FIGURE 4.26

Images captured at 8-bits may exhibit uneven gradients such as the bands seen across a monochromatic blue sky.

FIGURE 4.27

The Panasonic HPX250 camcorder records in 10-bits to a P2 memory card. Ten-bit cameras capture very smooth gradients and four times more accurate color sampling than traditional 8-bit systems such as XDCAM, AVCHD, or HDV.

IS YOUR CAMERA A DOG?

FIGURE 4.28

I consider two main areas when assessing a camera's worthiness: its performance and its operation, which can be just as important.

- *Does the camera feel comfortable in your hand?*
  Is its shape and bulk ergonomically agreeable? Is the camera well centered and balanced? Does the camera permit easy operation from a variety of positions? Does the camera have a blind side? Can you see approaching objects over the top of the camera?

- *Are the controls well placed?*

  Is focus and zoom easy to access with bright witness marks in the useful shooting range from 6 to 8 feet (1.5–2.5 m)? Are buttons and controls robust and appropriately sized for your hands? Is the zoom action smooth and capable of glitch-free takeoffs and landings? Are audio meters visible from afar and not obscured by the operator? Are external controls (or WiFi) provided for setting routine parameters like time code, frame rate, and shutter speed?

- *Is the camera versatile? Can it operate worldwide?*

  At 24, 25, 30 and 60 FPS? Is both PAL and NTSC output supported? Is 1/100th second or 172.8° shutter selectable for shooting 24p in 50-Hz countries? Or 150° shutter for shooting 25p in 60-Hz countries?

- *Does the camera feature the output options you need?*

  USB, FireWire, SDI, HDMI. Is the HDMI output supported by your monitor at full frame without cropping?[13] Are the plugs and jacks most subject to stress firmly anchored to the camera chassis and not soldered directly to a PC board?

- *Is the camera rugged enough for the intended application?*

  Shooting news? Action sports? Wildlife? Is the camera adequately protected against moisture and dirt? Can it operate reliably in a range of temperatures and conditions? Can the lens housing support an external matte box? Does the mounting surface feature both $3/8 \times 16$ and $1/4 \times 20$ threads?

- *Is the swing out viewing screen practical for use in bright daylight?*

  Does the electronic viewfinder (EVF) allow easy focus? Are focus assists provided, and are they available when recording? Is the focus readout in the viewfinder clear and intuitive?

- *Is the camera insulated from handling and operating noise, for example, from the zoom motor?*

  Is the on-camera mic properly directional and placed sufficiently forward? Are XLR inputs provided and placed to the rear of the camera so as not to entangle the operator?

- *Is the power consumption reasonable?*

  Can the camera run for 4 to 5 hours continuously? Does the camera provide onboard power to a monitor or light?

- *Does the camera feature built-in neutral density[14] filters?*

  Does the camera offer a sufficient range for effective control of exposure?

- *Does the camera feature an interchangeable lens?*

  Is the locking mechanism secure? Is a range of lenses available? Can backfocus be set quickly? Does the camera maintain backfocus through the shooting day? (See Chapter 6.)

FIGURE 4.30

Many of today's camcorders are poorly balanced. This model is weighted substantially to one side making handheld operation inconvenient and wearying over time.

FIGURE 4.29

Compare the Aaton (left), a masterpiece of handheld design to the boxy RED model (right).

---

[13] See Chapter 8 for discussion of FireWire, Serial Digital Interface (SDI), and High Definition Multimedia Interface (HDMI).

[14] Neutral density filter used for exposure and depth of field control. See Chapter 9.

FIGURE 4.31

A badly designed latch makes access to the camera's memory cards unnecessarily awkward especially in winter with gloved hands.

FIGURE 4.32

Larger camcorders may block the operator's view of potentially dangerous objects approaching from the blind side. This camcorder features a low profile and excellent operator visibility.

FIGURE 4.33

The micro buttons are inconvenient for shooters with Bart Simpson–sized hands.

FIGURE 4.34

The lack of real estate in compact camcorders requires significant compromises. This slide switch inconveniently controls iris and convergence in a 3D camera.

FIGURE 4.35

Cable connectors are subject to stress and must be anchored securely to the camera chassis.

FIGURE 4.36

The viewfinder must be large enough to see critical focus and the frame edges. Most camcorders have viewfinders that are too small and lack sufficient resolution.

FIGURE 4.37

The top handle should feature ample mounting points for a light, a microphone, and a monitor.

(a)

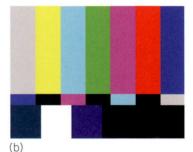

(b)

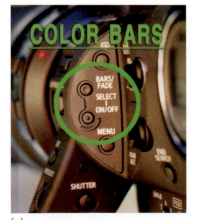

(c)

FIGURE 4.38

Frequenting the bars (a)? Record 30 seconds of bars and tone before rolling on a program. The bars (b) capture the state of the camera at the time of recording and helps ensure consistent audio and video levels throughout a production. Color bars are usually enabled (c) via a button at the side of a camera. Drilling down through multiple menus to select one's bars is a waste of a life.

DOES YOUR CAMERA PASS THE 10-MINUTE RULE?

Some cinematographers believe that deciphering the controls of an unfamiliar camera should not take more than 10 minutes. When a camera is well designed, it does not impose an operational burden, so the shooter's attention can be focused properly on his craft.

The ARRI Alexa is a tour de force of camera design with simple functions and menus in an easy-to-read display. The camera's display panel glows red when recording so the status is immediately obvious from across a set. The major buttons and controls are conveniently laid out and backlit for low-light operation. The camera is well balanced with I/O ports and plugs placed for easy access. Every detail is considered to help a crew move swiftly and efficiently. A great camera is not just about performance!

FIGURE 4.39

Owing to a simple design and layout the ARRI Alexa allows shooters to focus more on what really matters!

DOES YOUR CAMERA PURR LIKE A KITTEN?

FIGURE 4.40

So you've found a camera that passes the ten-minute rule, the buttons and controls are in the right place, and you feel good about the world and the operational efficiency of your machine. So what about its performance?

FIGURE 4.41

- *Consider optics first. And last.*
  Given the high resolution of today's cameras, the quality of optics most determines the quality of images. To achieve good optical performance one need not invest in pricey exotic lenses. Camera makers now routinely apply sophisticated digital correction to the mediocre optics built into low- and mid-price camcorders. Thus, the camera (usually under $10,000) with a noninterchangeable lens may perform significantly better than a comparable model with a swappable lens; the latter arrangement is best avoided in this price range, unless you have a $10,000-plus lens to go with it.

- *Processing sophistication.*
  Modern camcorders employ sophisticated processing to help produce artifact-free images. In cameras like the RED that capture RAW data the complex task of producing a viable image is off-loaded to an external device.

- *Color space*
  Cameras recording 4:2:2 sample the blue and red channels at 50% resolution; cameras recording 4:2:0, AVCHD, HDV, XDCAM, and so on also sample the blue and red channels at 50% but *skip every other red/blue line.* The green *luminance* channel in digital video is seldom compressed. (Read more about color sampling and color space later in this chapter.)

- *Shutter type*
  Traditional CCD (analog) cameras utilize a *global shutter*, which like a film camera exposes the entire frame at the same instant. Most CMOS (digital) sensors scan pixel by pixel line by line, and so introduce a time differential, which when panning or tracking, can lead to a sloping of vertical lines, aka *rolling shutter* or *jello-cam.*

- *Performance-related camera features*

  1. *Variable Frame Rates (VFR)*
     This feature reduces or eliminates *stutter* or *strobing* while capturing fast-moving objects. VFR is used creatively for fast- and slow-motion effects, to render wildlife captured at high magnification at normal screen speed, to add weight to actor's performance, and/or to capture scenes in very low light.

  2. *Shutter control*
     A camera's *coarse shutter* settings of 1/50th, 1/60th, 1/100th second, and so on may be used to increase or decrease motion blur or to eliminate flicker from out-of-sync light sources such as neon or fluorescents when shooting abroad. A camera's *fine shutter, also known as clear-scan or synchro-scan*, can prevent rolling in CRT computer screens and nonconforming TVs and other displays.

  3. *Gamma, matrix, and knee settings*
     These image control adjustments help communicate the mood and genre of your story. See Chapter 9 for detailed discussion.

  4. *Detail control*
     The *detail* or *edging* placed around objects can detract from your camera's perceived performance. News and nonfiction programs may benefit from a higher detail setting whereas dramas usually fare better and appear more organic with reduced detail.

BE SENSOR-TIVE

The CCD[15] is an analog system; the more light striking the CCD, the more electrons that are smoothly and continuously displaced, sampled, and digitally processed. The *charging* of a CCD mimics traditional photographic emulsion,[16] a *global-type shutter* exposing the sensor's entire raster in the same instant.

In most modern cameras equipped with high-resolution CMOS imagers, shooters face a new and potentially more serious disruption to the visual story. CMOS sensors are digital devices composed of rows of pixels that in most cameras are scanned in a progressive or interlaced fashion. The *rolling scan* of the sensor surface containing millions of pixels can take a while, and so we can often see a disconcerting skewed effect when panning or tracking in scenes with strong vertical elements.

Although digital CMOS or MOS[17] cameras are subject to *rolling shutter* artifacts, not all shooters will experience the *jello* effect. It really depends on the nature of the material and the frame. You won't see the vertical skewing in a static interview with the CEO or in the still life of a fruit bowl on a set at NAB. But the risk is real when shooting action sports or aerial shots from a helicopter, so the savvy digital shooter must be well aware.

FIGURE 4.42

High-resolution CMOS sensors consume only 20% of the power of a comparable-sized CCD. The MOS imager, developed by Panasonic, is said to feature improved brightness and smoothness comparable to a CCD.

FIGURE 4.43

The shutter in some CMOS type cameras produces an objectionable skewing effect when tracking or panning across scenes with pronounced vertical elements. CCD-type cameras do not exhibit such artifacts.

FIGURE 4.44

The rolling shutter interacting with a photographer's strobe light may create a truly bizarre effect. A portion of the frame may contain the discharging flash while another section may not. Many cameras now contain a flash band corrector that overwrites the offending frame with parts of the preceding or following frame. In the future, viewers may be more accepting of such anomalies!

[15] A CCD sensor moves an electrical charge to an area where the charge can be processed and converted into a digital value.

[16] Back to the future! One can argue that film is the only true digital technology. A grain of silver is either exposed or not exposed, similar to a bit that is either a conductor or not a conductor, a 0 or a 1. The binary nature of film emulsion seems as digital as digital can be!

[17] Many Panasonic cameras now feature MOS type imagers designed to suppress the uneven color and brightness of conventional CMOS sensors. CCD imagers do not exhibit such variations.

FIGURE 4.45

A rolling shutter may be quite apparent in DSLRs equipped with large CMOS sensors. This model features a 22.3-megapixel (5760 x 3840) sensor, the equivalent of almost 6K resolution in video parlance. DSLRs describe imager resolution in total pixels whereas video cameras only refer to horizontal resolution. This arrangement better accommodates the various frame heights associated with film and video: 2.35:1, 1.85:1, 16:9. 4:3, and so on.

(a)

FIGURE 4.46

CMOS sensors eliminate the CCD vertical smear often seen in urban night scenes.

DAMAGED PIXELS

(b)

FIGURE 4.47

A CCD camera aboard an aircraft at high latitudes may incur cosmic ray damage, which appears later as immovable white or violet dots on screen. In some cameras, the damaged pixels may be masked during auto-black balance (ABB). CMOS sensors are much less susceptible to cosmic ray damage during long international flights.

FIGURE 4.48

Although the performance of digital sensors has improved, many top cameras continue to employ lower noise CCD type (analog) imagers. The Sony F35 utilizes a Super 35mm CCD.

FIGURE 4.49

With improved processing and scanning strategies, today's HD cameras fitted with CMOS sensors exhibit fewer serious artifacts such as rolling shutter.

SIZE MATTERS, SORT OF

In stories that truly captivate the size and type of a camera sensor should not be a major concern. Still at a given resolution, the larger imager with more surface area allows correspondingly larger pixels, which translates (usually) into better *dynamic range* and improved low-light sensitivity. It also enables a shallow *depth of field*, a look fashionable among shooters these days. The longer focal-length lens required to cover the large sensor makes it easier to establish a clearly defined focal plane, which is central to many current shooters' storytelling prowess.

Although a larger sensor offers advantages, the trade-offs may not always be worth it. When shooting wildlife with telephoto lenses, the shallow depth of field can be frustrating and lead to soft unfocused images. Cameras equipped with sensors larger than two thirds of an inch, may be more difficult to transport and hold, owing to the increased weight and bulk of the body and lenses.

Cameras featuring large sensors with a huge number of pixels may also require high compression[18] and/or a dramatically higher data load, which can be crippling from an operational, workflow, and data storage perspectives.

Today's camera sensors range in size from 1/6 of an inch to 1 3/8 inches (35 mm) or larger. Like most everything else in this business, the numbers are not what they seem: When referring to a 2/3-inch imager the actual diameter is only 11 mm, less than half an inch, whereas a 1/2-inch sensor has a diagonal of 8 mm, less than a third of an inch. The discrepancy dates back to the era of tube cameras, when the outside diameter of a 2/3-inch sensor *inclusive* of its mount really *did* measure two thirds of an inch.

FIGURE 4.50

Audiences don't study resolution charts and neither should you! The Canon shoots high definition at 1920 × 1080. The RED Epic shoots 5K at 5120 × 2700 resolution. Which camera is "better"? Which camera is right for the job?

---

[18] See the discussion of **Compression** fundamentals later in this chapter.

THE RESOLUTION RUSE

For many shooters, the illogical numbers game rules the roost, because cameras are frequently judged these days not on performance or suitability for a project but by which offers the largest imager with the most pixels. American cars and trucks were once sold this way: The vehicle with the largest engine was deemed invariably the most desirable.

We discussed how feature films and other programs destined for the cinema must display enough picture detail to fill the large canvas; soft, lackluster images with poor dynamic range and contrast will alienate the viewer by conveying an amateur feeling. Remember your implied message as a shooter: If you don't value the story enough to deliver compelling images, why should your audience value the story enough to invest its time and attention?

Viewers' perception of resolution is determined by many factors, a camera sensor's native resolution being only one. Of greater importance is the exercise of good craft, especially how well we capture and maintain satisfactory contrast. High-end lenses low in *flare* and *chromatic aberration*[19] produce dramatically better images regardless of a camera's manufacturer or sensor type.

FIGURE 4.52

Similar to fine-grained film, HD sensors with diminished pixel size also sacrifice some low-light sensitivity in exchange for increased resolution. Larger sensors with larger pixels tend to have better dynamic range.

FIGURE 4.53

Clipping, compression anomalies, lens defects. At high resolutions, the viewer sees it all—the good, the bad, and the ugly!

FIGURE 4.51

The converging lines in the reference chart suggest how resolution and contrast work together. With improved contrast, the converging lines appear more distinct and higher resolution.

[19] See Chapter 5 for in-depth discussion of lens flare and chromatic aberration.

The proper use of accessories such as a matte box or sunshade is also critical to prevent off-axis light from obliquely striking the front of the lens and inducing flare. Simple strategies like utilizing a polarizing filter when shooting exteriors can substantially improve contrast and therefore perceived resolution.

HUMAN LIMITS TO PERCEPTION OF RESOLUTION

HD in some form or GOP length[20] is here. But why did it take so long? Clearly one problem was defining HD. Is it 720p, 1080i, or 1080p? Is it 16:9, 15:9, or even 4:3? Many viewers with widescreen TVs simply *assume* they are watching HD. This is true especially for folks experiencing the brilliance of plasma TV for the first time. If it looks like HD, it must be HD, right?

The popular demand for larger sensors and higher resolution is fundamentally flawed. Indeed, most viewers are hard-pressed to tell the difference between standard-definition and high-definition images at a 'normal' viewing distance. In a typical U.S. home, the viewing distance to the screen is about 10 feet (3 m). At this range, the average viewer would require a minimum *96-inch* display (fixed pixel plasma or LCD) before perceiving an increase in resolution over standard definition.[21] In Japan where living rooms are smaller, HDTVs higher resolution is more apparent, and so, unsurprisingly, HD gained much faster acceptance there.

> ### VIVA LA RESOLUTION
>
> Can you read this? Sure you can. Now move this page 10 feet away. The text is still high resolution at 300 dpi or more, only now the print is too small and too far away to be readable. So there is a practical upper limit to resolution and how much is actually discernible and worthwhile. Do we need the increased detail of HD? Yes! But how much resolution is ideal, and how much resolution is enough?

FIGURE 4.54

The short viewing distance in stores helps sell the superior resolution of HDTV. Viewers at a more typical viewing distance at home can usually perceive little improvement in definition until they buy a bigger TV or move closer to the screen!

IS THE END GAME NEAR?

The camera sensor in terms of resolution may be approaching its practical limit. Our primary viewing areas, in front of a computer, mobile device, or home TV, aren't getting larger, nor are the screen dimensions at the local multiplex. Fundamentally, there is only so much resolution that we can discern on small screens and mobile devices.

Most shooters will acknowledge the need for a 4K-resolution camera sensor for digital cinema applications. Although an 8K-resolution sensor may be required to produce a 4K-resolution image

---

[20]GOP refers to Group of Pictures. Read on.
[21] Schubin, M. (2004, October). HDTV: High & Why. Videography. Retrieved from http://www.bluesky-web.com/high-and-why.html.

free of artifacts, shooters and manufacturers seem inclined finally to halt the current madness and not go much beyond 4K resolution for the original image capture. In the future, we will likely turn to increased bit-depth or a higher frame rate for enhancement of our images.

FIGURE 4.55

For most applications, including digital cinema. this 4K model may represent the practical upper limit for camera resolution.

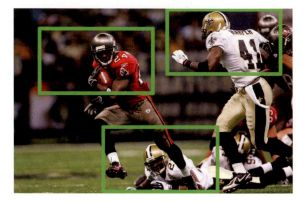

FIGURE 4.56

Intraframe switching? For broadcast coverage of sports, a 4K camera provides the ability to extract multiple 1920 × 1080 frames.

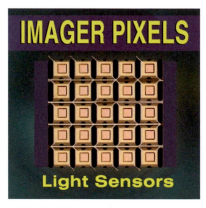

FIGURE 4.57

Camera sensor pixel arrangement in rows.

FIGURE 4.58

In a three-chip camera the green sensor is moved one-half pixel out of alignment relative to the blue and red sensors. The offset is intended to capture detail that would otherwise fall inside the grid, that is, between the regularly spaced pixels.

PIXELS IN A GRID

We've all heard the endless discussions of *film* versus *video looks*. A video sensor resolves focus and edge contrast differently than does film. Film allows a smooth transition from in to out of focus objects due to the randomness of the film grain and the more complete coverage that allows. By comparison, the regular pixel pattern of a sensor is interspersed with gaps so the transition between sharp and not sharp is abrupt and images look more *video-like*— without a shooter's thoughtful intervention.

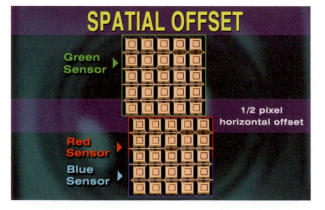

Engineers have long recognized the shortcomings of a discontinuous grid pattern. Although pixels arranged in rows ensure low-cost manufacturing, the regular arrangement thwarts the sampling of detail falling *between* the rows. This relative inability to capture *high-frequency* detail may produce a bevy of objectionable artifacts, including a pronounced, chiseled effect through sharply defined vertical lines.

To suppress such defects in single sensor cameras, engineers employ an *optical low pass diffusion filter.* The slight blurring attenuates the fine detail in high-resolution scenes, which has the counterintuitive effect of *increasing* apparent sharpness and contrast.

FIGURE 4.59

In scenes that contain mostly green tones (as well as in scenes that contain no green at all), a large portion of the image is not offset, increasing the likelihood of artifacts appearing in the finer details.

THREE-CHIP VERSUS SINGLE-CHIP

The three-chip camera utilizes a beam splitter or prism behind the lens to divert the green, red, and blue (RGB) image components to the respective sensors. The result is three discrete color channels that can be precisely tweaked according to the taste and vigor of the camera manufacturer, the compression engineer, or the savvy video shooter.

FIGURE 4.60

(a)

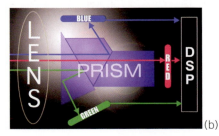

(b)

FIGURE 4.61

Dominating the professional broadcast world for years, three-chip cameras employ a prism behind the lens to achieve color separation. The strategy allows for maximum control of the individual RGB channels at the price of increased complexity.

FIGURE 4.62

Single sensor cameras do not utilize spatial offset. An optical low-pass diffusion filter (OLPF) is used instead to suppress high-frequency artifacts. Many DSLRs do not use an OLPF and are therefore subject to severe image defects in areas of fine detail.

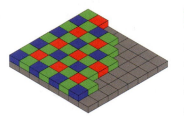

FIGURE 4.63

The traditional single sensor camera utilizes an overlying filter called a Bayer mask to achieve the red–green–blue separation.

CLEANING THE OLPF

FIGURE 4.64

Single sensor video cameras and some DSLRs utilize an OLPF to reduce high-frequency artifacts. Use caution when removing dust from the OLPF. A 10X loupe and hurricane air bulb may facilitate the job. Never use Dust Off—the propellant will ruin the filter's delicate crystal surface!

The three-sensor approach has notable shortcomings. Due to differences in energy levels, the red, green, and blue color components navigate the dense prism glass at different speeds. The camera's processor then must compensate and recombine the component colors as if they had never been split—a task of considerable complexity. Single-chip models without the prism are simpler and cheaper to manufacture, but require an overlying Bayer mask[22] or other technology to achieve the necessary RGB color separation.

---

[22] A Bayer mask contains a filter pattern that is 50% green, 25% red and 25% blue, mimicking the ratio of rods and cones in the human eye. It is named after its inventor, Eastman Kodak's Bryce E. Bayer.

WHY IS COMPRESSION NECESSARY?

We saw how more samples per second produce a smoother, more accurate representation of the ana-log curve that defines our *perceived* experience on Earth. Of course, if we had our druthers, we'd shoot and record all programs with as many bits as possible, and why not? *Uncompressed* recordings with *all* its samples intact obviate the need for guesswork during playback, thus averting the defects and picture anomalies that inevitably arise when attempting to reconstruct the abbreviated frames.

We often work with uncompressed *audio*, as most modern cameras can record two to eight chan-nels of 48-kHz 16-bit PCM.[23] Uncompressed audio may be identified by its file extension. If you're on a PC you're most likely working with .wav files; if you're on a Mac you're probably handling .aif files. There isn't practically much difference. It's mostly a matter of how the samples are arranged and are alluded to in the data stream.

Bear in mind that uncompressed audio (or video) does not necessarily mean a superior recording. At a low sample rate and shallow bit-depth, a telephone recording may well be uncompressed, but it can hardly be considered *good* audio.

CHART: UNCOMPRESSED AUDIO SAMPLE RATES

Telephone = <11,025 samples per second
Web (typical)/AM Radio = 22,050 samples per second
FM Radio/ some HDV/DV audio = 32,000 samples per second
CD Audio = 44,100 samples per second
ProVideo/DV/DVD = 48,000 samples per second
DVD-Audio/SACD/feature film production = 96,000 samples per second

FOR PRACTICAL REASONS

Let's say that in a moment of unexplained weakness, we want to release the 92-minute classic *Romy & Michele's High School Reunion* (1997),[24] *uncompressed* on single-sided single-layer DVDs. The ca-pacity of a disc is 4.7GB. The uncompressed stereo audio track[25] would fill about one fourth of the disc, approximately 1.1GB. It's a big file but doable. Fine.

Now let's look at the big kahuna. Uncompressed standard definition video requires 270 Mbps. At that rate given the movie's run time of 5,520 seconds, we could fit less than *135 seconds* of the glorious work on one DVD. So for the entire movie, we're talking about a boxed set of approximately 41 discs for the standard-definition release!

---

[23] Pulse Code Modulation (PCM) is frequently listed in camera specs to denote uncompressed audio record-ing capability. PCM 48 kHz 16-bit stereo requires 1.6Mbps. Many HDV and low-cost HD camcorders record compressed (MPEG, Dolby Digital, or AAC) audio. Recording compressed audio or PCM at sample rates less than 48 kHz is not advisable for video production.

[24] Kemp, B. (Producer), Mark, L. (Producer), Rothschild, R. L. (Producer), Schiff, R. (Producer), & Mirkin, D. (Director). (1997). Romy and Michele's High School Reunion [Motion picture]. USA: Touchstone Pictures.

[25] PCM 48-kHz 16-bit stereo audio at 1.6Mbps.

Venturing further into the macabre, let's consider the same title transferred to DVD as *uncompressed HD*. At the staggering rate of *1,600 Mbps*, each disc would run a mere 22 seconds, and the size of the collector's boxed set would swell to a whopping 253 discs! Loading and unloading that many discs every half a minute is tantamount to serious calisthenics. Clearly it makes sense to reduce the movie's file size to something more manageable and marketable.

REDUNDANCY, REDUNDANCY

What do compressors want? What are they looking for? The goal of every compressor is to reduce the movie file size in such a way that the viewer is unaware that some samples (indeed *most* samples, about 98% for a DVD!) have been deleted.

Compressors work by identifying *redundancy* in the media file. A veteran shooter may recall holding up a strip of film to check for a scratch or to read an edge number. He may have noticed that in a given section, one frame seemed hardly different from the next. In other words, there seemed to be *redundancy* from frame to frame.

Video engineers also recognized that redundancy occurred *within* the frame. Consider a winter landscape in New England, a group of kids playing in the snow under a slate gray sky. An HD camcorder framing the scene divides the idyllic tableau into blocks as small as 4 × 4 pixels, the camera compressor evaluating each block across the monochromatic sky and sensing little difference from block to block.

So the data and bits from the redundant blocks are deleted, and a message is placed in a *descriptor* file instructing the playback device when reconstructing the frame to repeat the information from the first block in subsequent blocks. To the shooter, this gimmickry is dismaying because the sky is not in fact uniform, but actually contains subtle variations in color and texture. So I'm wondering as a shooter with a modicum of integrity: *Hey! What happened to my detail?*

FIGURE 4.65

In a strip of film, one frame appears hardly different from the next or previous frames. Compression schemes take advantage of this apparent redundancy to reduce file size.

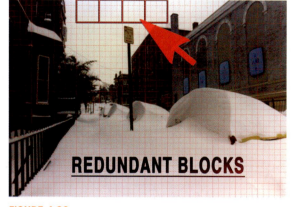

REDUNDANT BLOCKS

FIGURE 4.66

The HD compressor divides the frame into blocks as small as 4 × 4 pixels. The blocks in the sky are deemed "redundant"; their pixel data is replaced with a mathematical instruction to the player to repeat the values from a previous block when reconstructing the frame.

FIGURE 4.67

Compression can be ruthless as samples inside a block are subject to *quantization*, a profiling process by which pixels of roughly the same value are rounded off, declared "redundant," and then discarded. Such shenanigans can lead to the loss of detail and artifacts when playing back a compressed file. (Images courtesy of JVC.)

YOU DON'T MISS WHAT YOU CAN'T SEE

The imperative to reduce file size leads engineers into the realms of human physiology and perception. The eye contains a collection of *rods and cones*. The rods measure the brightness or *luminance* of objects; the cones measure the color or *chrominance*. We have *twice* as many rods as cones, so when we enter a dark room, we can discern the outline of the intruder looming with a knife but not the color of dress she is wearing.

Engineers understand that humans are unable to discern fine detail in dim light. Because we can't see the detail anyway, they say, we won't notice or care if the detail is discarded. Thus, the engineers look to the shadows primarily to achieve their compression goals, which is why deep, impenetrable blacks are such a problem for shooters working in highly compressed formats such as HDV.

When considering the notion of *color space* engineers mimic the ratio of rods and cones in the human eye. Accordingly, your camera shooting 4:2:2[26] samples a pixel's *luminance* ("4") at twice the rate of its *chrominance* as measured in the blue and red channels. The 4:2:0 color space used in formats such as AVCHD and XDCAM further suppress the red and the blue sampling—because you'll never notice, right?—in order to achieve a greater reduction in file size.

---

[26]The "4" in 4:2:2 indicates the full resolution *luminance* value of a pixel sampled four times per cycle: 4 × 13.5 million times per second in SD; 4 × 74.25 million times per second in HD.

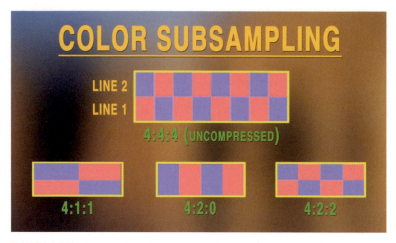

FIGURE 4.68

Owing to the eye's relative insensitivity to red and blue we need not sample for most applications at full-resolution RGB. Although the luminance bearing the green component is invariably sampled at full resolution because the eye is most sensitive to mid-spectrum wavelengths, the blue and red channels are sampled at only one-half resolution, that is, 4:2:2. When recording 4:2:0, the red and blue channels are alternately sampled at 50%, skipping every other vertical line.

FIGURE 4.69

In a dark room, the color information in the dress is difficult to perceive. It is therefore deemed "irrelevant" and may be discarded. Or so the thinking goes.

INTERFRAME VERSUS INTRAFRAME COMPRESSION

In formats like DV, DVCPROHD, and AVC-Intra, compression is applied *intraframe* only, that is, *within* the frame. This makes sense since the capturing of discrete frames is consistent with the downstream workflow that requires the editing, processing, and pretty much everything else including color correction, at a frame level.

To further reduce file size and storage requirements, AVCHD, HDV, and DVD-Video, utilize *interframe* as well as intraframe compression. In these more compressed formats, the *minimum decodable unit* is not the frame (as in film and most professional formats) but the *group of pictures (GOP)*, composed usually of 15 frames reduced by hook and by crook to a single reference *intra* or *I-frame*. Within the GOP, the fields, frames, and fragments of frames deemed redundant or irrelevant are discarded, and no data is written. Instead, a mathematical message is left in the GOP *header* instructing the player how to resurrect the missing frames or bits of frames based on embedded cues.

Bidirectional and *predictive frames* enable long-GOP formats to *anticipate* and *complete* action inside the group of pictures. This scheme of I, B, P frames seeks to identify and fill in events, by referencing the previous I-frame; the forward-looking P-frame and B-frame looking forward *and* back to track changes inside the GOP interval.

H.264, also known as *AVC (Advanced Video Codec*[27]*)*, utilizes a system of bidirectional prediction that looks ahead or back over an *entire* video stream, substantially increasing the processing and encoding times. H.264 may be implemented as either long GOP, as in AVCHD cameras, or *intraframe*, as found notably in Panasonic AVC-Intra models.

FIGURE 4.70

Although the frame is the minimum decodable unit for most pro video, the GOP is the basic unit for HDV, AVCHD, and XDCAM cameras that utilize interframe compression. A GOP size of 15 frames is typical—retaining only one complete frame about every half second!

FIGURE 4.71

As pedestrians enter and leave the GOP, the background building is revealed and must be interpolated. Clues recorded during encoding enable a player to reconstruct the missing portions of frames by referencing the initial I-frame—the only complete frame in a GOP. AVCHD cameras utilize long-GOP H.264 to achieve a dramatic reduction in file size.

---

[27] A **co**mpressor/**dec**ompressor, or "codec," is a strategy for encoding and decoding a digital stream.

MINIMUM DECODABLE UNIT

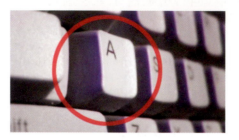

FIGURE 4.72

A computer's minimum decodable unit is the *byte*, the 8-bit sequence that defines each stroke or key on a 256-character keyboard. In pro video, the minimum decodable unit is usually the frame. In formats such as XDCAM HD/EX, HDV, and DVD-Video, the minimum unit is the *GOP*. Most NLEs must decompress the long-GOP formats in real time to enable editing at the frame level. A fast computer and use of an intermediate format such as Apple ProRes or Avid DNxHD is normally used to facilitate this.

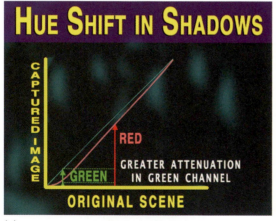

(a)

(b)

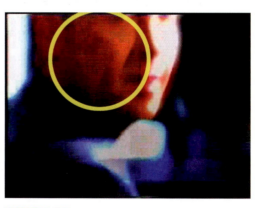

FIGURE 4.74

Compression anomalies like macroblocking are more noticeable in the shadows so the shooter should look there first for trouble. Cameras displaying such artifacts, especially in the facial shadows, should be rejected.

FIGURE 4.73

In low light, owing to the uneven compression, some cameras attenuate green wavelengths more than red, so shadow areas acquire a warm cast. Hue shifts are more likely to occur in Caucasian skin due to the predominant red tones.

SELECTING A FRAME RATE

Beyond the requirements of a network or client, the choice of frame rate is a function of the story. For news or sports captured at 30 or 60 FPS, the higher frame rate reflects the feeling of immediacy in a world of breaking stories, city council meetings, and endless police chases. The 30-FPS look is ideal for reality TV, corporate programs, and documentaries, when a clean, contemporary feel is desired.[28] Thirty frames per second allow easy down-conversion from HD to NTSC[29] and the Web, where video streaming at 15 FPS is the norm.

For dramatic applications, 24p offers the shooter a more filmic look rooted firmly in the past tense. Reflected in the actors' slightly truncated movements 24p communicates the sense of the classic storyteller seated by a campfire captivating his audience. In a show's first images the 24p flicker across a screen says, "*Oh, let me tell you a story . . .*"

Beyond the feel and story implications of 24p the frame rate provides ideal compatibility with display platforms such as DVD and Blu-ray. Given the near-universal support for 24p in postproduction, the shooter-storyteller can capture, edit, and output 24p without incurring the wrath of NTSC artifacts or encoder snafus stemming from the *2:3 pulldown*[30] inserted to produce a 29.97 FPS video stream.

WHY THE GOOFY FRAME RATES—OR WHY 24P ISN'T 24P?

In video as in much of the modern world there seems to be a paucity of honesty. So when we say 30p, we really mean *29.976* progressive frames per second; when we say 24p, we usually mean *23.976* progressive frames per second; and when we say 60i, we really mean *59.94* interlaced fields per second. This odd frame rate business is the legacy of 1950s' NTSC, which sadly instituted a 29.97 frame rate and not a more cogent and logical 30.00 FPS.

You may recall how we faded a light up and down for one second and we all shared and marveled at the seeming analog experience. We understood our eye *actually* witnessed the event as a series of 15 (or so) snapshots per second, but the signal processor in our brains applied *error correction*, interpolated the "missing" frames, and produced the perception of smooth, continuous *analog* motion.

The error correction we apply is evident in a child's flipbook. Flip through the book too slowly and we see the individual snapshots. But flip through a bit faster and our brains are suddenly able to fuse the motion by fabricating the *missing* samples.

---

[28] For general broadcast, 30 frames per second provides optimal compatibility with 60 Hz facilities. In 50 Hz countries, 25 FPS is the broadcast standard for standard- and high-definition TV.

[29] **The National Television Standards Committee (NTSC)** met in 1941 to establish the frame rate and resolution for broadcast television. Although a 525 line/60 field standard was adopted, one member Philco championed an 800-line standard at 24 FPS. NTSC is often humorously referred to as *Never Twice the Same Color.* It is used most notably in the United States, Canada, and Mexico.

[30] The term *pulldown* refers to the mechanical process of "pulling" film down through a projector. A *2:3 pulldown* pattern enables playback of 24p video at 30 FPS (actually 29.97 FPS) on a NTSC television. The blending of frames and fields leads to a loss of sharpness when encoding to DVD and Blu-ray.

In the early days of cinema in the nickelodeons of 1900, silent films were normally projected at 16 to 18 FPS, which is above the threshold for most of us to see continuous motion but is not quite fast enough to eliminate the *flicker*, a residual perception of the individual frame samples. Audiences in 1900 found the flicker so distracting that moviegoers more than a century later still refer to this past trauma as going to see a *flick*.

Seeking a solution engineers could have simply increased the frame rate of the camera and projector and thereby delivered more samples per second to the viewer. But this would have entailed more film and greater expense. As it was, the increase in frame rate to 24 FPS did not occur until the advent of sound in 1928, when talking pictures required the higher frame rate in order to achieve satisfactory audio fidelity.

When film runs through a projector, each frame is drawn into the gate and stops. The spinning shutter opens and the frame is projected onto the screen. The shutter continues around and closes again, and a new frame is pulled down. The process is repeated in rapid succession, which our brains fuse into a continuous motion.

To reduce flicker, engineers *doubled* the rotational speed of the *shutter* so that each frame was projected *twice*. This meant that viewers at 16 FPS actually experienced the visual story at 32 samples per second; compare this to the viewers of today's 24 FPS movies who see 48 samples per second projected at the local multiplex.

The imperative to reduce flicker continued into the television era. Given the 60-Hz main frequency in North America and the need for studios, cameras, and television receivers to all synchronize to it, it would have been logical to adopt a 60 FPS standard, except, that is, for the need to sample every frame twice to reduce flicker.[31]

So engineers divided the frame into odd and even *fields* producing an interlaced pattern of *60 fields* or the equivalent of 30 frames per second. Fine. Thirty frames per second is a nice round number. But *then* what happened?

With the advent of color in the 1950s, engineers were desperate to maintain compatibility with the exploding number of black-and-white TVs entering the market. The interweaving of color information in the black-and-white signal produced the desired compatibility but with an undesirable consequence: Engineers noted a disturbing audio interference with the color *subcarrier*, which they deduced could be remediated by the slight slowing of the video to 29.97 FPS.

This seemingly innocuous adjustment is today the ongoing cause of much angst and woe. When things go wrong as they tend to—bad synchronization, dropped frames, an inability to input a file into the DVD encoder—we always *first* suspect a frame rate or a time code snafu related to the 29.97/30 FPS quagmire. Even as we embrace HD, the need persists to *down-convert* programs to NTSC or PAL for broadcast or DVD. Thus, we continue to struggle mightily with the legacy of NTSC's goofy frame rate, particularly as it pertains to timecode. I discuss the NTSC's dueling timecode systems in Chapter 8.

So herein lies the rub: Given NTSC's 29.976 FPS standard, it makes sense then to shoot 24p at 23.976 FPS, with the six-frame boost to standard definition being very straightforward, and thereby avoiding the mathematical convolutions that degrade image quality. Alas, NTSC's odd frame goofiness lives on!

---

[31] In audio, this dual-sample requirement is known as *Nyquist's Law*. When CD audio was being devised in the 1970s engineers looked to a young child with unspoiled hearing. Determining a maximum perceived frequency of 22050 Hz, engineers doubled the value to reduce *flicker* and established the 44100 Hz sample rate standard for CD audio.

THE MANY FLAVORS OF 24P

For shooters with aspirations in feature films and dramatic productions the advent of 24p was a significant milestone with improved resolution and a more cinematic look. Before 2002, cost-conscious filmmakers engaged in various skullduggery like shooting 25 FPS PAL[32] to achieve the desired progressive look and feel. That changed with the introduction of the Panasonic DVX100 that offered 24p for the first time in a camcorder recording to DV tape.

SHOOTING 24P FOR DVD AND BLU-RAY

Since DVD's introduction in 1996 movie studios originating on film have encoded their movies at 24 FPS for native playback on a DVD player. Relying on the player to perform the required conversion to standard definition at 29.97 FPS, the shooter can pursue an all-24p workflow and avert NTSC's most serious shortcomings, while *also* reducing the program file size by 20%— not a small amount in an era when producers are jamming everything and the kitchen sink on a DVD or Blu-ray disc.

FIGURE 4.75

Every DVD and Blu-ray player is inherently a 24p device. This is a compelling reason for many shooters to originate in 24p.

SO YOU'RE SHOOTING 24P

During the last decade, camera manufacturers have devised various schemes to record 24 FPS. The Panasonic DVX100 recording to tape offered *two* 24p recording modes, which continue to be relevant in solid-state P2 and AVCCAM models. In *standard* mode, images are captured progressively at 24 frames per second (actually 23.976) then converted to 60 interlaced fields (actually 59.94) using

---

[32]**Phase Alternating Line (PAL)** is an NTSC-derived television system adopted in Europe and much of the 50 Hz world in the 1970s. PAL operates invariably at 25.000 frames per second and so averts NTSC's ugly frame rate intrigue. Some folks cite PAL's superior 625-line resolution compared to NTSC's 525, but the NTSC has more fields/frames per second. Some industry pros and stand-up comics in North America refer to PAL as "Pay A Lot."

a conventional *2:3 pulldown*. After recording to tape or flash memory and capturing into the NLE,[33] the editing process proceeds on a traditional 60i timeline.

In 24pA (advanced) mode, the 24-frame progressive workflow is maintained from image capture through output to DVD, Blu-ray, or hard drive. The camera scans progressively at 24 frames per second, but the 60i conversion to tape or flash memory is handled differently. In this case, the 24p cadence is restored in the NLE upon ingestion by removing the extra frames inserted temporarily during capture to facilitate capture and monitoring at 60i.

For shooters reviewing takes with their directors, it is important to note that playback of 24pA footage displays a pronounced stutter due to the temporarily inserted frames. This is completely normal and is not to be construed as just another cameraman screw up!

FIGURE 4.76

Every manufacturer handles 24p differently. Canon's inscrutable "24F" format derives a progressive scan from an interlaced imager—a complex task! Some Sony 24p cameras output "24PsF," comprised of two identical (segmented) fields per frame. Although 24p playback with pulldown appears smoother, the 24PsF video may seem sharper.

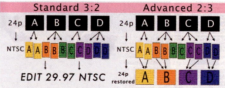

FIGURE 4.77

In 24p standard mode, progressive images are captured at 23.976 FPS and then are converted to 29.976 FPS (60i) by adding 2:3 pull-down. The process merges every second or third field and contributes to 24p's slightly stuttered film look. Footage recorded in 24p standard mode is treated like any other 60i asset in the NLE timeline. Images captured in advanced mode are also scanned progressively at a nominal 24 FPS, but in this case, entire frames are inserted to make up the 29.976 time differential; these extra frames are then subsequently removed during ingestion into the NLE. In this way, the shooter can maintain a favorable 24p workflow and avert the NTSC interlacing artifacts when encoding to DVD, Blu-ray, or digital cinema.

[33]**NLE** = nonlinear editor, such as Avid, Final Cut Pro, and Adobe Premiere Pro, among others. Older linear editing systems required assembly of images and sound in a predetermined sequence, making frequent revisions and updates awkward and inefficient.

FIGURE 4.78

Freed from the shackles of videotape and a mechanical transport solid-state camcorders are able to record individual frames just like a film camera. Recording only the desired "native" frames reduces by up to 60% the required storage when recording 24p to flash memory.

IF SD STILL LIVES WITHIN YOU

It doesn't make you a bad person. Maybe HD just isn't your thing. Or maybe you're leery of HDV's high compression, the 6 times greater bandwidth, or AVCHD's long-GOP construction that can instill convulsions in the NLE timeline. Maybe the tapeless workflow seems too daunting, or you're shooting a cop show late at night and you need the low-light capability that only your old SD camcorder can deliver—about two stops better sensitivity on average than a comparable-class HD or HDV model.

FIGURE 4.79

Standard definition still rules the roost in many parts of the world. The adoption of HD for broadcast in countries in Africa is a decade away—at least.

ATTENTION LAGGARDS!

Until recently, when our stories originated invariably on videotape, we felt a comfort in the tangible nature of the medium. We knew tape well, even with its foibles, and had a mature relationship with it, like a 30-year marriage. At the end of the day, we might have griped and sniped at our long-term partner, but then it was off to bed after supper and television and all was well with the world.

(a)

(c)

(b)

FIGURE 4.80 a,b,c

We could see it, feel it, watch the innards turning. The mechanical world of videotape was comforting, until, uh—it wasn't.

(d)

FIGURE 4.80d

I think we've had quite of enough of you, thank you.

FIGURE 4.81

Who has the tapes? Production folks nervously pose this question after every shooting day. With tapeless cameras, the manner of handling and safeguarding original camera footage is critical.

ONCE UPON A TIME

In an era of blue-laser recording and flash memory, the dragging of a strip of acetate and cobalt grains across an electromagnet seems crude and fraught with peril. Condensation can form and shut a camera down. A roller or a pincher arm can go out of alignment and cause the tape to tear or crease, or produce a spate of tracking and recording anomalies. And there is the dust and debris that can migrate from the edges onto the tape surface and produce ruinous dropouts.

Today's tape shooters no longer face quite the same perils. Although clogged heads and the occasional mechanical snafu still affect some recordings, the frequent dropouts from edge debris are no longer a serious risk if we use master-quality media.[34]

TALE OF DV TAPES

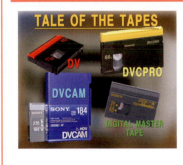

Apart from the physical cassette and robustness of the media, there is no quality difference among DV, DVCAM, and DVCPRO formats. It is not advisable to mix brands of tape as the lubricants used by different manufacturers may interact and cause head clogs or corrosion leading to dropouts. Be loyal to a single brand of tape if you can!

FIGURE 4.82

[34] A **dropout** is a loss of data caused by the lifting of a record head from the tape surface as a result of dirt or debris. **Read errors** have multiple causes, including deteriorated tape, worn record or playback heads, or elevated tape hiss that can obscure a signal.

We should always exercise care when handling videotape. Carelessly tossing loose tapes into the bottom of a filthy knapsack is asking for trouble. Shooting in unclean locations such as a factory or along a beach amid blowing sand can also be conducive to dropouts as grit can penetrate the storage box, the cassette shell, and the tape transport itself.

Dirt and other contaminants can contribute substantially to tape deterioration over time. The short shelf life of MiniDV tapes (as little as 18 months) should be of concern to producers who routinely delete original camera files from their drives, and rely solely on the integrity of the camera tapes for backup and archiving.

FIGURE 4.83

No swallowed tapes in this puppy! And this camcorder has a 5-year warranty!

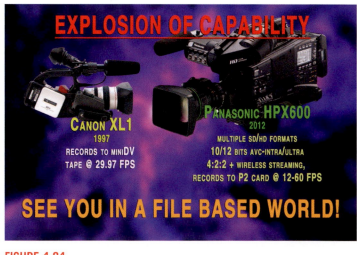

FIGURE 4.84

Table 4.2 The most popular HD, 2K, and 4K formats at a glance.

FORMAT	Resolution	Data Rate	Raster Size	Aspect Ratio	Audio
HDV	720p/24/25/30/60 1080i/50/60 1080p/24/25//30	19.2 Mbps 25 Mbps 25 Mbps	1440 × 1080 1280 × 720	16:9	MPEG-1 L2 PCM MPEG-1 Level 2 MPEG-1 Level 2
AVCHD	720 × 480 NTSC 720 × 576 PAL 720p/24/50/60 1080i/24/50/60	< 24 Mbps	1440 × 1080 1920 × 1080	4:3/16:9 4:3/16:9 16:9 16:9	1–7.1 PCM 1–7.1 PCM 1–5.1 ch. AC3 1–5.1 ch. AC3
AVC-INTRA 100 AVC-ULTRA 200	720p/24/25/50/60 1080i/24/25/50/60	50/100/ 200 Mbps	960 × 720 1280 × 720 1440 × 1080 1920 × 1080	16:9	1–4 ch. PCM
DVCPRO HD	1280 × 720 1080i/50 1080i/60	40–100 Mbps	960 × 720 1440 × 1080 1280 × 1080	16:9	1–4 ch. PCM
XDCAM HD	1080i/50/59.94 1080p/23.98/ 25/29.97	< 35 Mbps	1440 × 1080	16:9	1–4 ch. PCM
XDCAM EX	720p/23.98/25/ 29.97/50 59.94 1080i/50/59.94 1080i/50/59.94 1080p/23.98/ 25/29.97	< 35 Mbps	1280 × 720 1440 × 1080 1920 × 1080 (effective) 1920 × 1080 (effective)	16:9	1–2 ch. PCM
DVD-VIDEO	720 × 480 720 × 576	< 9.8 Mbps		4:3/16:9	PCM / AC3 / DTS
BLU-RAY	720 × 480 NTSC 720 × 576 PAL 720p/23.976/24/ 50/59.94 1080/23.976/24/ 50/59.94	< 36 Mbps	720 × 480 720 × 576 1280 × 720 1440 × 1080 1920 × 1080	4:3/16:9 4:3/16:9 16:9 16:9 16:9	PCM / AC3 / DTS

EDUCATOR'S CORNER: REVIEW TOPICS

1. Discuss the relative merits of shooting progressive versus interlaced. For what applications might shooting 50i or 60i be appropriate? Live TV? Broadcast?
2. Consider the factors that have an impact on perceived resolution. Is greater resolution always better? Under what conditions might *less* resolution be desirable?
3. How does camera sensor size impact workflow and the images you present to the world? Explore the notion of more or less depth of field. Consider the aesthetic and practical aspects of shooting with a narrow focus.
4. Explain the two (2) major ways to improve digital recordings. Why does more compression increase the risk of noise and objectionable artifacts?
5. Explain 4:2:2 and 4:2:0 color sampling. How does a 10- or 12-bit workflow substantially improve the quality of images?
6. Consider your next camera. Identify eight (8) features that are important to you in terms of performance and operation.
7. Salespeople have been saying this for years: Digital is better than analog. Do you agree?
8. Discuss the advantages, if any, of long-GOP formats like XDCAM EX and HDV compared to *intraframe only* compressed formats like ProRes and AVC-Intra. Why do camera makers continue to promote 8-bit formats when 10-bit recording systems are superior in performance and workflow?
9. Why is 24p not 24 FPS? Why is 30p not 30 FPS? Why is 60p not 60 FPS? What's going on? Explain this calmly without histrionics or vitriol.
10. Please list ten camera and/or postproduction *codecs* with which you are familiar. Indicate the associated bit rates for each. Are the formats long GOP or I-frame only? Consider the rudiments of compression. What do encoders look for when determining what pixel information to discard?
11. Compression is bad. Do you agree?
12. Finally, is the world an analog mess or a digital mess? Cite three (3) examples to support each perspective.

The DSLR Story

5

It came as a surprise to nearly everyone that DSLRs might be used for serious work. It wasn't supposed to happen like this—not by a long shot. The DSLR only came about because the news wire services no longer wanted to send both still and video camera people to the same event.

Today the pro shooter must look at the DSLR in a different light, for as much as it doesn't feel or act like a true video camera, the ersatz camcorder has nonetheless emerged as a serious tool in the shooter's burgeoning bag of tricks.

FIGURE 5.1

The DSLR plays a serious role for shooters of every stripe. I used a Canon 5D to shoot the web demos for *Moonrise Kingdom* (2012).[1]

FIGURE 5.2

The DSLR has profoundly influenced the shape and capabilities of video cameras. The large sensor Panasonic AF, RED Epic, and Canon EOS are effectively souped-up DSLRs.

A MATTER OF PERFORMANCE

We all know that a DSLR can produce very compelling video images. We *also* know that the DSLR is capable of producing the most hideous amateur-looking video images. The fact is if you stay within a DSLR's narrow dynamic range, and limited color gamut, you should do fine, or even better than fine. But venture too far into the darkest night or the brightest day, and you better watch out. A bevy of ugly artifacts is never far away.

[1]Anderson, W. (Producer & Director), Bush, E. (Producer), Cooper, M. (Producer), Dawson, J. (Producer), Hoffman, S. (Producer), Peissel, O. (Producer), . . . Yacoub, L. (Producer). (2012). *Moonrise Kingdom* [Motion picture]. USA: Indian Paintbrush.

FIGURE 5.3

In the right hands, the DSLR can produce remarkable and compelling images, such as this one from *The Girl Who Could Not Fly* by Chris Morgan, Tanzania, 2012.

The DSLR's reduced sampling does not in itself produce inferior images, but it does increase the *risk* of pictures that are soft or clipped, that lack contrast, or exhibit noisy shadows. If you can handle the risk, are cognizant of it, and can work with the camera's operational and performance compromises, then proceed. Embrace the DSLR for the economy and filmmaking prowess it offers. Embrace it with all the gusto in your being.

IT'S NOT A VIDEO CAMERA

The DSLR is designed to yield the best possible *still images*. It was never intended to capture superior audio and video; indeed, the price difference between the two types of cameras underlies many DSLR compromises and limitations.

FIGURE 5.4

Which camera makes sense for you? The DSLR is inexpensive and features a large sensor with a wide range of available lenses. It is also subject to overheating, the zoom is not a true zoom and lacks servo control, the CF card connector pins are prone to bending or breaking, the camera has no proper audio capability and connectors, and usually lacks timecode support and full-raster HDMI monitoring.

(a)    (b)

FIGURE 5.5

The heat sinks in a true video camera (a) direct excessive heat away from the sensor. To achieve low noise, DSLRs without the proper heat sinks or heat dissipation must necessarily limit the processing load. The size and shape of a still camera (b) works against efficient heat management, which in turn limits a camera's continuous runtime.

MORE THAN LOW-LIGHT CAPABLE

The large pixels in a DSLR are light sensitive in the way large-grain bromide crystals are triggered more readily in high-speed film emulsion. The Canon 5D's double-frame sensor is twice the size of a 4-perf 35mm cine sensor, and this greater size has its benefits—and drawbacks.

FIGURE 5.6

The DSLR center-crops HD video to 1920 × 1080, reducing the significance of a sensor's total pixel count.

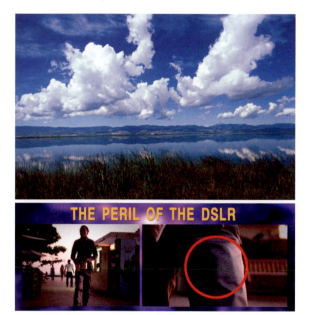

FIGURE 5.7

DSLRs designed to produce the sharpest still images do not utilize an optical low pass filter (OLPF) and so are susceptible to severe moving video defects like moiré.

FIGURE 5.8

The Nikon D800 was one of the first DSLRs to be fitted with an OLPF. The filter placed in front of the sensor reduces moiré by absorbing ultraviolet and infrared light. The use of a low pass filter is controversial due to the trade-off in resolution. Unlike an ordinary camera diffusion filter, the OLPF affects fine detail only.

LOAD SHEDDING

If you're shooting video with a still camera you need to understand the implications. The DSLR's low data load spread over a huge raster places enormous stress on an image. Omitting huge numbers of samples, skipping every other sensor line, or utilizing ham-fisted long-GOP compression, do not great pictures make!

FIGURE 5.9

To minimize the heat that contributes to noise, the still camera uses line skipping and other questionable practices to reduce the processing load. More sophisticated models rely on improved algorithms to reduce the data burden.

It is vital to recognize a DSLR's narrow dynamic range. This means avoiding blown-out overly bright windows in a dark interior set, and deep impenetrable shadows in high-contrast daylight exteriors or at night.

DSLR shooters must employ adequate fill to lift weak shadow areas to avoid *blockiness* and noise. Besides the routine use of a mirror or passive fill card, I also may use a TIffen Soft/FX or Schneider Digicon to tighten the shadows at the bottom of the camera's characteristic response curve.

FIGURE 5.10

Blotchy shadows may appear in highly compressed DSLR images especially in low light.

FIGURE 5.11

Act of Valor (2012). A sizable portion of the movie's $12 million budget went to ameliorating the shortcomings in the DSLR images and workflow.

FIGURE 5.12

The DSLR shooter constantly seeks ways to fill weak shadows and reduce noise. Mirrors or bounce cards can be effective. So can an on-camera LED or ring light to fill the facial shadows of actors' close ups.

Owing to many DSLRs' notorious line skipping, these cameras may exhibit noticeably reduced vertical resolution. The tilting of the camera therefore in high-detail scenes should be performed with care to minimize aliasing artifacts, which may be especially apparent on a big screen.

Keep in mind that the load shedding in a DSLR is really a form of *cost* shifting, because the shortcomings of the camera along with its low price are frequently offset by the additional costs incurred in post-production. The 2012 feature *Act of Valor*, shot largely with the Canon 5D, attests to the large sums that can be expended in post-production to address high-compression artifacts, noise, frame rate, focus, and other issues.

FIGURE 5.13

DSLRs do not possess sufficient on-board processing to shoot 24 FPS RAW, even to an external device. To capture 1080p HD RAW, a 36-megapixel sensor is needed, about 18 times what is currently allocated to produce HD video in a typical DSLR.

SETTING UP

Proper setup of the DSLR is critical to gain control of a camera's capabilities and potential drawbacks. MANUAL operation is imperative, and indeed, most DSLRs link the *Movie Mode* to the "M" setting. A slow shutter of 1/50th or 1/60th second is vital to infuse motion blur into the frame. Remember in progressive mode, we don't have the benefit (or liability) of *field* blurring that is intrinsic to interlaced capture.

A default ISO value of 160 has been typical for most DSLRs. With the advent of updated models from Canon, Nikon, and others, the shooter has gained two stops more exposure, so ISO 640 may be considered *normal*. Shooting at less than a camera's "normal" ISO may unnecessarily deepen shadows and lower black levels, so proper awareness and perhaps an external neutral-density filter may be in order.

FIGURE 5.14

These settings represent a typical configuration for shooting Canon 5D video. Later models, including the Canon 6D, feature greater manual control over audio levels, exposure, and other key parameters.

FIGURE 5.15

It takes a lot of processing to wrap a plastic edge around in-focus objects. Turning sharpness down to zero takes a load off the DSLR and may help address noise and heat issues. On the left, the look is much more organic. Note that small-screen presentations on a mobile device may require a harder edge.

Use NEUTRAL PICTURE PROFILE. Some manufacturers may call it something else. The idea is to capture as flat an image as possible in order to preserve maximum shadow detail and gradations in the original image. The Neutral Picture Profile in Canon cameras is analogous to the CINELIKE-V setting in Panasonic models; this allowing maximum flexibility in postproduction by producing what is in effect a low-contrast camera original.

Turning SHARPNESS down to zero (but not off) produces more tasteful, organic-looking images and substantially reduces the processing load in a DSLR. *Sharpening* in-camera puts great stress on the codec to maintain strong edges, which effectively expends bits preserving *false* detail rather than *actual* detail. The sharpening algorithms in-camera also tend to be less sophisticated than what is commonly available in Adobe After Effects, Boris FX, and other postproduction software.

Speaking of which, the sharpening and tweaking of contrast in postproduction must be considered in light of the anticipated delivery vehicle. DVD, Blu-ray, mobile devices, and the Web have different sharpening requirements, especially if scaling *after* sharpening is also required.

Shoot dialed down; recover in post. It's a good mantra for DSLR shooters.

JELLO-CAM

A major downside of the DSLR is the *jello* effect from the *rolling shutter.* I discussed this phenomenon in Chapter 4 as the digital sensor in most DSLRs scans pixel by pixel, line by line from the top down, and so introduces a time differential, which when panning or tracking can lead to an unnatural sloping of vertical lines.[2]

It isn't just a matter of limiting quick pans. Buildings and walls may appear warped or grotesque with a rapidly moving camera. The effect may not be noticeable in a forest, say, given the trees and

FIGURE 5.16

Once you become sensitized to the rolling shutter, there is no turning back. You are doomed. The sloping lines will drive you nuts.

[2]The Sony PMW-F55 introduced in 2013 utilizes a global shutter in conjunction with a Super 35 CMOS sensor. Could this be the end of *jello-cam?* Is this the harbinger of things to come? One can only hope.

foliage and the viewer having no fixed sense of sizes or shapes. But follow an actor through a narrow urban street or capture his point of view down an office hallway, and suddenly the walls and columns weave and lean like a drunken sailor. More disturbing are the faces of actors, especially women, who appear distorted. The sickening effect is hardly conducive to one's future career prospects!

NARROW DEPTH OF FIELD: BLESSING OR CURSE?

For decades, shooters have used selective focus to appropriately direct viewer's attention inside the frame. However, a whisker-thin depth of field can be disturbing as in the case of an actor whose nose tip appears sharp but whose eyes are slightly soft.

FIGURE 5.18

Concerts and sports and wildlife programs usually benefit from a smaller camera sensor and increased depth of field.

FIGURE 5.17

Can't afford a proper set or background? The DSLR's narrow focus can make quick work of in-frame distractions.

FIGURE 5.19

Orson Welles famously used deep focus in *Citizen Kane* (1941). DSLR shooters should bear in mind that the current shallow depth of field fad is just the fashion!

FIGURE 5.20

Despite the large assortment available, most lenses designed for still cameras are poorly suited for video applications. See Chapter 6.

The sensor of a full-frame DSLR extends over the equivalent of eight perforations (in film parlance), which may produce a very narrow focus with a normal lens.[3] The DSLRer shooting wide open may struggle to find and keep critical focus in a scene, or else he or she might *stop down* to increase the depth of field and gain additional operating margin that way.

Of course, the smaller stop is achieved by adding light. Do you see what's happening? The large sensor deemed so desirable by shooters entails substantial compromise simply to achieve sufficient depth of field for routine operation.

Aesthetically, the full-frame shallow focus look can also seem unnatural, since audiences conditioned over the decades are accustomed to the look and feel of cinema's 4-perf 35mm; the 8-perf DSLR look may induce discomfort or can even alienate the traditional large-screen movie viewer. For that reason, the Super 35 or Micro 4/3-size sensors may be better suited for feature film projects, offering the perspective of a larger imager while still allowing a practical and reasonable DOF. On the other hand, if you're doing a show about eyelashes, you may very well want the whisker-thin depth of field offered by a full-frame DSLR.

THE OPERATIONAL CHALLENGE

Every camera has its share of operational compromises, and the DSLR, owing to the fact that it isn't a video camera in the first place, has more than most with respect to ergonomics, focus, audio connectivity, and workflow.

FIGURE 5.21

Special rigs are available to accommodate the DSLR's unwieldy profile. This setup was used to shoot the 2010 season finale of the popular U.S. television show *House*.

[3]A full-frame SLR normal perspective lens is 50mm. A 1/3-inch camcorder's normal lens is 7mm. The shorter focal length lens has more depth of field. Simple. See Chapter 6.

(a)

(b)

FIGURE 5.22

As shooters we often face challenging environmental conditions. The best DSLRs have seals to protect against rain, snow, and grit.

FIGURE 5.23

Oh man. Tiny buttons everywhere with cryptic graphics! The DSLR's layout of controls leaves a lot to be desired.

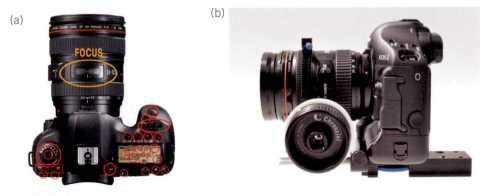

(a)

(b)

FIGURE 5.24

Oh, more buttons. And soft buttons too. Following focus? The range of focus covers barely a one-eighth turn of the lens barrel. A precision follow focus (b) can help.

FIGURE 5.25

Zooming in or out to frame a scene? The DSLR's vari-focal lens is not a true zoom. It requires critical refocusing when changing focal lengths.

SEEING WHAT WE'RE DOING

In bright daylight, the DSLR's LCD screen may be obscured and difficult to see. For this reason, the shooter usually opts for an external monitor connected via HDMI. This output is sadly hobbled in some cameras and does not reproduce a full-size monitored image.

Fortunately, this is changing with the latest DSLRs that output a 1920 × 1080 raster. Although there exist multiple versions of HDMI,[4] the camera should allow HD monitoring in virtually all cases.

FIGURE 5.26

Reviewing takes on a DSLR's tiny screen can be futile, especially in daylight. A dedicated high-resolution monitor is required.

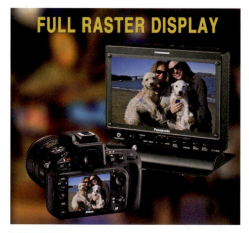

FIGURE 5.27

The latest DSLRs output full-raster HD to an external monitor.

---

[4]As of 2013, there were six different versions of HDMI: HDMI Ethernet Channel, Audio Return Channel, 3D Over HDMI, 4K × 2K Resolution Support, and a new Automotive HDMI. Stay tuned. That is only Version 1.4. Next up is Version 2.0 supporting 4K resolution at 60 FPS.

UNSOUND THOUGHTS

Audio is the underbelly of a DSLR. Most models do not allow manual control of levels, the preamps and limiters are primitive, and the feeble 1/8-inch mic input is prone to failure. For most folks, capturing production audio to a DSLR is a nonstarter, which means in nearly every case, shooting *double system*, that is, recording to an external device like a Zoom or Tascam. The audio separated from the picture is synchronized later using a tool like *PluralEyes* that compares the waveforms of the production audio with a reference track captured in-camera.

THE UNLOCKED AUDIO MESS

In professional camcorders, the audio is locked to picture via time code. In the DSLR, for reasons of economy and load management, the audio and the video are allowed to drift, the amount varying from camera to camera. The drift is not consistent, and usually not more than one or two frames, depending on the length of the scene. Some DSLRers shoot a reference at the beginning of each day to ascertain that day's drift. Because the audio recorded to camera is used to align the production sound, the synchronization in-camera is critical. *PluralEyes*, for all its elegance, is useless if it is syncing to the out-of-sync camera audio.

If shooting *double system* it is advantageous to roll and *cut* the camera and recorder at about the same time. Although this is not always possible especially in documentaries, it is worthwhile to capture a roughly equal amount of audio and video. It makes handling of a show's footage much more efficient and facilitates archiving down the road.

Speaking of organization the sound recordist should be sure to press STOP rather than the PAUSE button when capturing to the external recorder. Pressing STOP forces the recorder to create a new file, which can be a big time saver when working with PluralEyes or other automated syncing software.

Although most shooters are loath to do it, the prenaming of clips in the recorder can help with organization as well. Appending the date to each file ensures that a unique file name is captured for each scene. This is to avoid each day's files having the same names, which can be annoying.

Shooters should take particular care when shooting double system at 24 FPS. Different cameras require audio recorded at different speeds. Newer DSLRs usually specify 23.976 FPS—or 29.976 FPS. It is critical to conduct sync tests prior to the first day of shooting. In this particular minefield, no one likes surprises, and there tend to be plenty when shooting double system with a DSLR.

As a practical matter, be sure to record proper head and tail slates and feed a *guide track* into the camera for reference inside the NLE or for use as a possible backup. I will revisit the subject of shooting double system in Chapter 12.

FIGURE 5.28

Good sound makes our pictures look better! Recording to an external machine circumvents the camera's weak onboard audio. The flimsy 1/8-inch mini-jack is ongoing menace.

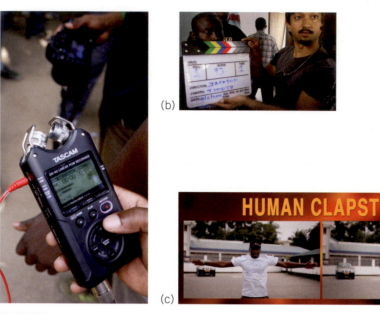

(a)   (b)   (c)

FIGURE 5.29

Capturing audio (a) to a separate recorder? Be sure to capture 48-kHz .wav or .aif files and record a guide track into the camera. You'll need a clapperboard (b) or other reference to facilitate the lineup of picture and sound inside the NLE. Some lowbrow shooters use a handclap or series of jumping jacks to assist the postsynchronization efforts.

FIGURE 5.30

When shooting double system we may encounter a sync discrepancy of one or two frames depending on the length of a scene. Over 30 minutes, the audio may be three frames out of sync!

FIGURE 5.31

To forestall synchronization problems we can run the output from the recorder into the camera mic input. Although this ensures a precise line up of picture and sound, the mismatched levels will blow out the camera audio unless we use a 25dB attenuating cable. This cable conveniently accommodates a second set of headphones!

FIGURE 5.32

If the performers in a long shot appear out of sync consider this: Audio lags at a rate of one frame for every 14 meters (45 ft) from the camera. This discrepancy is in addition to the inherent drift of a DSLR's internal audio.

GETTING TO WORK

With each new generation, the DSLR is becoming more sophisticated and video capable, with increased manual control over audio levels, exposure, shutter, and key imaging parameters. At the same time, the cameras are increasingly reflecting the IT world, integrating camera setup, operation, and streaming into a slew of wired and wireless devices. This trend appears to be driving the industry as more professional WiFi-enabled video cameras enter the market.

This DSLR has already impacted the world media scene in profound ways. The camera's inconspicuousness, low cost, and ability to capture compelling images and immediately disseminate those images around the world, has once again placed enormous power in the hands of the video shooter. Our challenge then, more than ever, is to use this power wisely.

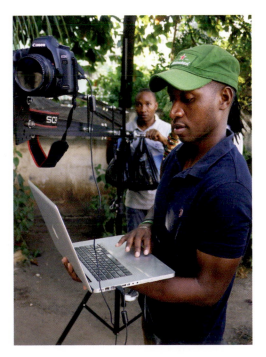

FIGURE 5.33

The DSLR is easily integrated into the file-based system we use every day.

FIGURE 5.34

Convenient software for the laptop or iPad controls camera setup and operation, helps organize files and folders, and manages proxies and script notes.

FIGURE 5.35

The integration of timecode into DSLRs still requires the use of synchronizing tools such as PluralEyes.

FIGURE 5.36

This Micro Four-Thirds DSLM (Digital Single Lens Mirrorless) camera records 1080p50 or 60 FPS at 72 Mbps with intraframe compression. That sounds a lot like a video camera to me!

FIGURE 5.37

The DSLR accesses places where pro video cameras are loath to tread. In Dhaka, UN Development officer Mahtab Haider uses a colorful gamcha to reduce the camera's visibility in crowds. From Tahrir Square to Times Square, keeping a low profile is often critical to one's success.

FIGURE 5.38

The DSLR camera has transformed how stories are told and by whom. This new world order embracing potentially tens of millions of viewers is only now starting to come into focus.

EDUCATOR'S CORNER: REVIEW TOPICS

1. Identify three (3) ways how the DSLR has influenced the design of proper video cameras. Consider workflow in addition to performance and operational aspects.

2. Many DSLR shooters prefer a shallow depth of field. How does narrow focus help or hinder a shooter's effectiveness as a camera operator and storyteller?

3. Is the DSLR "good enough" for the kinds of stories you intend to tell? List five (5) factors that may influence your decision to use a DSLR for your next production.

4. Discuss three (3) areas of concern when using a DSLR on a feature film. Do the same caveats apply to a documentary?

5. What are the advantages of finalizing image sharpness, detail, and contrast, in post?

6. Describe the procedure for recording DSLR double system.

7. The optical viewfinder is a major advantage for DSLR shooters, who use it to light and compose their scenes. Other than cost, are there any benefits to an electronic viewfinder?

8. Finally do *you* know the significance of the cryptic icon buttons in Figure 5.23b?

Your Window on the World

6

The camera lens is your window on the world, the element through which every aspect of the visual story must flow. Any way you grind, shape it, or filter it, your camera's optics are critical to your success as an effective shooter-storyteller.

It matters little, from the viewer's perspective, which manufacturer's logo is emblazoned on the side of your camera, which format or compression ratio appeals to you, or whether you record to tape, disc, or hard drive. The quality of optics matters most when it comes to creating compelling images. Your lens dear shooter is where and how the visual story meets the road.

In Chapter 3, we looked at how the lens focal length can contribute to or detract from the intended story. The telephoto lens, by compressing screen space, can dramatically increase the apparent size of crowds, or even *create* crowds, by strategically stacking objects one behind another inside the frame. A short focal length or wide-angle lens has the opposite effect, expanding a scene's apparent scope by drawing nearby objects closer and pushing background objects farther away. For these reasons, the wide-angle lens is used extensively for broad vistas and landscapes and, in action sports, to increase the visual impact of objects passing close to the camera.

FIGURE 6.1

The extreme "fisheye" exaggerates the apparent speed and motion of the skateboarder close to the camera. The Century Xtreme features a 180° horizontal field of view!

The *fisheye* has long been the darling of the skateboard crowd. Its superwide perspective creates severe distortion, exaggerating the height and the speed of a skater's leaps and tail grinds—an effect consistent with the intended storytelling. A short focal length lens also helps minimize the shake of a handheld camera, which is especially useful when shooting extreme sports from the nose of a surfboard, for example, or the handlebars of a motocross racer.

(a)

(b)

FIGURE 6.2

Lost in Venice. The wide angle (a) establishes my son's forlorn place in the iconic cityscape. The telephoto (b) isolates him from the background and helps convey his disorientation in an unfamiliar city. Which story is correct? As a storyteller, your choice of focal length should reflect a subject's mental state and point of view.

CONTROL YOUR SPACE

To communicate the desired story, the viewer must understand the geography of a scene, the location and the relative proximity of the players, and the direction of movement. The use of the telephoto lens can make a pursuer seem closer, the exploding boxcar more perilous, and the car door opening into the path of a biker more menacing. The wide lens expands space, pushes objects back into a scene, and so minimizes these perils.

(a)

(b)

FIGURE 6.3

The wide angle captures the emptiness of a Parisian park (left) and the desolation of an urban street after dark (above).

FIGURE 6.4

In San Marco Square, the boy and pigeons appear to share the same space owing to the perspective of a telephoto lens.

FIGURE 6.5

The long lens draws the towering billboard into this Los Angeles street scene.

FIGURE 6.6

The compression of screen space can increase tension and drama. This is Robert De Niro in Heat (1995).

TO FLATTER OR NOT TO FLATTER

It's not a matter of framing a close-up any way you can, because a wide angle in close up can capture an actor with the same relative screen size as a telephoto from farther away. The story implications of lens choice cannot be overstated; a short telephoto lens usually produces the most flattering representation of an actor's features at a normal shooting distance of 6 to 8 feet (1.5–2.5m).

FIGURE 6.7

Novice shooters may love the effect but your narcissistic star will hate you forever. The wide-angle lens in close up grotesquely distorts facial features.

FIGURE 6.8

The long telephoto lens unnaturally flattens an actor's face; the ears and nose appearing in the same plane undermines the intimacy we usually try to foster with our viewers. In this signature scene from *Tootsie* (1982),[1] Dustin Hoffman appears transformed as a woman emerging from the crowd. The extreme flattening afforded by the 1,000mm lens heightens the impact of this pivotal story moment.

FIGURE 6.9

A short telephoto or portrait lens offers the most flattering perspective when shooting talent.

MAXIMIZE USE OF THE STORYTELLING TOOLS

Just as the violinist uses a full bow for maximum expression and impact, so should the shooter exploit the full range and capabilities of his tools. In documentaries, I often use the zoom at full wide angle to establish a scene or capture essential action, and then jump in closer, *much* closer, to frame the details and close-ups that propel the story.

In most cases, I'm not talking about actually *zooming*! The great advantage of a zoom lens is the ability to quickly *reframe* without having to stop to reposition the camera or otherwise interfere with the action.

Shooters investing in a new camera should seek a model with a sufficient wide-angle. Many camcorders with integrated lenses offer too narrow wide-angle coverage. When shooting with a 1/3-inch-format camera, you should have at least a 4.5mm wide-angle, the SLR full-frame equivalent of 28mm, in order to provide proper coverage.

If your camera has an inadequate wide-angle, you might consider an adapter to increase coverage 30% to 40%. The practical use and the optical quality of such adapters vary considerably. Some permit partial or total zooming; others don't. Some create severe *barrel distortion* like a fisheye; others don't. What works depends on the story you're trying to tell. Only you the master of your storytelling domain can make this determination.

---

[1]Pollack, S. (Producer & Director), Evans, C. (Producer), Richards, D. (Producer), & Schwary, R. L. (Producer). (1982). *Tootsie* [Motion picture]. USA: Columbia Pictures Corporation.

FIGURE 6.10

Juxtaposing the wide angle with the full telephoto catapults the viewer spectacularly into the story! These scenes were shot with a Panasonic HPX250 fitted with an integrated 22X zoom.

USE YOUR FULL BOW

28 MM ------------> 616 MM

(a)   (b)

FIGURE 6.11

Wide-angle adapters with large front elements may create a front-heavy camera and complicate the mounting of a matte box and filters. To keep things simple and compact look for a camcorder with a sufficient, built-in wide-angle.

GO LONG FOR THE TOUCHDOWN

While a proper wide-angle with sufficient coverage is essential, the same might also be said for the telephoto, which offers the perfect complement. The instant narrowing of field of view (Figure 6.10) from 28mm to 616mm can be effective, even thrilling, to audiences.

The zoom lens is a marvelous thing and can be a valuable assist when needing to recompose quickly, say, between questions in an interview. In documentaries, the lack of predictability means we must reframe often to ensure good coverage or to exclude unwanted elements such as a boom pole protruding into the frame.

It's tough for many shooters, but it's a discipline worth learning. If you zoom *only* when the story demands it, you'll be a far better shooter. Zoom for emphasis, yes, to sell a point or to milk a contrite ax murderer's confession, but remember the zoom *always* reflects a story's motivation. The zoom (as opposed to a *dollying in or out*) is very unnatural, an optical trick that will draw the viewer's attention. Maybe this is OK. Maybe it isn't. So once again, the story is our guiding light, the lens through which we see and *feel* every creative decision.

FIGURE 6.12

When transitioning between shots, a hard cut is always preferable to zooming, unless motivated by the story or a character's point of view.

Table 6.1 Optical zoom ranges for popular HD cameras.

Some manufacturers' claims regarding optical zoom range should be taken with a grain of pulverized pumice.	
Canon HF11	12X
Canon XH-A1s	20X
Canon XL-H1s	20X
Canon XF305	18X
JVC GY-HD200B (stock)	16X
JVC GY-HD250 (stock)	16X
JVC GY-HM100	10X
JVC GY-HM710 (stock)	17X
Panasonic AG-HMC40	12X
Panasonic AG-AC90	12X
Panasonic AG-HVX200A	13X
Panasonic AG-HPX250	22X
Panasonic AG-HPX370 (stock)	17X
Sony HVR-A1	10X
Sony HVR-Z5	20X
Sony PMW-EX1	14X
Sony PMW-EX3 (stock)	14X

BEWARE OF DUBIOUS CLAIMS

Just as most of us wouldn't buy a car based on its horsepower rating alone, so we shouldn't automatically opt for a camera with the most pixels, best *minimum illumination*,[2] or the longest zoom range. What is the zoom range of a lens, anyway? 12X? 15X? 22X? Truth is, any lens can be a 50X or more

---

[2]There is no common standard to measure a camcorder's *minimum illumination*. Beware of such claims (usually specified in *lux*) that do not adequately consider a camera's performance in very low light.

if we, or the manufacturer disregard any notion of performance. Just omit a stop on the lens barrel—and *voilà!* Suddenly we have a longer zoom lens for next year's NAB show!

An overly optimistic zoom range has craft implications as well as these lenses typically exhibit poor performance at high magnification. Scenes lacking in brilliance and contrast can disrupt the visual flow and stick out like a sore thumb.

FIGURE 6.13

The optical zoom range of a lens can be any value—if performance is not considered. The 12X zoom on this Sony feels more like 6X to me.

FIGURE 6.14

The loss of light and contrast at high magnification is apparent in cheaper zoom lenses.

WHAT DO YOU WANT FROM ME?

The ideal lens is fast, lightweight, and low cost. In general, the faster the lens and the longer the zoom, the more massive it must be. The manufacture of precision lenses requires hours of skilled labor and hand finishing, which translates into high cost.

Have a moment? Ask your lens some hard questions:

- *Are you wide enough?*
  Avoid models with an insufficient wide-angle lens. A 28mm SLR equivalent is suitable for most shooters. Don't rely on pesky supplemental adapters, which can cramp your style.
- *Are you close enough?*
  Macro zooms may sacrifice some performance but are worth it. Close focus to 3 feet (0.9 m) or less is desirable. Better still is the ability to focus to the front of the lens, a feat only possible in cameras with noninterchangeable optics—another reason to avoid low-cost models with interchangeable lenses.

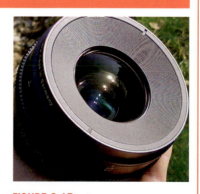

FIGURE 6.15

Any way you grind it, great lenses don't come cheap!

- *Are you as honest as the zoom is long?*
  Some manufacturers play fast and loose when representing the magnification range of a zoom lens. Performance must always be considered when assessing these claims. Loss of contrast and light transmission of two stops is common at extended focal lengths. Look for *vignetting* at minimum focus, in macro mode, and when shooting at full wide angle.
- *Do you breathe more than an obscene phone call?*
  One-piece camcorders generally compensate for breathing of focus. Set your camera zoom at full wide angle, rotate the focus ring, and check for noticeable shift in image size. Such lenses may be problematic in narrative productions that require precise follow focus.
- *Do you have lens distortion over the barrel?*

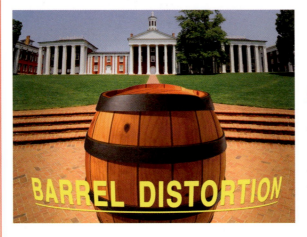

FIGURE 6.16a

Unless you're a skateboarder, a flat field with upright verticals is usually desirable. Look for inward curving of posts and walls near the frame edges in wide-angle scenes—a sign of inferior optics combined with insufficient in-camera correction.

- *Can you stay on track please?*
  Do images remain centered throughout the zoom range? Must you adjust the camera up and down, left and right, while zooming to compensate?
- *Do you have the smarts to find and hold focus?*
  In low-light and low-contrast scenes? At 24 FPS? Do images stay sharp in auto and manual modes throughout the zoom range?

FIGURE 6.16b

Are enough steps provided in the servo matrix to ensure continuous sharp focus at full telephoto?

OPTICAL VERSUS DIGITAL ZOOM

It hardly matters that no one in the history of humankind has ever used a camera's digital zoom.[3] Manufacturers continue to tout the "feature" by pasting an impressive-sounding number on the side of their cameras: 400X Digital Zoom! 500X Digital Zoom! 700X Digital Zoom! Wow!

Whereas optical zoom magnifies the actual photographed image, the digital zoom simply blows up the captured pixels to fill the frame.

(a)

(b)

FIGURE 6.18

The digital zoom at high magnification has limited usefulness.

FIGURE 6.17

700X?? Whoa! Some folks are impressed by such numbers. You don't have to be one of them.

FIGURE 6.19

An optical 2X extender incurs a light loss of two stops and markedly lowers contrast. Use with care.

GOING WIDER AND LONGER

There are times when we should take advantage of the widest, most distorted fisheye we can find for a program, say, on mind-altering hallucinogenic drugs. There may also be times in Formula 1 racing or in a sci-fi epic when only the longest 1,200mm telephoto lens will do. These lenses are not subtle, and because we usually try to be unobtrusive in our visual storytelling, we must use caution when resorting to optics with extreme points of view.

---

[3] I'm exaggerating a bit. Some cameras utilize the 2X digital zoom as a focus assist, and some shooters prefer the digital zoom in lieu of an optical extender especially in low light.

For news and reality shows, the wide-angle zoom is a daily workhorse. It's versatile in uncontrolled spaces like the kitchen in *Gene Simmons: Family Jewels* or in the rear seat of a racing pet ambulance for *Animal Cops*. It adds drama and stability to the shipboard calamities on *Deadliest Catch* and can dramatically increase the grandeur and fluidity of Tiger Woods's swing at the U.S. Open. In short, these lenses provide the coverage and ooh-and-ahh shots that producers demand and keep us working. I love my wide-angle lenses!

But there's trouble afoot in superwide and ultra-wide optics. Aside from the aesthetics and whether the extreme perspective is helpful or hurtful to the visual story, the lenses tend to be heavy and bulky. As 2/3-inch zooms have widened from 5.5mm more than a decade ago to 4.3mm today, their increased weight and girth have introduced a bevy of headaches, including *vignetting*,[4] breathing and tracking issues, and uneven illumination across the frame.

Some light falloff to the corners may be apparent in even the best optics. At full aperture and wide angle, the falloff is especially noticeable in high-speed lenses and when shooting with a matte box as the off-axis light reaching the corners of the frame is further attenuated.

Adding to these woes is the growing trend toward cameras with large CMOS-type imagers. Some CMOS designs utilize recessed photo sites like little "buckets" deep enough to block angled light from reaching the sensor surface resulting in a noticeable light fall off at the edges of the frame.

The demand for wider, lighter, and faster lenses has unleashed a spate of conflicting demands on manufacturers. Naturally, we want the most versatile lens we can find. We want top performance with a constant f-stop, a flat field with no vignetting, and superb contrast to the corners. Toss in a 2X extender, internal and macro focus, and the cams and followers to make it all work, and pretty soon we're talking about *real* complexity. Now if they could just make it inexpensive as well, we'll be all set!

FIGURE 6.20

How wide is wide enough? Terry Gilliam's warped view of the world in *Brazil* (1985)[5] serves to shrink the protagonist into his environment.

FIGURE 6.21

In the climactic scene from George Lucas's *THX 1138* (1971),[6] the extreme telephoto captures the cathartic escape from an oppressive subterranean world.

---

[4] *Vignetting* may be defined as a falloff of brightness or saturation at the periphery of an image. Some vignetting may be acceptable short of *portholing*, a more obvious impression of looking through an actual porthole.
[5] Cassavetti, P. (Producer), Milchan, A. (Producer), & Gilliam, T. (Director). (1985). *Brazil* [Motion picture]. United Kingdom: Embassy International Pictures.
[6] Coppola, F. F. (Producer), Folger, E. (Producer), Sturhahn, L. (Producer), & Lucas, G. (Director). (1971). *THX 1138* [Motion picture]. USA: American Zeotrope.

FIGURE 6.22

Some cameras with integrated lenses can focus to the front element, greatly increasing the shooter's storytelling options.

(a)

(b)

FIGURE 6.23

Show me a world I haven't seen before! The unusual perspective afforded by a 360° lens can help you do just that.

TALE FROM THE TRENCHES

The mediocre lenses that accompany most prosumer cameras pose a challenge to shooters vying to do first-class work. The trade-off in optical quality shouldn't be surprising given the manufacture of top-quality optics is a mature technology requiring costly and sophisticated processes. The few dollars that manufacturers allocate for the lens in an entry-level camera does not buy a whole lot.

So let's forget the virtues of CCD versus CMOS, HD versus 4K, 5K, or 6K resolution. You've thought way too much about your camera's minimum illumination rating, 14-bit DSP, and 4:2:2 or 4:2:0 color space. The truth is that the quality of optics, Dear Fixated One, is your camera's most critical attribute—in terms of what viewers can see and appreciate on screen.

I recall reviewing the JVC GY-DV500. The $5,000 camcorder was fairly impressive at the time despite a look that tended toward the brassy and harsh. But fitted with a $10,000 lens, the camera no longer just looked decent; it looked great! Such is the power of superb optics that can transform the look of virtually *any* camera.

Logically, there's no way you'll find a $25,000 broadcast lens on a $2,500 camcorder. We can hope, of course, and some camera makers encourage the notion by silk-screening the names of legendary optics makers around the lens barrel. But don't be fooled. When you spend only a few thousand dollars on a camera, there is something you're not getting. And that is, more likely than not, a lens that you can proudly hang your lens shade on.

Of course, we want a lens that is lightweight and fast, has a long zoom range, and has a close-focus capability that is also low in cost. Problem is these demands are often at odds with each other. Extending the zoom range, for example, tends to work against greater speed. And greater lens speed tends to work against maintaining low weight.[7]

Considering the compromises inherent to any complex lens, we shouldn't be surprised by the shortcomings in low-cost optics. Poor or nonexistent lens coatings, chromatic aberration, lack of sharpness, and weak contrast to the corners, are significant drawbacks that can have a negative impact on our images, especially when viewed at high magnification on a big-screen plasma TV or cinema screen.

FIGURE 6.24

Your lens is not an afterthought—it should be your first thought! What kind of images does your simian demand?

FIGURE 6.25

The lowly optics in prosumer camcorders can be the source of great consternation. In recent years, manufacturers employing digital in-camera correction have significantly improved the performance of these lenses.

---

[7]Increased lens speed—that is, light transmission—is largely a function of lens diameter, which translates usually into increased lens weight and mass. Most shooters prefer lighter weight lenses and equipment.

WHY LENSES LOOK CHEAP

In my camera and lighting seminars, I sometimes use a resolution chart to demonstrate how a thin layer of nose grease can *enhance* the performance of a cheap lens. The grease, if applied finely enough on the front element, can serve as a crude lens coating, improving light transmission and reducing flare.

Normally, when light strikes a hard glass surface, a portion of the beam is reflected. This loss of light is compounded in lenses with many elements, leading to a reduction in *lens speed.* More and better coatings reduce the light loss to as little as one-tenth of 1%, enabling complex lenses to be made smaller and lighter while still maintaining efficient light transmission.

Superior coatings are expensive, so it's no surprise that consumer camcorders come up short. The increased internal reflections, aka *flare*, can significantly reduce the contrast and sharpness in these cameras, irrespective of sensor resolution or compression format.

The quandary for shooters is thus: Our HD-, 2K-, or 4K-resolution camcorders can resolve amazing picture detail, which we presumably want. At the same time, the cameras also resolve more lens *defects*, which we presumably do not want. This points to the need for better optics, if for no other reason than we see and resolve more lens problems at higher resolutions.

The most objectionable lens defects are chromatic aberrations, which are found to some degree in all lenses regardless of price or sophistication. Chromatic aberrations (CAs) also referred to as *shading* artifacts appear along the edges of over-exposed light sources such as streetlights, or along the horizon line at dusk. The fringing is usually more apparent at the long end of the zoom, where the aberrations are magnified. CA has always been a problem, but standard definition's ragged edges effectively covered most defects. HD's smooth, well-defined edges offer no such refuge. For HD shooters, CA is the main reason that cheap lenses look cheap.

FIGURE 6.26

Rubbing a layer of nose grease over the front of a cheap lens may improve its speed and performance! High-quality lenses with advanced coatings obviate the need for such crude and demeaning tactics.

SAY NO TO SMALL F-STOPS

The bending of light through a pinhole-size aperture produces a multitude of tiny light sources, which can create internal reflections and increase flare. Under such conditions, bright daylight scenes appear washed out and lacking sharpness and resolution. One-third-inch and smaller sensor cameras may exhibit severe diffraction at f5.6 and smaller apertures. Larger sensor cameras and DSLRs also exhibit a lowering of contrast but not until f11 to f16.

FIGURE 6.27

This scene recorded at minimum f-stop appears washed out due to severe diffraction.

It is important to maintain a proper f-stop because shooting at f5.6 or higher with a 1/3-inch HD camcorder will yield images no better than standard definition! For this reason, some entry-level camcorders automatically apply neutral density to avoid the narrow apertures that can lead to the loss of resolution and contrast.

FIGURE 6.28

With tiny apertures, the edges of the iris appear to glow and act as tiny light sources that scatter the light and lower contrast. Poor lens performance is a good reason to shoot early or late in the day, when wider apertures can be employed.

WHY ONE-PIECE CAMCORDERS MAKE BETTER PICTURES

Some shooters will have it no other way: They want a camcorder with an interchangeable lens. They want the flexibility to mount long, short, wide, or whatever optics they please, as the need and the job arises.

The premise seems reasonable, yet we know from research that only a small percentage of shooters take advantage of their camera's interchangeable lens capability, and when they do, they simply replace one cheap lens for another. For most shooters with sub-$10,000 cameras, a swappable lens system is hardly worth it, given the substantial performance compromises.

Fact is modest camcorders with fixed lenses perform better than similar-class camcorders with interchangeable optics. The Panasonic HPX160, for example, fitted with a whopping 22X integrated lens doesn't exhibit nearly the breathing of focus one might expect. Why? Because the breathing of focus, tracking errors, and chromatic aberrations are mapped out and digitally corrected in-camera. This level of performance is simply not achievable with inexpensive interchangeable optics.

CHROMATIC ABERRATION COMPENSATION

In some cameras, *Chromatic Aberration Compensation* (CAC) may improve the apparent performance of an interchangeable lens. A *CAC lens* fitted to the Panasonic HPX600, for example, provides a unique signature; the camera identifying the make and model lens then applies an average correction from a *Lookup Table* (LUT). CAC does not correct for *tracking errors*, *soft focus*, or *flare*,[8] but it does suppress the CA *fringing* that tends to plague inexpensive optics especially at high magnification. The latest generation zoom lenses from Canon and Fujinon all support CAC, a feature well worth looking for when considering a camera fitted with a modest interchangeable lens.

---

[8] *Tracking* describes a lens' ability to remain centered on an object while zooming. *Breathing* reflects the inability of a lens to maintain critical focus while zooming. *Flare* refers to the level of internal reflections in a lens that reduce contrast and sharpness.

FIGURE 6.29

High-definition cameras are fabulous! They resolve greater picture detail and fill our viewers' minds with endless wonder. Unfortunately, they also resolve more lens defects. CAC helps reduce the visibility of color fringing in high-contrast areas of the frame.

FIGURE 6.30

CA is the main reason cheap lenses look cheap! CA is not art!

FIGURE 6.31

CAC is applied automatically from a library of LookUp Tables (LUTs) stored in a camera's memory. Look for CAC to become common in future 2K- and 4K-resolution cameras.

MAKING PEACE WITH YOUR NOT-SO-HOT LENS

To compensate for mediocre optics, camera makers will resort to cheap tricks, such as ratcheting up a camera's *detail level* to create the illusion of increased sharpness. In Chapter 9, we'll see how a reduced detail level can contribute to a more organic, less electronic look. Caution should be exercised, however, when setting the camera detail too low, as this may produce muddy, lifeless images especially given a lens that lacks good contrast in the first place.

We mentioned the *ramping* or darkening that often occurs at the long end of many zooms. We cited also the lack of proper lens coatings that contributes to flare and loss of contrast. Beyond carping and the shedding of a few drops of lens fluid, is there anything we shooters can do to improve the performance of a mediocre lens?

HOW SWEET IT IS

Our camera's cheap lens may look okay on a small monitor, but on a large screen, the lens tells a different story. Luckily, some improvement in performance is possible by identifying a lens' *sweet spot*. The fact is that most cameras' optics can perform rather well at a specific focal length and f-stop.

The best way is find a lens' sweet spot is to shoot a test scene and display the result on a large plasma or cinema screen. Large-screen projection immediately reveals serious problems such as breathing of focus, loss of contrast, poor tracking, and other faults. On the big screen, you can run, but you can't hide. Most shortcomings are painfully obvious under such scrutiny.

You can also evaluate a lens by referencing a monitor capable of displaying at least 1,000 lines of resolution. Such a monitor is one of the best investments you can make; the precision it offers is useful to shooters in many aspects of production. High-resolution monitors connected via the serial digital interface (SDI)[9] eliminate the laborious setup once required of older analog displays.

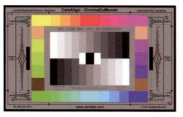

FIGURE 6.32

The Chroma Du Monde chart (left) is the standard of the industry for referencing color and resolution. You can improvise your own chart (right) using sections of newspapers taped to the wall.

FIGURE 6.33

Respiratory problems? The package lens that accompanies an entry-level camcorder often has mild to severe breathing issues; a change in focus should not produce a significant shift in field size, nor should zooming produce obvious changes in focus.

---

[9] Serial Digital Interface (SDI) is commonly found on professional camcorders. A single cable carries uncompressed red, green, and blue data streams that are interweaved in a *multiplexed* signal.

FIGURE 6.34

Place your camera's crosshair maker over an object and zoom in. Does the object stay centered? If so, *très bien*!

FIGURE 6.35

The backfocus should be checked daily to ensure sharp images, especially since a camera's tiny viewfinder is incapable of providing this reassurance. The style of backfocus adjustor varies from lens to lens.

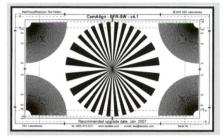

FIGURE 6.36

Setting backfocus: a star chart's fine grid appears to snap in and out of focus on a high-resolution display.

LAYING DOWN WITH YOUR LENS

Evaluating your lens is critical to developing your prowess as a shooter-craftsperson. Use this procedure to assess zoom lens performance for a camera fitted with *interchangeable* optics and engraved footage markings:

1. Start with the camera on a tripod focused on a distant object. I prefer a telephone pole, but any object with a clear vertical edge will do. Set the lens to INFINITY and check the setting. Can your camera find sharp focus? Cameras and lenses that focus past infinity should be rejected. I recently shot a car commercial with a lens that tracked okay but focused a bit past INFINITY. This bizarre behavior drove my assistant nuts and ruined several takes.
2. Now place your camera and tripod 6 feet (1.7 m) from a wall. Use a tape measure and be sure to measure from the imager's focal plane. Many cameras indicate this point on the camera body. If not, you'll have to estimate.
3. Next use a reference chart if you have one, or you can retrieve yesterday's newspaper from the recycle bin and tape several pages to the wall. Be sure the center and all four corners of the frame are covered. At 6mm focal length on 1/3-inch-type cameras, the image will approximately cover an area 5 feet wide by 3.5 feet high (1.5 m × 1.1 m).
4. Set up two lights at 45° to the wall. Angle the lights to avoid hot spots and zoom in fully. Focus critically and check the lens barrel for accuracy. Some lenses may not have a 6 foot (1.7 m) reference, so you may have to estimate or use a different distance. Any discrepancy should be noted to assure accurate focus and follow-focus during production.

5. Now zoom out slowly while eyeing the monitor. Note the breathing of focus in the newspaper text. Most lenses will soften slightly. Watch for sharp sections and note any sweet spots. If your camera is so equipped, you can record these points on the external focus ring. Also note any off-center shifting, because tracking can be a problem in cheaper lenses.
6. *Check backfocus!* I'll repeat this: **check backfocus!** A zoom lens needs to be checked daily. Incorrect backfocus may not allow your camera to focus to infinity. It may also produce soft images at full wide angle at maximum aperture. Heat, cold, shock, and routine handling can affect this measurement measured in millionths of an inch, which means the backfocus can be easily disturbed in the course of a shooting day. You can use a *star chart* available at low or no cost from the major lens manufacturers or from DSC Labs (http://dsclabs.com/). The gradient patterns and fine lines in the star appear to snap in and out of focus on a high-resolution display, a great help for conducting routine backfocus checks.

DUBIOUS FOCUS, ZOOM, AND ONION RINGS

Because precision lenses are expensive, some manufacturers look here first to cut corners. Focus rings in particular may be either nonexistent or shoddily constructed, thus denying the shooter the ability to set and follow precise focus.

FIGURE 6.37

C'mon, guys! What's with the miniscule markings? A cine-style lens features large bright witness marks that can be seen and logged by an assistant or script supervisor from across a crowded set.

CINE-STYLE LENSES

There are times when a camera's cheap *package* lens will not suffice regardless of a shooter's expertise. At such times, it's logical to turn to cine lenses as a viable alternative. Cine and cine-style lenses employ superior coatings, finely machined gears, and the finest optical glass. Light transmission, resolution, and contrast are usually dramatically better than the low-cost fare a shooter might be used to, with cine lenses' stated specs regarding speed and zoom range in general more accurate and honest.

Cine lenses have operational advantages as well. Besides the more visible focus, zoom, and iris markings, commercial-grade optics feature integrated follow-focus gear rings. Film shooters are used to such functionality, but until recently, this capability was rare for the modest digital shooter.

Keep in mind that vintage film lenses are usually poorly suited for digital use. Owing to the random nature of film grain, the *bob and weave*, and the registration errors in the gate of a film camera, serious lens defects such as chromatic aberration were effectively concealed. Compare this to the stationary high-resolution CCD or CMOS sensor that reveals unabashedly all defects large and small.

Of course, as in all things, story is the final arbiter of creative and technical decisions, so it's important to recognize the advantages of working with film lenses in a digital environment. These lenses may infuse a dreamlike quality that might be *exactly* what your story demands!

SOURCE OF ENCHANTMENT AND FRUSTRATION

Owing to their relative low price and range of available focal lengths, still camera lenses have become popular for a range of professional applications. This is despite the operational and performance compromises associated with them. Most SLR lenses do not offer sufficient *barrel rotation* for following focus at a normal working range from 6 to 8 feet (2.2–2.7 m). Some lenses provide barely a 1/8 turn of the lens barrel to cover the full range of focus from minimum distance to infinity.

EXCESSIVE DEPTH OF FIELD

A shortcoming of small-format camcorders is the relative inability to capture images in clearly defined planes. Because large sensor cameras and DSLRs require a longer focal length lens to cover a *normal* field of view many shooters take advantage of the shallower depth of field to help guide viewers' attention inside the frame.

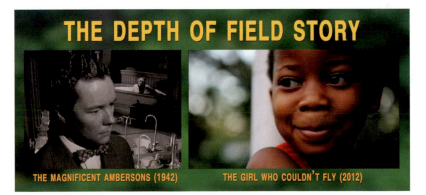

FIGURE 6.38

The scene from *The Magnificent Ambersons* (1942)[10] illustrates how deep focus can unify elements in multiple planes. The DSLR has contributed to the currently popular shallow depth of field look.

[10]Moss, J. (Producer), Schaefer, G. (Producer), Welles, O. (Producer & Director), Fleck, F. (Director), & Wise, R. (Director). (1942). *The Magnificent Ambersons*. USA: RKO Radio Pictures.

FIGURE 6.39

A narrow depth of field helps if we don't have much of a background to work with!

FIGURE 6.40

A 7.3mm lens on a 1/3-inch camcorder offers the same "normal" perspective as the 50mm lens on a full-frame DSLR camera. The longer "normal" focal length explains the reduced depth of field in cameras fitted with large sensors.

FIGURE 6.41

The diagonal measure of a sensor's imaging area determines the "normal" focal length.

WHY HIGHER F-STOPS PRODUCE MORE DEPTH OF FIELD

A higher f-stop/smaller aperture allows more in-focus rays (a) to reach the camera sensor, resulting in greater depth of field. A lower f-stop/larger aperture has the opposite effect (b) producing less depth of field.

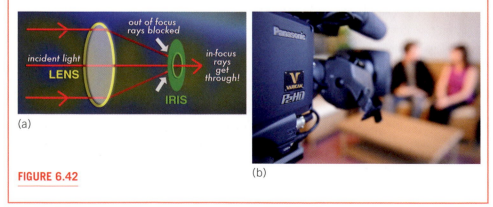

FIGURE 6.42

LENS ADAPTERS

Before DSLRs and large-sensor camcorders, the 35mm lens adapter was the solution of choice for achieving a narrow depth of field. Most lens adapters employed a spinning or oscillating ground glass, so maintaining sharp focus was an ongoing challenge. There is little advantage these days to utilizing a lens adapter that results in a loss of resolution and two stops of exposure. If a reduced depth of field look is required, we have at our disposal now a range of large-sensor options that can achieve the desired look much more economically—and efficiently.

FIGURE 6.43

The 35mm adapter mounted on a small-sensor camcorder preserves the narrow depth of field of a cine lens.

EDUCATOR'S CORNER: REVIEW TOPICS

1. Explore the notion of screen space and how lens choice impacts the apparent size and proximity of objects. Consider particularly how lens choice affects an actor's facial features.

2. List the features that might be offered in the ideal lens. Which attributes matter most given your intended application? What compromises in design, features, or price are you willing to make?

3. Explain how too much or too little depth of field may impact the visual story. Discuss the techniques you might use to direct a viewer's attention appropriately inside a frame with deep depth of field.

4. Fast lenses are preferable to slow lenses. Do you agree?

5. Longer zooms are preferable to shorter zooms. Do you agree?

6. Cameras with integrated lenses may perform better than cameras with interchangeable optics. How might the inability to swap lenses have an impact on the stories you're likely to tell?

7. You're shooting the D-Day landing à la *Saving Private Ryan*. Consider the lens that best conveys the story as the GIs hit the beach. Will you use the wide-angle lens up close, or the telephoto from farther away? Which choice best communicates the desired intensity in the film?

8. Your generous uncle passed away and left you $10,000 to purchase new equipment. How much of this sum would you allocate for the camera? How much for the lens? Would you select a camcorder with an integrated lens? Explain the various considerations in the context of the stories you intend to tell.

The 3D Shooter

7

In a sense, we've always shot 3D. Since the dawn of photography, the challenge to shooters has been how to best represent the 3D world in a 2D medium. Because the world we live in has depth and dimension, our filmic universe is usually expected to reflect this quality, by presenting a lifelike setting within which our screen characters can live and breathe and operate most transparently.

FIGURE 7.1

Knowingly or not, 2D shooters regularly integrate a range of depth cues to sell the 3D illusion. The highlights in the billiard balls and the soft focus background are suggestive of a scene that has dimension, that is real, that exists.

FIGURE 7.2

The converging lines at the horizon contribute to this scene's strong 3D quality.

FIGURE 7.3

Shooters in 2D and 3D usually seek to maximize the texture apparent in a scene. Texture is a powerful depth cue because only objects with dimension exhibit it.

FIGURE 7.4

In 3D, the texture in the face is emphasized so care must be taken to suppress any unwanted detail. Sometimes the detail in the face is the story!

THE ESSENCE OF 3D

We take two pictures, one from each eye, and put them together in the same frame. Think of it as a multicamera shoot with two cameras' images appearing simultaneously on one screen.

And therein lies the difference between a cinematographer and a *stereographer*. The 2D shooter is concerned foremost with the sanctity of the *frame;* the cinematographer uses focus, composition, and lighting to properly direct the viewer's eye while defending the frame's edges from elements that can detract from or contradict the intended visual story.

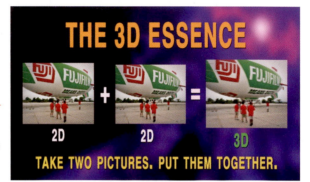

FIGURE 7.5

The 3D shooter places the left and right images atop each other and hopes viewers will accommodate the fusing of the two into a single stereo image.

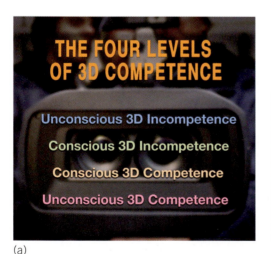

(a)

(b)

(c)

FIGURE 7.6

Picking up a camera for the first time, the new 3D shooter feels reassured by its familiar size and shape and proceeds to shoot unwatchable rubbish. Sobered by the experience, the shooter becomes aware of how much he doesn't know. With practice, the shooter gains competence, but he or she must consciously apply the requisite skills until after many years and 10,000 experiences, the craft becomes automatic. The same stages of learning apply to other skills, such as playing a violin or operating a standard-transmission car. (b) *Violin Player* (c. 1640) by Dutch Golden Age painter Molenaer-Jan-Miense.

The stereographer is primarily concerned with the *window*. Unlike in 2D, the 3D viewer has the option of exploring objects at various planes *behind* the window; *at* the window aka the *screen plane*; or in *front* of the window in what may be regarded as the viewer's personal space.

The skill required to manage this extra dimension requires a new way of seeing and capturing the world, and so for us accomplished in the 2D realm, it is truly disheartening to have to *unlearn* 90% of what we know. Forget the over-the-shoulder shots and the bread-and-butter close-ups. The 3D medium is a different beast that requires a vastly different set of skills.

Keep in mind we are not *really* shooting 3D—we are shooting stereo. In real life, 3D is immersive like walking down the aisle of a 7-Eleven and being enveloped by the trail mixes and Little Debbie cakes. We are transported by the allure of the merchandise and the magic of the place that sweeps over and around us.

The format we call *3D* is not nearly so immersive, but it can still create intimacy as audiences experience characters in front of the screen and feel the personal interaction.

FIGURE 7.7

The 2D shooter places a ***frame*** around the world and instructs the viewer to "Look at this! This frame and everything in it are important." The 3D shooter establishes a ***window*** through which the audience may experience multiple scenes simultaneously in front of, at, or behind the screen plane.

FIGURE 7.8

Shooting 3D requires a new way of seeing and capturing the world. It's easy to assume we know more than we do.

3D IS A TECHNICAL TRICK

There's nothing real about it. Audiences create the stereo image in their brains by fusing the two images presented on screen. Most go along with the ruse, but here's the rub: The front of the brain understands it's only a movie and there's nothing to fear. But the *back* of the brain, the primitive part responsible for our survival and physical well-being, isn't so sure. The primitive brain reacts with fear at our fellow species members running around with their heads or body parts chopped off, when they are not in focus, or wrapped in red; these conditions, hardly notable in 2D, provoke an involuntary *automatic* response in 3D. The two parts of the brain in conflict can and do induce headaches, nausea, and even epileptic fits. No 2D filmmaker beyond Kevin Smith has the potential to wreak such wrenching pain on viewers. Because 3D toys with the animal portion of the brain, technical snafus can have a serious impact on the 3D story. Left and right images that are vertically misaligned or are rotated off axis are especially difficult for the primitive brain to reconcile. The one-piece camcorders from Panasonic use a bevy of built-in servomotors to control these errors, a major advantage over the complex mirror rigs used commonly on high-end productions.

FIGURE 7.9

The stereo shooter must understand the physiological implications of the medium. About 12% of audience members are unable or unwilling to form the 3D image.

(a)

(b)

FIGURE 7.10

The injection of red into a 3D scene invokes instant fear and elevates the blood pressure of an audience. As a shooter, you cannot alter this response because on a primitive, unconscious level, the threat is real. The animal brain associates red with fire, blood, and gore—and impels us to run like hell.

(c)

DEPTH CUES, ANYONE?

Understanding the physical layout of the world protects us from the perils of daily life. Whether we're crossing a busy street or ducking a 100-mph fastball, it's fortunate for us that this portion of our brains operates on autopilot; the threats to our survival require an instantaneous response unslowed by a conscious thought process.

FIGURE 7.11

Facing the menace of marauding college students or a speeding rickshaw, we constantly assess the depth cues in the world around us for imminent approaching danger.

FIGURE 7.13

Folks with one eye can still have good depth perception and operate a motor vehicle, despite some loss of peripheral vision and ability to navigate in tight spaces.

FIGURE 7.12

MONOSCOPIC DEPTH CUES

Monoscopic cues like linear and aerial perspectives contribute significantly to our perception of a third dimension. The direction and character of shadows and their relative size are also strong communicators of depth. We know for example that the actor in Figure 7.15 is much smaller than the train in the distance. If the actor appears larger in frame, it must be because the train is very far away. Such sizing cues communicate a strong sense of depth.

In Figure 7.16, one actor partially blocks the other. We know, from the way the world works, that the more distant actor is likely still in one piece, the unseen part of his body hasn't disappeared but is *occluded* by the closer actor. Occlusion cues are monoscopic and so do not require the muscular effort of fusing two separate images, which may over time contribute to viewer fatigue.

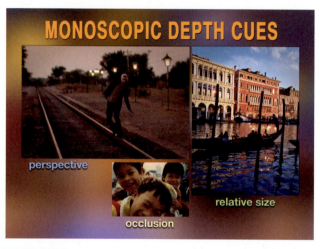

FIGURE 7.14

FIGURE 7.15

The relative size of the train and actor effectively communicates a third dimension.

FIGURE 7.16

An object partially blocking another object conveys depth. No physical muscular effort required.

Increasing the number of *monoscopic* depth cues can help produce a more comfortable viewing experience. We can place objects of a familiar size and shape around the set, or move the camera laterally along a slider rail. A tracking camera produces an abundance of motion depth cues, which help an audience acclimate to the strange and unnatural stereo environment.

FIGURE 7.17

The viewer assumes that the stones at the top and bottom of the frame are the same size. If the stones don't appear that way in the scene, it must be because they are receding into the distance.

(a)

(b)

FIGURE 7.18

The perception of depth is influenced by our knowledge of the world. We know the beach ball is round, so we don't need a stereo view to understand its shape. We know the configuration of the shoebox and the coin without seeing around the objects. As part of my Brisbane workshop (b) in 2010, my students considered ways to integrate a familiar monoscopic depth cue, the beach ball, into a scene.

FIGURE 7.19

We see the interplay of highlights and shadows and understand this object is real. Only 3D objects exhibit such texture.

FIGURE 7.20

Motion cues are powerful communicators of depth. The aircraft flying at hundreds of kilometers per hour appears stationary in the sky. How can this be? Your audience understands how fast planes really fly. It can only mean that the aircraft is very far away.

FIGURE 7.21

A moving camera multiplies the number of easy-to-read depth cues. A slider rail or Steadicam work well in 3D!

STEREOSCOPIC DEPTH CUES

Whereas monoscopic cues are sufficient to protect us from threats beyond 15 meters (50 ft), our ability to process *stereoscopic* depth cues is essential to shield us from more immediate dangers. In other words, there is a limit to the depth information that a single eye can provide. Beyond 15 meters, there are no stereoscopic cues because our eyes are not separated sufficiently to see around objects at such distance.

How close is the girl to the car at left?

FIGURE 7.22

This girl selling tissues in the streets of Cairo is very close to the car at left. But how close? The stereo view sees slightly around the car and reveals her true peril.

Stereoscopic cues are powerful because they provide input that cannot be gleaned from a single eye's perspective alone. The successful 3D shooter understands how to moderate the use of stereo *revelations* by using monoscopic cues wherever possible to communicate depth.

Keep in mind that shooting 3D well is a matter mostly of applying the brake, of *holding back* the depth in a scene before giving it a *little* gas and *rarely* a *lot* of gas. With 3D, you have the power to entertain and to create the most amazing stories, or you can make people wretch. Whatever you want. It's your choice. What kind of 3D shooter are you?

thin section of background visible by one eye but not the other.

FIGURE 7.23

WHAT A REVELATION!

LEFT EYE

RIGHT EYE
Amount of side view is function of object size and distance

FIGURE 7.24

The detail revealed at the sides of objects cannot be re-created in postproduction. This is why 3D shooters have to get it right: The amount of depth in a scene is fixed at the time of image capture.

FIGURE 7.25

Shooting 3D is mostly brake—with a little gas. Continuously hotfooting it will leave your audience writhing in pain.

INTERAXIAL VERSUS INTEROCULAR

Let's keep it straight: *Interocular* distance refers to the separation of the eyes; *interaxial* distance refers to the separation of the camera lenses. A 3D camera's interaxial distance has a significant effect on the perceived shape and size of objects. A narrow interaxial allows objects to approach the camera more comfortably and enables closer perspectives, but the reduced stereo effect may require shorter focal length lenses to restore the proper roundness. Conversely, a wide interaxial enhances the 3D at greater distances, but a telephoto lens is required to flatten the field slightly and mitigate the unnatural stereo revelations.

Cameras fitted with a 60mm interaxial are said to be *orthostereoscopic* because they closely approximate the human perspective at 3 to 15 meters (10–50 ft). For shooters accustomed to working at a more typical 1.5- to 2.5-meters (6–8 ft), a narrower interaxial from 25 to 45 mm is usually preferred in combination with a shorter focal length lens.

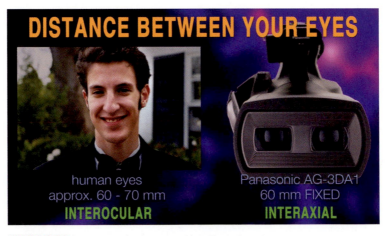

FIGURE 7.26

Interocular? Interaxial? Although some shooters use the terms interchangeably your stature as a 3D shooter and craftsman will be enhanced by the use of the appropriate reference.

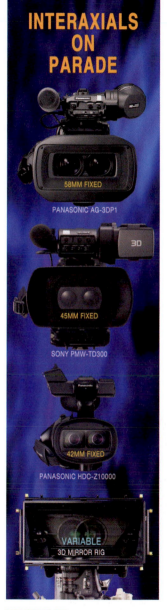

INTERAXIALS ON PARADE

58MM FIXED

PANASONIC AG-3DP1

45MM FIXED

SONY PMW-TD300

42MM FIXED

PANASONIC HDC-Z10000

VARIABLE
3D MIRROR RIG

FIGURE 7.27

Which interaxial makes sense for you? 58mm? 42mm? 28mm? The implications on the 3D story can be profound.

FIGURE 7.28

Human beings cannot perceive much stereo beyond 15 meters (50 ft), so expansive scenes such as cityscapes can be captured just as well with a 2D camera for 3D presentations.

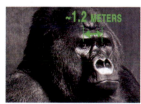

(a)   (b)

FIGURE 7.29

Whose point of view are we in? An audience peering through King Kong's eyes perceives the city like a toy model because Kong's wide interocular distance allows him to see around buildings that humans normally cannot.[1] If a human is able to see around a building 2 miles away, the brain assumes the object must be a miniature.

---

[1] I have no idea what King Kong's interocular distance might be. The 1.2 meters I've suggested is speculative.

(a)   (b)

FIGURE 7.30

3D producers often demand that every shot exhibit depth, so sports, such as football/soccer played over a large field, fare poorly in stereo as distant players look like little toy dolls! Honestly, take a look around. Gaze into the heavens. Some things in 3D, as in life, ought not to show depth.

(a)   (b)

FIGURE 7.31

An audience seeing through a mosquito's eyes is not able to see around objects it would normally expect to so objects appear huge! The fella to the right of Herman Munster (Fred Gwynne) is the great Brooklyn Dodgers manager Leo Durocher. Mr. Durocher's eyes are not sufficiently separated to see around Mr. Munster so Mr. Munster looks massive—which he is!

WHERE TO SET THE SCREEN PLANE

James Cameron, the 3D filmmaker and King of the World, puts it simply: *You converge on the money.* If Tom Cruise is in your scene, you converge on Tom Cruise. If you're shooting a Mercedes commercial, you converge on the Mercedes. In 3D, the viewer's eyes go to the screen plane first, the plane of convergence, so it makes sense that the bulk of your storytelling should be focused there.

So audiences converge their eyes on the screen and then hunt around for other objects in front of or behind the screen. This seeking and fusing of images across multiple planes occurs across every cut in a 3D movie, presenting a potentially significant disruption to the flow of the finished stereo program.

For this reason, shooters try to avoid large shifts in the position of objects relative to the screen. One way to achieve this is to feather the amount of depth in and out within a scene during original photography. The strategy can ease the bump across 3D transitions and obviate the need to perform substantial *horizontal image translation (HIT)*[2] in postproduction.

Most 3D *plug-ins* have a HIT capability to adjust the overlap of the left and right images. Note that repositioning of the screen plane via HIT does not affect the actual *depth* as the occlusion revelations in a scene are *baked in* and can't be altered.

Also, in cameras that originate in 1920 × 1080, there is no ability to perform HIT without blowing up the frame slightly to accommodate the shift in pixels. This is why 2K-resolution cameras (or greater) are preferred for 3D production, the 2048 horizontal resolution allows for a 10% horizontal *translation* without loss of resolution when outputting to 1920 × 1080, the preferred display format for most 3D movies and programs.

FIGURE 7.32

NLE platforms usually require a plug-in for stereo editing. Left–right separation, vertical gap, rotation, and magnification can be adjusted in the plug-in settings.

FIGURE 7.33

Viewing 3D, the eyes converge first on the screen then explore objects lurking in other planes. Objects in front of the screen in the audience (negative) space may have humorous implications, which might not be desirable in a drama.

---

[2]*Horizontal Image Translation* is a process of shifting the left- and right-eye images to improve the apparent position of the screen for more comfortable viewing. HIT can also alleviate excessive parallax in original camera footage.

Squinting in close-up   Relaxed gaze in landscape

FIGURE 7.34

Just as in life, converging on objects too close to the eye or camera can induce pain and fatigue.

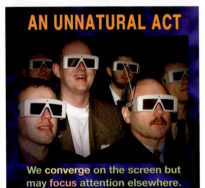

AN UNNATURAL ACT

We converge on the screen but may focus attention elsewhere.

FIGURE 7.35

3D takes advantage of a loophole in our physiology that allows us to separate focus from convergence. For some folks, this takes practice.

FIGURE 7.36

The 3D shooter's first order of business: Where is the screen plane? Where do I converge?

FIGURE 7.37

The audience's eyes go first to the screen plane across every cut.

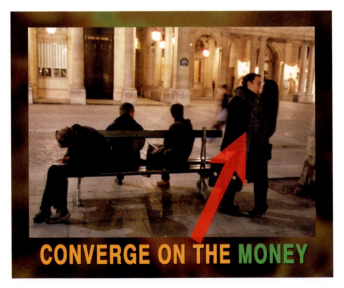

CONVERGE ON THE MONEY

3D CAMERA SETUP

The essential functions are familiar—white balance, exposure, shutter, and focus. With respect to scanning mode, it is best to avoid the interlaced formats, which may complicate color correction and post processing and impede the viewer's merging of the left and right images that contain a temporal separation. Although shooting in progressive mode at 24, 25, 30 or 60 FPS is preferable it may not always be possible for broadcast applications.

With the advent of *The Hobbit: An Unexpected Journey* (2012)[3] presented at 48 FPS, increased attention is being paid now to shooting 3D at a higher than normal 24 FPS. Although resolution is important, it is not nearly as critical as frame rate to realizing a compelling viewer experience. The impact of *3D HFR (High Frame Rate)* is felt notably in the smoothness of motion and the ease and willingness of audiences to merge the left and right images. The film has raised significant issues however with respect to genre and viewer perceptions. I discuss some of these at the conclusion of this chapter.

3D requires matching photography in each eye. This is automatically done for us in one-piece 3D camcorders—but not always. Vertical misalignment can still be problematic especially with longer focal length lenses. Most 3D camcorders have a manual adjustment to correct the error.

FIGURE 7.38

Integrated 3D camcorders feature an intricate series of servomotors that lock the left and right imaging systems together. The matching is a delicate balancing act especially given the complexity of a zoom lens!

[3] Blackwood, C. (Producer), Boyens, P. (Producer), Cunningham, C. (Producer), Dravitzki, M. (Producer), Emmerich, T. (Producer), Horn, A. (Producer), … Jackson, P. (Producer & Director). (2012). *The Hobbit: An Unexpected Journey* [Motion picture]. USA: New Line Cinema.

FIGURE 7.39

When white balancing a 3D camera, be sure the white reference covers both lenses! Interestingly, when superimposing a pair of images this far out of whack, the brain selects the properly balanced left eye and disregards the right!

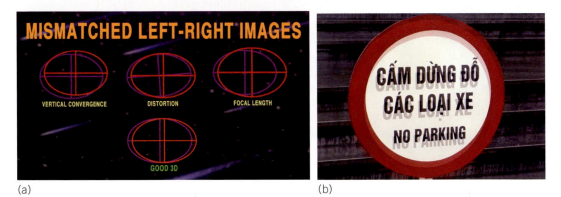

(a)   (b)

FIGURE 7.40

The vertical gap apparent in (b) is among the most objectionable of stereo defects. Vertical misalignment can be manually corrected in some cameras.

AVOIDING TOLERANCE ISSUES

On one hand, it is vital to see as much 3D as we can to develop a proficiency at spotting defects like vertical registration errors or excessive parallax. On the other hand, we know that shooting 3D is a lot like using drugs. Over time, we need more to feel the same effect, as we become acclimated to the 3D *gimmick* and are able to fuse increasingly higher levels of stereo. Keep in mind that our viewers are not nearly as addicted or as proficient at viewing 3D.

When operating a 3D camera, it is important to see our work in stereo from time to time to test our assumptions and confirm all is well, but we should not be making critical imaging decisions based on a small monitor's stereo image. A monitor's view can be misleading and should not be referenced by the shooter or client as an accurate representation of the final work. Seeing a compelling image on a small monitor only means the stereo image looks good on *that* size monitor. It has no bearing on the viability of the stereo image on larger (or smaller) screens.

The camera finder or monitor should be set to *mixed* mode to ascertain the position of the screen plane, where the overlapping left and right eyes appear as a single image. It is important to disable *peaking* and EVF[4] to more clearly see the outline of the overlapping the left and right channels. Switch to the *base view* (left eye only) to frame, focus, and follow action. Don't forget to focus. That's important.

FIGURE 7.42

The 3D Assist in some monitors provides a grid to check for excessive parallax.

FIGURE 7.41

Shooters must learn to assess proper parallax from the mixed image—not the 3D view.

FIGURE 7.43

Do not rely on a 3D monitor for shooting. It only reflects how the stereo will look on *that* size screen!

FIGURE 7.44

Proper parallax is assessed while monitoring the *mixed* left and right images.

---

[4]The electronic viewfinder (EVF) peaking in most cameras may be disabled via an external switch or control.

SCREEN SIZE MATTERS

The human adult's eyes are approximately 65 mm apart. This means to avoid the pain and discomfort of splaying the eyes outward the separation of the left and right images *regardless* of screen size cannot exceed 65 mm (2.5 in.). On a tablet or mobile device, the 65 mm separation represents a relatively high percentage of the screen area, which means small-screen viewers are able to enjoy greater depth than large-screen viewers in a cinema, where the 65 mm represents less than 1% of the projected image.

For this reason, 3D shooters must know and take into account the largest anticipated screen size, even at the risk of losing depth on smaller displays. In order to preserve a consistent look across multiple platforms, James Cameron was said to have prepared *34* different versions of *Avatar* (2009)[5] for different screen sizes, distribution formats, and display devices.

If in doubt about the ultimate display venue, it's always better to err in favor of the larger screen. The conservative approach may also help preserve one's broadcast options. SKY TV currently restricts 3D programming to 2% separation in positive space and only 1% in negative space. That's fewer than 20 pixels of parallax in front of the screen!

FIGURE 7.45

Most audiences have limited proficiency when viewing 3D. A conservative approach to setting parallax can help smooth the public's transition into this alien universe.

FIGURE 7.46

Be considerate. Regardless of screen size, 65 mm is the maximum amount of left–right separation that we can comfortably handle.

[5]Cameron, J. (Producer & Director), Breton, B. (Producer), Kalogridis, L. (Producer), Landau, J. (Producer), McLaglen, J. (Producer), Tashjian, J. (Producer), … Wilson, C. (Producer). (2009). *Avatar* [Motion picture]. USA: 20th Century Fox Film Corporation.

PARALLAX: GETTING IT RIGHT

We have various tools to help determine the proper separation of the left and right images. The integrated 3D camera features a *convergence control* that sets the relative position of the screen plane and amount of parallax. In Panasonic cameras, the convergence control is linked to a *3D Guide*, a numerical readout that indicates the distance range of objects that lie safely within the audience's comfort zone. The *comfort zone* is calculated mathematically and varies according to screen size, interaxial distance, lens focal distance, and focal length. At longer focal lengths, the comfort zone may be reduced to a few centimeters!

FIGURE 7.47

Like focus, the convergence may also need to be adjusted mid-scene to ensure actors do not venture to the wrong side of the screen!

FIGURE 7.48

(a) A 3D shooter must be cognizant at all times of the viewer's comfort. Unfused objects (UFOs) such as fists and beach balls that exit the comfort zone and race toward the viewer are time sensitive and may not linger in front of the screen (b) A comparable level of discomfort may also be realized from *hyperdiverged* objects behind the screen.

(a)

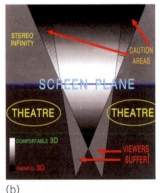

(b)

(a)   (b)

FIGURE 7.49

The 3D Guide (a) in Panasonic cameras features settings for 77- and 200-inch screens. This display indicates a comfort range for objects situated from 3.1 meters to infinity. Smartphone apps like this one (b) support a wide range of formats, sensor sizes, interaxials, and display venues.

SHOOTING 3D IN 10 EASY STEPS

1) Set white balance & exposure.

2) Enable 3D guide for largest **screen size.**

3) Select MIX.

4) Disable EVF peaking.

5) **Set convergence point.**

6) Confirm **Comfort Zone.**

7) Disable MIX to return to single-eye view.

8) Focus.

9) Check framing for **window violations.**

10) **Shoot.**

FIGURE 7.50

FIGURE 7.51

Allow actors to breathe! Placing the convergence point too close to an actor may lead him to fall out of the screen!

WINDOW VIOLATIONS

A *window or edge violation* occurs when a person or another object appears in front of the stereo window and is cut off by the window's edges. It's illogical that the screen window located *behind* an object is somehow able to obscure it. A window violation that truncates a human body is especially disturbing, because the primitive brain doesn't react well to detached heads and torsos hanging willy-nilly in space.

The seriousness of window violations is highly dependent on screen size. Audiences in front of a 20-meter cinema screen are more forgiving because they are less aware of the window edges. With the move to mobile devices and smaller screens, the impact and disturbing nature of window violations are much greater.

FIGURE 7.52

Not all window violations require remediation. An audience in a large cinema, not seeing the edges of the 3D volume, can be very forgiving.

THINKING ABOUT THE 3D STORY

If 3D is to flourish and become more than a gimmick, it is critical that the third dimension contribute to the emotional stakes of the story. Similar to how color may be used to track the emotional journey of a character, so, too, ought a character's three-dimensionality or *roundness* reflect in some way his filmic journey.

When planning a 3D production, the depth in each scene should be thoroughly explored from the points of view of the characters. The storyboard should consider the relative placement of objects and players in positive and negative space, and continuity should be carefully monitored on multiple planes understanding that the viewer's attention may not be limited exclusively to the screen plane.

Careful blocking of the actors allows the shooter to modulate the 3D intensity during the course of a production, restraining the amount of stereo when it is not needed for example in a dialogue scene, and letting go with greater abandon when it *is* needed in a chase or action scene. This level of control elevates the impact of the work and creates a more comfortable and satisfying audience experience.

FIGURE 7.53

The 3D storyboard details the usable depth in each scene and helps ensure a consistent position of the screen plane.

FIGURE 7.54

When blocking 3D scenes, we integrate as many monoscopic depth cues as we can to facilitate more comfortable stereo viewing.

FIGURE 7.55

Forcing a viewer to fuse excessively diverging images behind the screen is exhausting for a viewer and will lead to cries of anguish.

THE ROUNDNESS FACTOR

The 3D shooter, like shooters in general, understands the critical importance of treating actors well. When our actors, bride and groom, president of the republic, or CEO look warped or distorted, we as

FIGURE 7.56

The head and face of your 3D subjects must exhibit proper shape and volume. Grotesque distortion of a leading lady's visage is not a smart career move!

shooters suffer. We lose clients, we lose opportunities, and we lose income.

Preserving proper roundness is the 3D shooter's primary responsibility. In 2D, a long telephoto lens flattens the facial features of actors. The extreme wide-angle lens conversely produces *excessive* roundness in close-ups, conveying the not-so-flattering look of an ogre.

Sometimes the monster look is intentional, and the story demands such a treatment. In 3D, the distortion of the head and face is especially disturbing. To primeval men and women, the sight of an alien with a medicine ball for a skull spells danger. It means "*Run! Get away!*" The unfamiliar being from another world could be a serious predator.

3D camcorders with humanlike interaxials do a good job at preserving the proper roundness in the face. Utilizing a telephoto lens with these cameras reduces the roundness in the human form and produces the effect of a die-cut Colorforms[6] figure.

SHEDDING YOUR EVIL 2D WAYS

It happens all the time. I see shooters in my workshops crouching low for a ground-level shot or forcing the perspective of a handrail or staircase. I see them zooming in for a *choker* close-up,[7] shooting over the shoulder, or going handheld.

These strategies do not work because 3D engages a portion of the brain that is primitive, fearful, and literal. The *shakycam* of 1980s' MTV is problematic in the stereo world—and this is why: Look around wherever you are, in the college library, airport loo, or the aisle of a local bookstore where you're not going to buy this book anyway. What do you see?

Well, one thing, unless you're drunk, high on drugs, or live in Southern California, is that the walls aren't moving. To the primitive brain, a rocking and rolling room is powerful motivation to seek immediate more secure shelter.

3D THOUGHT PROCESS

Consider 3D EMOTIONAL STORY
Think COMPOSITION of 3D volume
Follow CONTINUITY in depth
Modulate 3D INTENSITY
Create 3D STORYBOARD
Avoid 3D GIMMICKS & UFOs

FIGURE 7.57

[6]Colorforms, invented in 1951 by Harry and Patricia Kislevitz, were part of a children's play set consisting of thin patches of vinyl that could be applied to a plastic laminated board to create imaginative scenarios.
[7]A choker close-up is just what it sounds like—a tight framing that cuts through an actor's forehead and chin.

Same deal with focus. In 2D scenes, soft focus can be an effective. It says to an audience, *"Don't look at this. It's not important to the story."* In 3D, the opposite applies. Wherever we are in the world, most everyone and everything we look at is *in focus*. If someone or something is *not* in focus, we perceive a potential threat and scrutinize the object *more* closely to decipher what the heck it is. The 3D audience, fearing for its safety, can't keep its eyes off out-of-focus objects!

The same can be said of areas in a scene that lack clear depth cues. Significant over- or underexposed areas are difficult for the primitive brain to process and let go of. Likewise, expansive surfaces such as a wall or a table that lack texture can be difficult to reconcile, as well as reflections in mirrors and glass and repeating patterns in waves and puddles.

FIGURE 7.58

Reverting to old 2D habits? Consider having someone spank you.

FIGURE 7.59a

The approaching walkway at ground level is coming out of the comfort zone. In 3D, the forcing of perspective in this way will induce severe pain.

FIGURE 7.59b

The repeating patterns in puddles make it difficult to assess the location of individual elements. Without clear depth cues, the viewer places these areas at the screen plane, which may not be logical.

FIGURE 7.59c

Out of focus 3D is usually not a good option. For this reason, small sensor 3D cameras are preferred owing to their inherent greater depth of field. James Cameron's *Avatar* was photographed with cameras fitted with 2/3-inch sensors!

FIGURE 7.59d

Large areas of over- or underexposure lack clear depth cues and should be ameliorated.

FIGURE 7.59e

Handheld 3D can be effective for action scenes and barroom brawls because the individual shots are brief and the viewer is not inclined to try to fuse the left and right images.

WOMAN MISSING TOP OF HEAD!

FIGURE 7.59f

The careless cropping of the head and other body parts in front of the screen screams, "Danger! Run for the exits!"

FIGURE 7.60

In 3D, the flat cutout of Mr. Edison looks like a flat cutout. Objects that are supposed to be 3D must actually be 3D!

THE FUTURE IS GLASSES FREE

Audiences do not like wearing glasses to view a 3D movie. Aside from the inconvenience and the bad fashion statement, the notion of wearing dark glasses in a dark theatre strikes many folks as counterintuitive. Indeed, second to the discomfort of the glasses themselves, audiences regularly cite the lack of screen brightness as the *other* serious impediment to enjoying 3D movies in a cinema.

3D glasses provide the left and right eye separation required to view stereo. Active glasses utilize an electronic shutter that synchronizes to a transmitter in the projector or monitor. For home use active glasses are usually preferred as they offer better off-axis viewing, a consideration for folks watching 3D while folding the laundry or preparing a spaghetti and meatball dinner.

3D GLASSES ON PARADE

ACTIVE   PASSIVE   ANAGLYPH

FIGURE 7.61

Active glasses offer brighter viewing than the passive type because viewers receive the full 1080p image in each eye. The active system also does not require a special screen, so images can be projected on any white wall in a gallery, classroom, or apartment.

Akin to normal sunglasses, passive 3D eyewear relies on polarizing filters with a left and right eye orientation that reduces brightness and resolution by 50% in each eye. Passive glasses without electronics are much cheaper to manufacture and require no battery or charging, and so are favored in commercial cinemas and public venues. A silver screen or monitor that preserves polarization for each eye is required to view 3D with passive glasses.

When no better system is available, the old *anaglyph* system provides an easy low-cost way to view stereo content. Anaglyph 3D encodes the left and right images using opposite colors usually red and cyan. When played back on a 2D laptop or TV screen, anaglyph 3D provides a simple way to check assumptions regarding parallax, position of the screen plane, and smoothness of transitions. Many editors operating without a stereo monitor go this route to occasionally check their work.

Eventually, glasses-free viewing will become the norm as large cinema screens give way to mobile devices as the primary means for displaying 3D content. Handheld displays grow brighter each year, and can be fitted with a *lenticular*[8] lens to achieve the required left–right separation, effectively placing *the 3D glasses* on the *device* rather than the viewer. Low-cost *autostereo* (glasses-free) TVs with a wide viewing angle are still at least several years away.

FIGURE 7.62

Incompatible eyewear among manufacturers have contributed to the public disillusionment with all things 3D. These newly minted shooters in Brisbane don't seem to mind their flashy new accoutrement.

DON'T EVEN *THINK* ABOUT ENJOYING A 3D MOVIE!

If you're a shooter learning the ropes and are out seeing a 3D movie with a date, don't just enjoy the movie or the date! It's time to get educated! Raise and lower your glasses frequently to check the parallax on-screen. When scenes work, note the separation, and when scenes don't work, note that too. Especially note that.

---

[8]A lenticular screen projects interlaced left and right images through tiny lenses embedded in an overlying film. Lenticular displays require precise viewer placement to ensure good 3D effect. Future lenticular TVs may track the viewer's position in front of the screen and adjust the dual images accordingly.

3D VIEWING ON A BIG SCREEN WITHOUT GLASSES?

This Magic Eye® stereogram conceals a three-dimensional scene behind a repeating pattern of roses. Are you able to de-synchronize convergence from focus to reveal the hidden image? A few of my students can from across a room without glasses!

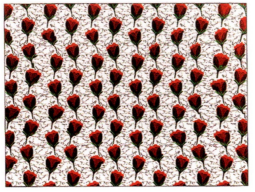

FIGURE 7.63

IS 3D HERE TO STAY?

In a 2012 poll, four out of five Americans expressed a negative or mostly negative view of 3D movies and TV.[9] By mid-2012, just 2% of the 330 million TVs in the United States could show 3D programs. *Avatar* was supposed to spur 3D's grand entrée into homes around the world. It didn't work out that way. Indeed any way you look at it, passively or actively, the stereo picture doesn't look good … *or does it?*

FIGURE 7.64

This camera's humanlike interaxial makes sense for small-screen displays that support greater parallax.

---

[9] Who's Watching? 3-D TV Is No Hit With Viewers; *USA Today*. (2012, September 29). Durham, NH: Leichtman Research Group.

(a)

(b)

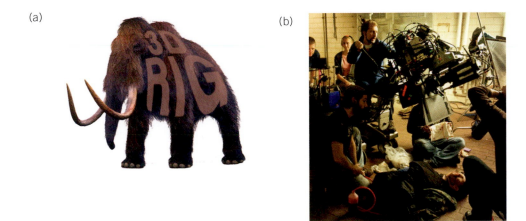

FIGURE 7.65

It's essential to learn all we can now about the $250,000 3D behemoth rigs because in a few years they will be gone.

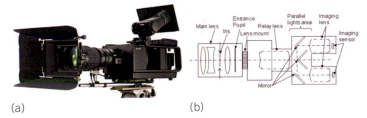

(a)   (b)

FIGURE 7.66

Less is more. It's true in lighting. It's true in life. And it's true in 3D cameras.

FIGURE 7.67

3D cameras with dual lenses employ complex technology to ensure a common optical axis, image size, and focus. This single-lens Sony prototype uses mirrors in place of shutters to create the left and right images. The simpler approach ensures better registration and precision at frame rates up to 240 FPS.

3D POSTPRODUCTION AND OUTPUT

The digital editing of stereo programs is accomplished using familiar tools. Final Cut Pro, Adobe Premiere, and Avid, allow for simple editing of the base view (left eye), with a *plug-in* automatically conforming the right eye for length, color correction, geometry, and so on.

Editors new to 3D understand that the pacing of stereo programs must be slower than 2D to accommodate *the moment of disorientation* across every cut, as audiences must each time locate the screen and any objects lurking behind or in front of it. The confusion across 3D transitions may be mitigated by adjusting the position of the screen plane while shooting or in post via a plug-in such as *Dashwood Stereo3D*. Its HIT function may also help address serious window violations by pushing

FIGURE 7.68
Use caution when editing to a stereo monitor. Besides developing a tolerance for overly aggressive 3D images, the pacing, parallax, and depth utilization indicated by the small screen may not be applicable to larger venues.

Edit LEFT EYE Conform RIGHT EYE

FIGURE 7.69
Digital editing is simple and straightforward—a major reason why 3D is going to stick around this time.

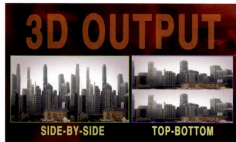

3D OUTPUT
SIDE-BY-SIDE   TOP-BOTTOM

FIGURE 7.70a
Whereas SbS sacrifices 50% of the horizontal resolution in each eye, top-and-bottom (T&B) foregoes 50% of the vertical resolution, which may be preferable for viewing sports with lots of lateral motion. Three-dimensional commercial discs utilize a frame packing strategy that stacks the left and right images in order to retain full resolution in each eye. A special encoder not widely available is required to prepare full resolution 3D discs.

FIGURE 7.70b
The SbS format is usually preferred for distributing one-off discs for screeners, demo reels, weddings, and small corporate projects.

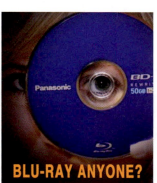

BLU-RAY ANYONE?

FIGURE 7.70c
Adobe Encore allows for limited BD authoring as well as encoding and burning of SbS and T&B discs on a Mac or PC. Burning a Blu-ray volume to recordable DVD media is possible, but not all BD players will recognize the disc unless encoded to an H.264 long-GOP "consumer" format.

the offending objects back into or behind the screen. As mentioned previously in cameras that shoot 1920 × 1080, there is no room to adjust the left–right eye overlap without enlarging one or both images and suffering some resolution loss.

Despite the 50% loss of horizontal resolution, *side by side (SbS)* is the most common configuration common format for delivering 3D content for broadcast, Web, and Blu-ray. Note that *3D Blu-ray (3DBD)* is a different format delivering full 1080p resolution to each eye. 3DBD requires its own player and a special encoder that is very expensive and not widely available. SbS or top-and-bottom (T&B) consumes no more bandwidth than does 2D HD, making SbS attractive to broadcasters and others working within narrow bandwidth constraints.

3D IS COMING—AGAIN!

This time we're not talking about *theatrical* 3D. That ship has sailed, and by almost all accounts, it's teetering and taking on water. If current trends continue and the major studios adhere to current plans, 3D feature films will account for no more than 10% of industry releases by 2015. Compare that to more than half of all studio product in 2011, which means any way you slice it, converge it, or horizontally translate it, 3D for the big screen is becoming a nonissue.

Notwithstanding the loss of public appetite for 3D movies and TV, the next 3D go-around will be much more virulent and far-reaching. The impending wave will have an impact on a broad swath of *nontheatrical* users, from corporate, industrial, and educational concerns to weddings and events, tourism, and short-form entertainment vehicles such as music videos and eventually episodic television. The catalyst for this transformation is the imminent introduction of 3D tablets and smartphones, that is, a 3D iPad, with potentially millions of portable stereo viewers entering the market virtually overnight.

Understand that I have no direct knowledge of Apple intending to release a 3D iPad, iPhone, or anything else. If I did, Apple would hunt me down, tie a pair of leaden Lisa computers to my feet, and toss me in the Sacramento River. I would die there and nobody would care. Still the stereo writing is on the wall. This time, 3D is for real and you can take *that* to the bank. Just be sure to leave your 3D glasses. You won't be needing them.

FIGURE 7.71

A flood of new 3D mobile devices will create a robust demand for nontheatrical applications from corporate and industrial training to remote learning and entertainment. This is the future baby!

2D TO 3D CONVERSION

Is it possible to shoot 2D and convert to convincing stereo later? It depends. Although good 2D to 3D conversion is expensive and only applies to big-budget productions, it is sometimes possible to achieve acceptable real-time results in some contexts, such as American football, owing to the relative ease of deciphering the spatial relationships among the players, field, and the frame edges. Unsurprisingly, close-ups are the most difficult scenes to convert on the fly, owing to the lack of *occlusion revelations* required for producing compelling stereo.

FIGURE 7.72

This real-time $40,000 converter exploits the monoscopic depth cues within a scene to produce stereo-like images.

EVOLUTION OF THE CRAFT

The Hobbit: An Unexpected Journey challenged the validity of many heretofore presumed stereo notions. Its high frame rate at 48 FPS appears at first unnatural and stilted like watching a rehearsal tape for a high school play. But after 10 minutes or so, audiences become acclimated to the new *hyperreal* look, and can then appreciate the 3D story and the clear, smooth images.

The movie challenged the long-term conditioning of viewers for whom a frame rate greater than 24 FPS communicates the look and feel of television, not cinema. As *The Hobbit* demonstrated there is no magic formula for shooting 3D. The out-of-focus backgrounds so vilified by 3D trainers such as myself were really not so bothersome on the big screen. Ditto for the moderate-to-fast cutting tempo, which audiences didn't seem to mind either.

So let's put it this way: 3D defects fall into two main categories: the aesthetic, such as the evolving use of soft focus and fast cutting, as the animal brain in us becomes more acclimated; and the technical, such as grossly mismatched left and right images, vertical disparities, or the inadequate brightness of a projector or a monitor. These latter defects are clearly problematic for audiences and really do inflict pain, especially when several of the most serious defects are combined!

FIGURE 7.73

The Hobbit: An Unexpected Journey challenged many aspects of the 3D craft from frame rate and soft focus to use of texture and pace of cutting. The wisdom of such techniques will continue to be debated as audiences are exposed increasingly to 3D content.

SHOW ME A WORLD I HAVEN'T SEEN BEFORE

The 3D perspective supports our greater mission to represent the world in a unique and captivating way. With tens of millions of mobile devices about to enter the market, the opportunities for 3D shooters will grow exponentially in the years ahead.

FIGURE 7.74

Be bold. Embrace 3D's alien universe with all the gusto within you.

FIGURE 7.75

Seek a new 3D horizon.

FIGURE 7.76

EDUCATOR'S CORNER: REVIEW TOPICS

1. Please explain the statement: *We've always shot 3D.*

2. Describe three (3) differences between a *videographer* and a *stereographer*. How does each type of shooter approach his or her craft differently?

3. List five (5) depth cues used commonly by 2D shooters. Do the same monoscopic cues work more or less effectively in a 3D environment?

4. Identify (3) factors that influence the placement of the screen plane.

5. Why is the ability to unlink convergence from focus so critical to 3D viewing and storytelling?

6. 3D is a technical trick that impacts the primitive brain. Identify three (3) conditions on screen that could trigger an automatic fearful response in an audience.

7. What might be the storytelling rationale for placing objects in negative space, that is, in front of the screen?

8. "3D is antithetical to effective storytelling. It constantly reminds us we are watching a screen and completely prevents emotional involvement." Do you agree? Please discuss.

9. Consider the *roundness* of objects and characters in a 3D story. From a camera perspective, list three (3) factors that impact the size and the shape of an actor's head and face in a scene?

10. Is it ever appropriate to blame the viewer for a bad 3D experience?

Story Command and Control

If we're singers, we modulate the tone and timbre of our voice. If we're writers, we temper our choices of words and phrases. And if we're shooter-storytellers, we control our images' look and feel.

For shooters using the simplest consumer camcorders, this chapter may seem moot because these models lack the rudimentary setup options. The cameras' imaging parameters—exposure, white balance, and focus—are controlled automatically according to the pre-proscribed dictates of omniscient engineers in far-off lands.

The demands imposed by the mass market have had a profound effect on the capabilities of entry-level cameras. In past generations, Kodak was said to have designed its popular Kodachrome® films with the *assumption* that mindless vacationers would leave the film in a car's hot glove box. This expectation of less-than-intelligent behavior played a key role in the product's engineering, and the same can be said for many consumer cameras today. Most low-end models are designed to require as little user brain-power as possible.

It's as if shooters want the technology to do the storytelling for them! Auto-focus, auto-exposure, auto–white balance—these aren't so much *features* as they are gimmicks, because relegating such choices to an automated process does not a gifted video shooter make!

The major camera manufacturers are finally transcending the auto-everything notion by enabling increased manual control of focus, white balance, exposure, and audio levels. Some cameras go further, allowing shooters to tweak *gamma*, *detail correction*, and the *color matrix*.[1] For the shooter coming to grips with the latest generation cameras, the creative options can be overwhelming and paralyzing.

FIGURE 8.1

Push this button. See what happens. The most compelling stories need a bit more of your input and guidance.

---

[1] See Chapter 9 for a discussion of key camera menu setup options.

AUTO-EVERYTHING: WHO NEEDS IT?

Auto-focus, auto-exposure, auto–white balance—what silly notions! How is *any* camera able to know what should be in focus, what *normal* exposure looks like, or how much red is supposed to be in a scene?

FIGURE 8.2

Capturing compelling visual stories requires rigorous control of your camera's imaging capabilities. Look for a camera that offers extensive manual control.

FIGURE 8.3

This menu toggle may have saved the manufacturer a few pennies, but its flimsy feel will drive you nuts, especially with gloved hands. Your camera must be rugged enough for your intended application.

FIGURE 8.4

The auto-everything toggle on the side of your camera is there for a reason—to be switched *off* !

DOWN WITH AUTO-EXPOSURE

Exposure is critical to establishing the desired mood, but what constitutes *proper* exposure? *Correct* exposure is ultimately a creative choice since deliberate *underexposure* can often add desired drama and mystery to a scene. Intentional *overexposure* can also play an effective storytelling role, say, in a sci-fi romance on the surface of Venus or of a traveler dying of thirst in the Gobi desert. The camera's auto functions generally preclude such treatments, so unless *your* story happens to demand a uniform middle gray, the camera's auto-exposure should be disabled. Consider the most annoying of all telltale amateur defects—the breathing of the camera's auto iris, as it continuously adjusts and readjusts mid-scene. When set to auto-exposure, your camera will interpret the world and everything in it as 18% gray. A solid white wall will be captured as gray even though it is not. A solid *black* wall will also register as gray even though it clearly is not. C'mon, engineers, get with the program! The world is a rich and vibrant place full of color and nuance. It is not 18% gray!

(a)   (b)

FIGURE 8.5

The world may be full of color, but your camera's auto-exposure assumes otherwise. Many shooters record a color strip or gray scale at the beginning of every setup. This can save time and money by providing a valuable grading reference later.

(a)

(b)

(c)

FIGURE 8.6

Earn your stripes! Your camera's zebras can help determine proper exposure. When set to 70%, a smidgen of stripes should be visible in a Caucasian face. Some cameras feature two sets of zebras with the ability to input custom values for each herd.

(a)

(b)

(c)

FIGURE 8.7

(a) Underexposure deepens shadows and buries the detail in the darker tones. (b) Overexposure produces washed-out blacks and a loss of detail. (c) Deliberate underexposure can add drama and intrigue to otherwise lackluster scenes.

FIGURE 8.8

When shooting in low light, try to include a strong source such as this freeway caution light to distract the viewer from the swirling noise in the unlit shadows.

YOUR CAMERA'S ISO

FIGURE 8.9

A camera's "native" ISO is fanciful at best because digital shooters, in effect, create their own virtual film emulsion from a long list of menu options.

A camera's ISO[2] rating is dependent largely on a shooter's tolerance for noise. Like film grain, some noise may be acceptable in one context but not another, and so a camera's ISO must necessarily be subjective. Some cameras including most Sony models apply substantial noise reduction, which may lead shooters to assess a higher ISO.

Camcorders that seem to exhibit a high ISO are usually tweaked for maximum shadow detail. In general, most cameras today may be rated at ISO 320, although some models with larger imagers relative to their resolution (such as the Panasonic AF100) may be rated higher. Standard-definition camcorders with relatively large pixels usually exhibit lower noise and a higher ISO—about two stops better on average than HD models.

ISO is influenced by user-inputted values like *gamma* and *gain* that impact a scene's gray scale. The rating suggests a camera's relative ability to produce a comparable image on film given the same exposure parameters.

THE CHINA GIRL

For years, the *China Girl*—who knows who she was or is, whether she's married or single, or actually more than one person—provided filmmakers with a common reference for Caucasian skin. The fact that a large part of the world's population is *not* Caucasian apparently eluded the designers of most motion picture films. The same bias apparently applies to video engineers who, like their film brethren, mostly live and work in countries in the northern latitudes, where the facial tones of the China Girl are the norm.

I'm not about to dwell on the political correctness of film emulsions, CCD or CMOS sensors, or the camera designer's cultural proclivities. Suffice it to say that a camera's auto-exposure is trying its hardest to render every face as though we all shared the flesh tones of the China Girl.[3]

---

[2]ISO is not an acronym but is in fact derived from the Greek word *iso*, which means "equal." The ISO rating reflects a film or video camera's relative sensitivity to light.

[3]In British television, the girl widely used as a reference was reportedly the daughter of BBC's head of video engineering. She still appears on the U.K. test card; however, she may well have grown up, married, and had children of her own.

FIGURE 8.10

This gal may not be from the Far East, but for decades, the flesh tones of an Asian woman served as a visual guide for filmmakers and laboratory technicians.

FIGURE 8.11

The Caucasian reference presumed by camera engineers fails to consider the range of skin colors in diverse populations.

FIGURE 8.12

The ethnocentric white globe of a professional cinematographer's exposure meter.

FIGURE 8.13

Note to humanity: We all share the same skin color regardless of race or ethnicity. The relative brightness of our skins, however, can vary considerably.

RIDING THE WAVEFORM

It used to be that a waveform monitor could only be found in a broadcast control room. Today, in many cameras and monitors, shooters have access to a simple waveform, which can warn of *clipping* or detail loss in a scene's brightest highlights. For green screen, a waveform is useful to ensure an even illumination.

(a)   (b)

FIGURE 8.14

The loss of detail in clipping highlights (a) contributes substantially to an overall amateur look. The waveform (b) built into some cameras can help fight this scourge.

FIGURE 8.15

From left to right: a dark scene possibly underexposed; a hot, "clipped" scene possibly overexposed; and a "normal" scene with a wide dynamic range that is possibly what you want. Any of the waveforms may be correct for the story you intend to tell!

I SHUTTER TO THINK ABOUT IT

Most video cameras have *two* shutters: a course variety for selecting the time: 1/25th, 1/50th, 1/100th second, and so on and a *fine shutter* for synching with a computer monitor or discharge lighting like fluorescents or neon when shooting overseas. With a slow shutter, shorter than 1/60th second, the increased blurring may add a slightly surreal look, whereas a faster shutter, greater than 1/60th second, produces a sharper image but with increased risk of stutter or *strobing* between frames. Varying the shutter speed (or angle) can have a dramatic impact on your visual story.

FIGURE 8.16

The motion blur induced by the slow shutter helps capture the hyperactivity of a New York City street.

FIGURE 8.17

By eliminating motion blur a fast shutter can produce an objectionable stutter, especially at 24p. Capturing this scene with a fast shutter and a higher than normal frame rate eliminates the risk.

THE STAGECOACH WHEEL EFFECT

Progressive video produces a series of still images that when played back quickly create the illusion of motion. If a wagon wheel spins at the same speed as the camera shutter at 24 FPS the wheel *strobes* and appears to be standing still. If the wheel turns at twice the rate of the camera, at 48 FPS, the wheel also appears to be stationary. However, the wheel spinning at, say, 45 FPS appears to be moving backward, because the slower wheel has not yet completed two full shutter rotations.

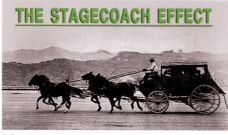

(a)

(b)

FIGURE 8.18

Some scenes are troublemakers. To avoid stutter or strobing when capturing a speeding stagecoach or when panning across a picket fence, use a slower shutter or wider shutter angle. A 210° shutter is usually sufficient to reduce the strobing risk (normal shutter = 180°).

FIGURE 8.19

The shutter can be a powerful creative tool. Some cameras express shutter "angle" in degrees, a reference understood by shooters accustomed to the mechanical shutter of a traditional film camera.

THE SYNCHRONIZED SHUTTER

The camera's fine shutter, aka *synchro* or *clear scan*, enables shooters to capture out-of-sync TVs, monitors, and other displays without the rolling bars and convulsions that can disrupt a visual story.

When shooting abroad, we may encounter a flicker in television screens, neon signs, and other discontinuous light sources. The shooter should be especially mindful of flicker from the fluorescent lights in supermarkets and many public places, as the noxious defect may not be readily apparent in a camera's tiny viewfinder.

FIGURE 8.20

A 1/100th second shutter eliminates the flicker from fluorescent sources when shooting 24p in 50-Hz countries. A shutter setting of 172.8° accomplishes the same goal without resorting to a faster shutter and concomitant loss of exposure.[4]

FRAME RATES AND YOUR STORY

Frame rate and the visual story go hand in hand. After determining the resolution (720, 1080, etc.), we select a *reference* frame rate. If we're shooting a feature intended for digital cinema, DVD, or Blu-ray, 24p is usually the best choice, from image capture through postproduction and output to optical disc. If our subject is news or sports and is destined for broadcast or the Internet, then 25p, 30p, or 60p makes sense, owing to the Web's 15 FPS de facto standard and the relative ease of down-converting material to that rate.

In high-end cameras that employ *intraframe* compression, 60p capture is usually limited to 720 resolution; there is no standard yet for 1080p60 acquisition, although cameras like the Panasonic AF100 are able to capture at this frame rate and resolution in a compressed format like AVCHD.

---

[4] Shooting 25p in the United States or other 60-Hz country? Set your camera shutter angle to 150°.

I mostly use non-standard frame rates in subtle ways, for example, when shooting a mood piece I may *overcrank* slightly by one or two frames to add weight to an actor's performance or to impart a dreamlike quality. Conversely, if shooting a car chase, I will *undercrank* by two or three frames to increase the apparent speed and peril of the pursuit. In either case, the effect is restrained and the viewer is quite unaware of the manipulation.

FIGURE 8.21

At high magnification, this flamingo would appear to move unnaturally fast if shot at "normal" speed. Capturing the scene at 40 FPS for 24 FPS playback produces a more natural look.

FIGURE 8.22

Slightly undercranking the camera can increase the drama of a chase. Shooting at 20 FPS or 22 FPS accelerates the action just enough to reinforce the peril while not making the scene appear artificially treated or comical when played back at 24 FPS.

FIGURE 8.23

Shooting at a slightly higher than normal frame rate can impart a dreamlike quality. This scene of my daughter at Mauna Loa, Hawaii, was shot at 30 FPS for 24 FPS playback. The extra frames slowed her turns and movements, adding weight to her performance.

FIGURE 8.24

A lower frame rate at night may help capture stunning cityscapes. The undercranked camera can dramatically improve a camera's low-light performance!

FOCUSING ON WHAT'S IMPORTANT

It would be easy to rant about the pointlessness of *auto-focus*—it's idiotic, intended for amateurs, it's the scourge of mankind—and for the most part, these comments are accurate. A camera's auto-focus should be avoided like Neil Diamond's 1992 *The Christmas Album*.[5] Selective focus and the appropriate guiding of the viewer's eye inside the frame is vital storytelling business, too important to leave to guileless engineers.

THESE GUYS ARE NOT ARTISTS

For some unknown reason, engineers believe that the center of the frame should always be in focus. Never mind the insights of the Old Masters and the Rule of Thirds. In most cameras, the shooter is saddled with this illogical conceit without the ability to target an alternative area of the frame.

Focus is fundamental to our craft. When we switch the camera from AUTO to MANUAL, we are affirming who we are as craftsmen and human beings. We must never surrender our craft to a soulless machine! Not now! Not ever! To focus manually we zoom in and bring the image into sharp glorious focus, then we pull back to frame our shot. We do this even in cameras without a dedicated focus ring by momentarily depressing the AUTO button. Just be sure to reframe afterward in a manner consistent with your storytelling goals and greater humanity.

FIGURE 8.25

Most cameras are designed to maintain focus at center-frame, which runs counter to many artists' notion of a compelling composition. As shooters, we direct the viewer's eye inside the frame by assigning relative importance to in-focus or out-of-focus objects. Only you the inspired shooter can make this determination!

FIGURE 8.26

Switch to MANUAL to avoid an irritating nonstop search for focus in the middle of scenes.

FIGURE 8.27

This camcorder's touch screen lets shooters target the desired auto-focus region of the frame.

[5]Diamond, N. (1992). *The Christmas Album* [CD]. New York, NY: Sony.

HD FOCUS CAN BE TOUGH!

The Society of Operating Cameramen has a slogan: *We see it first!* With the advent of HD cameras with miniscule viewfinders, one frustrated member half-jokingly suggested a new more appropriate motto: *We see it worst!*

In the HD trenches, we often struggle to find focus on a tiny low-resolution screen. Embarrassingly, our audiences will likely see the same image on a much bigger screen, perhaps in a theater at high magnification. It is truly disconcerting to think that our audiences have a clearer view of the scene than we do!

As craftspeople, it is critical to see what we're doing. One would think this should be a given in a business where seeing *is* everything, but it's clearly not the case. Heck, we will discuss to no end the merits of shooting 2K, 4K, or 6K resolution but something practical like the size and the quality of a camera's viewfinder and our eyes grow dim. It seems the *fantasy* of capturing great images is more appealing than *actually* having the means to do so.

New LCD and OLED[6] viewfinders are clearer and brighter but the challenge remains for shooters struggling with clumsy 1- or 2-inch screens. Manufacturers are aware of the focusing challenge and are trying various strategies to address the issue. Some cameras employ an *expanded view, bar,* or *histogram* as a graphical focus assist. The latter systems detect the high-frequency detail around objects in sharp focus. JVC camcorders utilize a three-color system, which serves up a monochrome image with in-focus objects *peaking*[7] and displaying a color fringe. All of these approaches share the same disadvantage: they are impractical for run-and-gun documentary applications.

For this kind of work, I use a simplified zone system and refer to the rangefinder readout in the camera's LCD. When shooting handheld, I support the camera from below and extend my forefinger to engage the focus while setting the approximate distance in the viewfinder rangefinder. Operating this way is fast and efficient, because I need not be concerned with *critical* focus except when fully zoomed in, or in very low light.

(a)   (b)   (c)

FIGURE 8.28 a,b,c

HD focusing on a tiny 1 or 2-inch screen is tough! Most cameras have a focus assist.

---

[6] Organic LEDs offer near-absolute black with a wide color gamut. With refresh rates 1,000 times faster than LCD, OLED viewfinders offer a smooth clear view devoid of lag, approximating the look and feel, it is said, of an optical viewfinder.

[7] To facilitate critical focus, most camera viewfinders feature a *peaking* function that boosts sharpness. The peaking level has no effect on the camera's recorded or output signal.

FIGURE 8.29

For documentaries, it is fastest and most effective to set focus by referring to the camera's rangefinder. Support the camera firmly on the palm of the hand and extend the forefinger to engage the focus ring.

FIGURE 8.30

The focus rings on older cameras were completely useless, spinning endlessly in both directions with little or no effect. Recent cameras like this one with a mechanical ring allow setting repeatable focus points—a welcome capability!

DON'T GET BURNED!

FIGURE 8.31

Beware! The midday sun can destroy your camera's viewfinder in a matter of seconds!

FOLLOWING FOCUS

For years, low- and no-budget shooters were hobbled by the inability to reliably follow-focus. When considering a follow-focus rig, look for a model with a large knob that can be easily grasped by a harried, rain-soaked assistant. Also look for a white marking disc that can be removed and recalibrated for other cameras.

High-quality accessories such as a precision follow-focus do not come cheap. Such a unit can easily run $1,500 or more, with the support rods, mounting plate, and drive gear.

So is it worth it?

I believe so. Top-end accessories such as a matte box and tripod will last for decades long after your shiny new *camera du jour* is relegated to a doorstop. If you're a serious shooter and intend to remain one for a while, it makes sense to invest in the best support gear you can afford. The superior craft that comes with proper support will serve you well long into the future.[8]

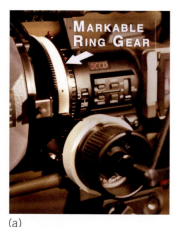

(a)

(a)

(b)

FIGURE 8.33

The focal distance for the Canon lens is measured from the red ring—not the imager plane!

(b)

FIGURE 8.32

The typical follow-focus engages a geared ring specific to a camera and lens.

FIGURE 8.34

The rocker control in many cameras is balky, making tasteful zooms difficult or impossible. This pro-grade controller enables well-feathered takeoffs and landings without the backlash or slop typical of cheaper units. Of course, the smart shooter refrains from zooming without a compelling reason to do so!

[8]See "Supporting Your Story" in Chapter 11 for further discussion.

WHITE BALANCE YOUR STORY

Our eyes can be remarkably adaptive perceiving white. We enter a supermarket lit by banks of fluorescents and don't notice the noxious green hue. We blow out the candles on our birthday cake and don't notice the warm orange cast. These out-of-balance scenes appear *white* because our brains do a lot of compensating—the green of the fluorescents is offset by a heavy dose of magenta, the orange of candlelight is infused with copious blue—all done without us ever being aware.

FIGURE 8.35

Excessive warmth may not be apparent to the eye. The camera is much less forgiving.

TO PRESET OR NOT PRESET

That is the question. For most documentary work, I recommend utilizing the camera's 3200 °K *preset* for interior tungsten and near-tungsten conditions and 5600 °K for daylight and near-daylight conditions.[9] Remember that white balance is a creative choice. Shooting under fluorescent lights is *supposed* to look a bit green. Shooting at sunset is *supposed* to look a bit red. Don't white balance these nuances out of your story!

In general, we need not be overly consumed with tweaking a camera's white balance. The popular editing tools from Apple, Adobe, Avid, and others, all have superb color correction capabilities that can perform minor tweaks and adjustments. Dramatic shifts in color, however, from day to night or from night to day are an entirely different matter because the massive boosting of an individual color channel can introduce noise and lots of it.[10]

MORE ABOUT WHITE BALANCE

To facilitate setting white balance under "average" conditions, most cameras feature *presets* for interior and exterior conditions. The interior setting is intended to capture scenes illuminated by standard studio lighting at 3200 °K,[11] the *color temperature* of a glowing tungsten filament suspended inside an airless glass bulb. This is the type of lamp used in pro lighting instruments from ARRI, Lowel, and others. The metal tungsten is used because when heated to 3200 °K, it emits an even spectrum of color—a near-perfect white light.

---

[9] Your camera's *white balance preset* is not the same as *auto white balance,* which is to be avoided like the plague.

[10] For more on color-correction techniques, check out *The Art and Technique of Digital Color Correction*, by Steve Hullfish (Burlington, MA: Focal Press, 2008) and *Color and Mastering for Digital Cinema* by Glenn Kennel (Burlington, MA: Focal Press, 2007).

[11] Color temperature is measured in degrees Kelvin after the British physicist who devised a system of quantifying differences in light emitted from objects heated to different temperatures. The Kelvin scale is identical to the Celsius system plus 273°.

FIGURE 8.36

Tungsten lamps produce a near-perfect white light at 3200 °K. Your camera's sensor and processor are designed to respond ideally under this type of illumination.

FIGURE 8.37

A typical white balance toggle features A and B position settings in addition to the interior/exterior preset.

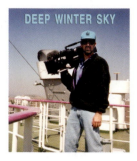

FIGURE 8.38

Scenes recorded under a clear blue sky may exhibit a noticeable cool cast, especially in the shadows. In winter, the color temperature in the shade may exceed 20,000 °K!

In nature, we find few light sources at 3200 °K. Incandescent household lamps exhibit a color temperature between 2600 and 3000 °K, which means scenes will appear unnaturally warm if the camera's tungsten preset is used with no further adjustment or filtration. Balancing the camera to a white reference in such cases adds the appropriate blue offset, which may *or* may not be what you want.

For exteriors, the camera applies a standard conversion by assuming a mixture of *skylight* and *sunlight* at a color temperature of 5600 °K. Fundamentally, the direct sun adds warmth, whereas the light reflected from a clear blue sky adds a noticeably cool cast.

FIGURE 8.39

Mixed illumination may be integral to a scene so you'll want to preserve the feeling. In most cases, the camera's white balance preset is the best way to handle it.

Color Temperature of Common Light Sources	
Artificial Light:	
Match flame	1700º K.
Candlelight	1850º K.
Sodium vapor streetlight	2100º K.
Household incandescent	2980º K.
Standard studio (halogen lamp)	3200º K.
Photoflood	3400º K.
Daylight blue photoflood	4800º K.
Fluorescent (Cool White)	4300º K.
Fluorescent (Warm White)	3050º K.
HMI	5600º K.
Xenon	6000º K.
Sunlight:	
Sunrise or sunset	2000º K.
One hour after sunrise	3500º K.
Early morning/late afternoon	4300º K.
Average noon (Washington, D.C.)	5400º K.
Midsummer	5800º K.
Daylight (mix of skylight and sunlight):	
Overcast sky	6000º K.
Average summer daylight	6500º K.
Light summer shade	7100º K.
Average summer shade	8000º K.
Partly cloudy sky	8000º–10000º K.
Summer/winter skylight	9500º–30000º K.

Source: *American Cinematographer Manual*, 6th Edition 1986.

FIGURE 8.40

SETTING MANUAL WHITE BALANCE

One way or another we must inform the camera what white *looks* like in our scene. To white balance manually, we can use as a reference any white surface such as a plain piece of paper or the back of a show card. Zoom in to fill the frame, then press and hold the camera's white balance button or dial. An icon in the viewfinder will blink, then go steady as the camera applies the requested compensation.

FIGURE 8.41

When balancing San Marco Square at dusk, we should compensate enough to alleviate the excessive warmth, but not so much as to remove all sense of place and drama. It's worth repeating: We don't balance our whites at the expense of the story!

THE ILLOGIC OF AUTO-WHITE

Our cameras are getting smarter, but how can any camera know what is supposed to be white in a scene? Left in auto mode the camera will continuously "correct" whether warranted or not. Warm sections of scenes will be *corrected* by adding blue. Cool scenes will get the opposite treatment, receiving an injection of red. We can imagine how the endless shifting color can wreak havoc in postproduction as we struggle to build a visually coherent sequence.

Auto-white is an anathema to good storytelling craft. *We* control how the camera sees the world, and the last time I checked, the world was not a morass of dull neutral tones. Yes, we must inform the camera what white looks like, use the correct preset, or set the white balance manually. However, we do it; remember that the *white* our story requires may well have a dash of warmth or coolness in it.

FIGURE 8.42

White balance goes a long way to communicate story. Warm or cool? Which is correct for this celebrity? This scene is from the 1st Annual Vietnam International Film Festival in Hanoi 2010.

The savvy shooter understands that white balance like other aspects of our craft is driven by the story imperative. Shooters for shows like *Access Hollywood* have become adept at capturing celebrities coming up the red carpet, rewhiting quickly in advance of a particular star by adding warmth or coolness to the star's *look* in accordance with the dictates of that evening's gossip mill.

Whiting the camera to a blue-tinted reference infuses the subject with a warm flattering glow. White balancing to a reddish source has the opposite effect, instilling a cool cast on an actor who may be playing a villain in his or her latest movie.

At first, the references carried by shooters were scraps of colored construction paper to match the particular stars. This is the Cameron Diaz. This is the Angelina Jolie. You get the idea.

Today we can purchase ready-made cards in a range of warm and cool tints. It's an easy and inexpensive way to control white balance and mood.

(a)   (b)   (c)

FIGURE 8.43 a,b,c

(a) Warm-hearted Julia Roberts. (b) Cool bad-guy Charlie Sheen. (c) Icy bad Nazi guy.

FIGURE 8.44

A tinted reference helps the shooter achieve a white-balance consistent with the desired story and mood. The effect may also be applied, albeit less conveniently, in the camera setup menu.

FIGURE 8.45

A camera's built-in vectorscope can alert the shooter to an overly warm or cool scene. The image at right might or might not be correct—depending on the story imperative.

(a)

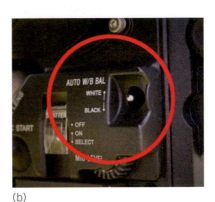

(b)

FIGURE 8.46

Auto Black Balance (a) ensures that proper color and shadow detail is recorded for each channel. In some cameras ABB can also help mask damaged pixels by borrowing data from adjacent undamaged photosites. ABB is usually initiated by a front toggle (b). In compact camcorders, ABB is performed automatically during start up or in tandem with Auto White Balance (AWB).

AUTOMATIC BLACK BALANCE

Automatic Black Balancing (ABB) should be performed periodically to ensure that blacks are free of color and are reproduced accurately. ABB resets the primary RGB colors to zero and is performed with the iris closed or lens capped. Many professional cameras close the iris automatically before executing ABB.

It is not necessary to perform ABB before every setup. However, the camera *should* be black balanced after a long period of inactivity, when the ambient temperature shifts substantially, when the shutter has been turned off, or if the camera is switched between progressive and interlaced scanning modes.

ABB should also be performed after a long flight as this may help mask dead or damaged pixels inflicted by high-altitude cosmic rays. This only applies to CCD cameras; CMOS or MOS models are not susceptible to cosmic ray damage, or at least not in the same way.

NO GAIN, NO PAIN

There is usually little to gain from increased *gain*. In CCD cameras the *gain* applies to the amount of signal amplification from the sensor.[12] When gain is raised the camera's ability to capture detail

---

[12] In CMOS sensors, the gain is applied at the pixel level on the surface of the chip. Regardless of sensor type, there is a concomitant increase in picture noise associated with elevated gain.

FIGURE 8.47

Undercranking the camera can create amazing images in low light. In Terrence Malick's iconic *Days of Heaven*[13] (1978), the actors slowed their movements to accommodate a 6 FPS camera for 24 FPS film playback.

FIGURE 8.48

Gain values ranging from –3dB to +18dB can be assigned to a camera's L/M/H toggle. I usually set the camera low gain to–3dB, middle gain to 0dB, and high gain to +3dB. Not all cameras feature a negative gain option.

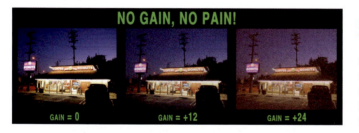

FIGURE 8.49

Be wary of shooting with high gain as this can dramatically increase noise and detract from the visual story. Some cameras including many Sony models apply noise reduction to offset the effect of elevated gain.

and grayscale in low light may improve, unfortunately, along with the background noise. When compressing later for output to the Web, DVD, or Blu-ray, this noise will be compounded potentially producing a maelstrom of ugly artifacts because the encoder is unable to separate the *unintended* noise from the *intended* image detail.

When shooting in low light, increased gain should be the last resort in order to achieve an acceptable range of gray tones. Most cameras offer gain up to +18dB, the noise at this level producing scenes usually suitable only for news or surveillance applications.

Each +6dB increase in gain nets a one-stop advantage in exposure. In cameras with a *digital super gain* up to +48dB, the camera boosts the signal in the digital domain where the noise can be more effectively isolated from the picture data.

Some shooters prefer working with *negative* gain, which may help obscure the noise in weaker shadow areas. Shooting at –3dB or –6dB has no effect on contrast or dynamic range; it simply reduces a camera's overall sensitivity, the equivalent in film-speak of employing a lower ISO.

---

[13]Brackman, J. (Producer), Schnieder, B. (Producer), Schneider, H. (Producer), & Malick, T. (Director). *Days of Heaven* [Motion picture]. USA: Paramount Pictures.

When shooting in very low light, I often *undercrank* the camera, that is, record at a slower than normal frame rate.[14] The strategy doesn't apply so much to dialogue scenes, but it can work well with newer generation camcorders that record discrete frames to solid-state memory. Undercranking at 12 FPS and slowing the scan rate of the imager effectively doubles a camera's low-light sensitivity (ISO).

KEEP THE NOISE DOWN

Although it's impossible to eliminate noise entirely, there are ways to reduce its visibility through proper camera setup, strategic use of physical and software filters, and controlled lighting.

Noise may be defined as random single-pixel bits of picture data that are always present but not necessarily apparent. Standard definition cameras with large pixels usually exhibit better shadow integrity with less noise than comparable-class HD cameras. In Chapter 9, I discuss how lowering the *Master Pedestal* can deepen the shadows and help conceal noise. The crushed look can be punishing, but if noise is the number one villain in your life, the victory-at-all-costs approach may be a way to go.

Dialing down a camera's *master detail (DTL)* helps reduce noise by blurring the edges of noisy pixels and rendering them less noticeable.

Raising a camera's *detail coring* can also help reduce noise by targeting and defocusing the pixels specifically in the deepest shadows where noise is most apparent. In some camcorders, the increased detail coring and noise reduction is applied as part of routine processing. This approach has its advantage, as images appear calmer without a shooter's direct input.

We must be careful, however, not to push detail coring too far because image detail is suppressed along with the noise residing in the same shadowy neighborhood. Use only enough coring to be effective, but not so much to render the shadows sterile and devoid of life. Note that raising the detail coring has little effect if the camera's DTL is already low. The coring option really only works at normal or elevated DTL settings.

Shadow noise can be especially objectionable in the faces of actors. For this reason, a lower *skin detail* level may be desirable to tamp down noisy pixels and reduce unwanted texture in the flesh tones. Of course, any substantial reduction in skin detail must be done with care to avoid an unflattering mushy look.

In news and documentaries, it is usually best to avoid the *cine gamma* modes that stretch the blacks and further exacerbate the noise in underlit conditions. Remember well-filled scenes are happy scenes where noise is not a concern or a serious storytelling impediment.

FIGURE 8.50

No guts, no glory! Shooting in low light opens yourself up to capturing your best stuff! Don't be afraid of the dark!

[14]Shooting at *less* than normal playback speed (24, 30, or 60 FPS) produces accelerated motion on screen; capturing a scene at higher than normal playback speed, that is, *overcranking*, produces a *slowed* effect.

THE TIMECODE SWAMP

Timecode provides a practical means of referencing and synchronizing audio and video throughout a production. In the PAL television system[15] used across Europe, Asia, the Middle East, and Australia, timecode is simple: Video moves along at 25.00 FPS, and timecode accounts for each frame on 1:1 basis. In the NTSC system, we deal with *two* timecode standards, owing to the discrepancy between the 30 FPS *nominal* frame rate and the 29.97 FPS *actual* rate. *Drop frame (DF)* and *nondrop frame (NDF)* timecodes have been around for decades, and they continue to be the source of misery and woe.

FIGURE 8.51

Beware of the timecode swamp. Timecode consists of four fields: hours, minutes, seconds, frames. A semicolon in software applications denotes drop-frame timecode.

FIGURE 8.52

Just as the earth doesn't spin precisely at 24 hours per day, NTSC does not operate at exactly 30.00 FPS. Drop-frame timecode compensates for NTSC's actual frame rate of 29.97 FPS by omitting 00 and 01 in the count every minute (except every 10 minutes). No video frames are actually dropped! As for the calendar, we compensate (with a few exceptions) every 4 years by adding an extra day— February 29.

FIGURE 8.53

The timecode swamp has sadly permeated the HD world. To enable easy conversion to standard definition, it is customary to shoot HD 29.97 FPS or 59.94 FPS with drop-frame (DF) timecode. When shooting 24p, the frame rate of 23.976 FPS and nondrop frame timecode usually applies.

---

[15]Phase Alternating Line (PAL) is a 50-Hz NTSC-like system with a raster size of 720×576. Introduced in Europe in 1967, PAL with the higher vertical resolution is superior to NTSC at 720×480. However, NTSC operates at a higher frame rate (29.97 FPS rather than 25 FPS) and so delivers more samples per second—a valuable consideration.

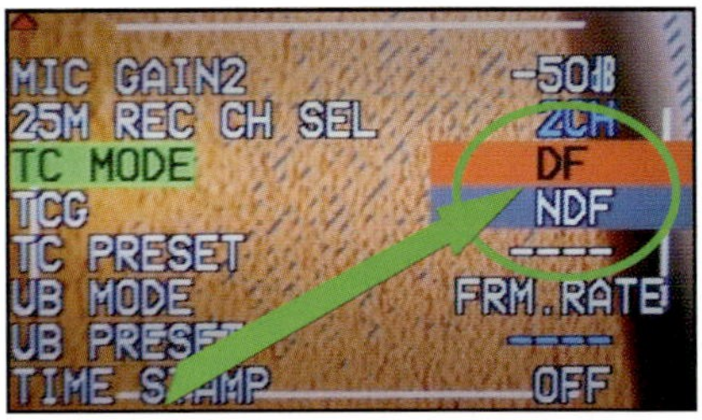

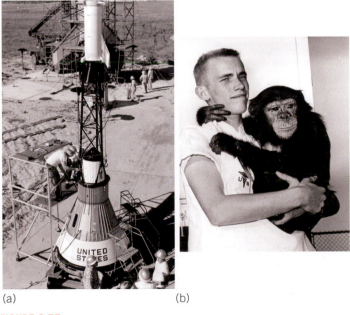

FIGURE 8.54

Broadcasters cuing programs for air usually prefer the running time accuracy of DF timecode. For closed-captions or subtitles, NDF timecode is the better choice, owing to the uninterrupted frame count. It doesn't matter which timecode mode is used as long as the workflow consistently reflects one or the other.

TIMECODE TAKES OFF

It was the best of times. It was the worst of times. Timecode arrived with the space program in the 1950s in order to reference flight anomalies beamed back from space. It made sense given the mission of the day: to divide timecode into hours, minutes, seconds and frames. The 1:1 system of counting frames over 24 hours associated each frame of video with a moment in real time. The system did not account for NTSC's *actual* 29.97 frame rate, however, which meant the timecode did not reflect *actual* elapsed time, a matter of critical importance to broadcasters looking to accurately cue programs and commercials in an era of live TV. Thus, the demand for an alternative timecode scheme based on the 29.97 FPS rate, instead of the 30 FPS approximation used by NASA and others up to that point.

(a)   (b)

FIGURE 8.55

The 1950s ushered in an era of space exploration—and timecode. To track anomalies in flight mission controllers embraced a 24-hour 30-FPS counting system.

WHEN YOU'RE FEELING OUT OF SYNC

When troubleshooting an out-of-sync condition always first suspect the matter of mismatched timecodes. Capturing DF footage as NDF or vice versa will result in program audio drifting out of sync at a rate of 3 seconds 17 frames per hour. This insight will save you hours and potentially earn you thousands of dollars as a troubleshooter over the course of your career. Please send your grateful payment to . . .

RUNNING FREE

When synchronizing multiple cameras the Free Run (F-RUN) setting continuously advances the timecode whether the camera is running or not. For single camera, the *Record Run* (R-Run) option is more practical because timecode only advances when actually recording.

FIGURE 8.56

Free Run (F-RUN)/Record Run (R-RUN) selector at side of camera.

SERIAL DIGITAL VERSUS HIGH-DEFINITION MULTIMEDIA INTERFACE

HDMI (High Definition Multimedia Interface) was originally designed to facilitate the interconnection of consumer devices and peripherals. In its many incarnations, HDMI interweaves uncompressed audio and video in a single cable at 8-bits per channel in the sRGB[16] color space. Although the reduced bandwidth and lack of timecode limits the applicability of the interface for serious production, many professionals utilize HDMI to connect to a monitor or wireless transmitter.

HDMI cables are notoriously flimsy and do not normally provide a solid connection due to the lack of a bayonet or other locking system. Secure HDMI connectors are available,[17] however, and can work in any ordinary HDMI camera socket, so be sure to look for them!

The more professional SDI *(Serial Digital Interface)* also outputs an uncompressed *multiplexed*[18] signal but, unlike HMDI, is not limited to 8-bits. This makes SDI or HD-SDI suitable for an all 10-bit workflow from origination in-camera through postproduction, color correction, and final output.

Circumventing the sometimes crippled capabilities of a camera's internal recording system the SDI output enables capture of superior images to an external device albeit not necessarily at 10-bits. The Panasonic AF100, Sony EX3, and Canon C300, output only 8-bits via SDI, leading to potentially compromised results. On the other hand, the 10-bit SDI output from cameras such as the Panasonic HPX255 or Sony F3 is capable of producing very high-quality recordings in a KiPro, a nanoFlash, or a similar unit.

---

[16]sRGB is analogous to the more frequently referenced *709* HDTV color space.

[17]Accell makes a locking HDMI connector that fits in any standard socket. The connector uses a shell expansion tab that works well. See http://www.accellcables.com/

[18]Multiplexing obviates the need for individual cables for video, audio, timecode and machine control.

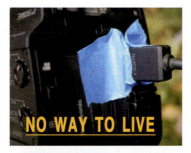

FIGURE 8.57

This is no way to live! Locking HDMI cables are available.

(a)

(b)

FIGURE 8.59

The AJA Ki Pro (a) is a versatile recorder capable of capturing uncompressed audio and video while up-, down-, or cross-converting from one HD or SD format to another. The popular nanoFlash (b) records SDI or HDMI signals to Sony XDCAM HD 422 using Compact Flash (CF) media.

FIGURE 8.58

A single SDI cable supports timecode, machine control, audio, and 10-bit video up to 1,485 Mbps-twice the bit rate of HDMI. A newer SDI variation dubbed 3G-SDI provides even greater bandwidth at 2,970 Mbps.

INTERCONNECTIVITY AND STREAMING

The transition to a file-based workflow has been dramatic, jettisoning videotape for solid-state memory, foregoing Firewire in favor of USB, and capturing discrete frames of data instead of video streams.

The camera has become a media hub and a server as interconnectivity via WiFi, USB, and Gigabit Ethernet grows in relevance, and content creators no longer need to offload video and metadata[19] for editing and processing. Camcorders are increasingly relying on remote control to accomplish this, employing proxy files in tandem with an Internet-enabled device like an iPad to transfer camera footage and edited programs via an FTP server.

---

[19] Metadata may be described as *data about data.*

FIGURE 8.60

The camcorder server allows wireless streaming, metadata support, and in-camera editing via a laptop or tablet. The editor utilizing the proxy video uploads the assembled program to a satellite truck or FTP.

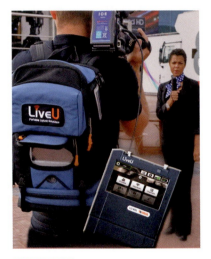

FIGURE 8.62

LiveU utilizes a wireless transmitter in combination with a cellular network to broadcast live video from almost anywhere in the world.

FIGURE 8.61

This camcorder records to an SD card in Slot 1 while transmitting video in real time via the Eye-Fi card in Slot 2.

MONITORING YOUR WORK

For most applications, an external monitor is essential for checking focus, color balance, framing, and composition. Achieving a solid black has been the bête-noire of LCD displays, because the fluorescent backlight projected through a liquid panel produces a murkiness that interferes with proper assessment of color and contrast. The newest displays reduce the murkiness by inserting a moment of black in the refresh cycle. This is a key advantage of doubling a monitor's refresh rate to 120 Hz, the improved shadows, deeper blacks and reduction in motion blur being advantageous for sports and other high-motion applications.

Organic light emitting diodes have dramatically improved the quality of images in camera viewfinders, monitors, and big-screen TVs. OLEDs utilize a shutter and series of filters with a response time of virtually zero, enabling near-absolute black with a wide color gamut and a contrast ratio of more than 1,000,000:1!

FIGURE 8.63

In low light or at night, an external display may offer the only clue to what you're actually capturing.

(b)

FIGURE 8.64

Some monitors offer a built-in waveform and vectorscope, with focus-in-red peaking (b) to assist finding critical focus.

MORE POWER TO YOU

Lithium-ion batteries are very efficient. Although they rarely last more than 5 years or 500 charging cycles, they're easy to maintain and don't lose much charge sitting in our travel cases or on a shelf waiting for the next call to duty. That's an advantage for the itinerant shooter; the self-discharge rate for lithium-ion batteries is half that of nickel-type batteries.

In every type of gadget and gizmo if it beeps, burps, or percolates, it's probably powered by a lithium-ion battery. From cell phones to cordless drills to the video cameras that pay our bills, we live in an era of lithium-powered everything. We like lithium. Go lithium!

But wait. Our friend who serves us so well has an onerous side. In 2006, a Wisconsin man went to bed one night and left his cell phone charging. The lithium battery in it overheated, exploded, and burned his doublewide to the ground!

A few years later, Fletcher Camera in Chicago replaced its entire inventory of lithium-ion batteries[20] with NiMH batteries after a *thermal runaway* wreaked havoc at a local sound stage. The flames from the exploding battery packs were said to have shot 10 feet into the air at a temperature of more than 1,000 °F!

Lithium-ion batteries can be especially hazardous aboard aircraft because superheated debris thrown off by a burning lithium cell can and has melted through the walls of aircraft cargo holds.

A battery may discharge in a slow trickle over a period of weeks or months, in a more moderate, controlled way as in the normal running of a camera or in an instantaneous release that could result in an explosion or fire. The latter result might be due to an internal short circuit, or the battery could be overcharged or physically damaged in some way. But once a cell goes *thermal*, there is no extinguishing agent that can stop it. As each cell breaks down, it fuels the next explosion. Given the number and size of batteries we pack for travel, a fire in one could quickly spread to others in the same case with disastrous consequences if this were to occur aboard an aircraft in flight.

Lithium-ion batteries require proper care. Running a battery too low prematurely ages the seals of the cells, which increases the explosion risk because a fully depleted battery coming back up quickly can produce enormous heat.

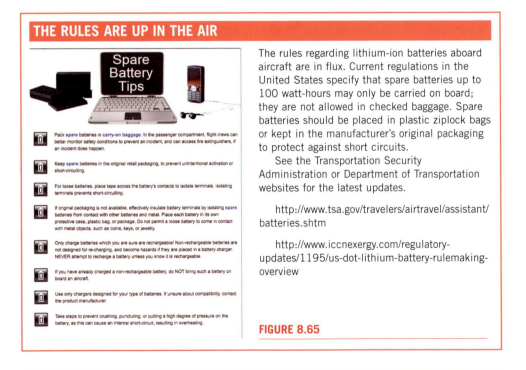

THE RULES ARE UP IN THE AIR

Spare Battery Tips

Pack spare batteries in carry-on baggage. In the passenger compartment, flight crews can better monitor safety conditions to prevent an incident, and can access fire extinguishers, if an incident does happen.

Keep spare batteries in the original retail packaging, to prevent unintentional activation or short-circuiting.

For loose batteries, place tape across the battery's contacts to isolate terminals. Isolating terminals prevents short-circuiting.

If original packaging is not available, effectively insulate battery terminals by isolating spare batteries from contact with other batteries and metal. Place each battery in its own protective case, plastic bag, or package. Do not permit a loose battery to come in contact with metal objects, such as coins, keys, or jewelry.

Only charge batteries which you are sure are rechargeable! Non-rechargeable batteries are not designed for re-charging, and become hazards if they are placed in a battery charger. NEVER attempt to recharge a battery unless you know it is rechargeable.

If you have already charged a non-rechargeable battery, do NOT bring such a battery on board an aircraft.

Use only chargers designed for your type of batteries. If unsure about compatibility, contact the product manufacturer.

Take steps to prevent crushing, puncturing, or putting a high degree of pressure on the battery, as this can cause an internal short-circuit, resulting in overheating.

The rules regarding lithium-ion batteries aboard aircraft are in flux. Current regulations in the United States specify that spare batteries up to 100 watt-hours may only be carried on board; they are not allowed in checked baggage. Spare batteries should be placed in plastic ziplock bags or kept in the manufacturer's original packaging to protect against short circuits.

See the Transportation Security Administration or Department of Transportation websites for the latest updates.

http://www.tsa.gov/travelers/airtravel/assistant/batteries.shtm

http://www.iccnexergy.com/regulatory-updates/1195/us-dot-lithium-battery-rulemaking-overview

FIGURE 8.65

---

[20] Nickel Metal Hydride (NiMH) batteries are not prone to fire or explosion and are therefore much safer for air travel. NiMH packs of the same physical size are heavier, less able to hold a charge, and produce only 60% as much power as lithium-ion-type batteries. A new generation of NiMH cells is currently in development.

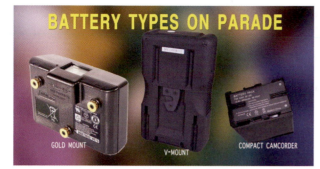

FIGURE 8.66

Full-size cameras in North America usually feature an Anton Bauer Gold Mount whereas cameras in Europe and Asia are generally fitted with a V-Mount. Simple adapters are available. The compact camcorder batteries from Sony and Panasonic are not interchangeable.

(a)

(b)

FIGURE 8.67

To avert a potential fire never completely exhaust a lithium-ion battery. Batteries from rental houses may be more prone to failure because they are likely abused and left on charge for long periods.

FIGURE 8.68

When not in use, your battery should live here. The trickle feature helps maintain optimal battery health, diminishing the risk of a calamity.

MANAGING VIEWFINDER CLUTTER

Focal distance, zoom percentage, date and time, battery condition, and umpteen other things all contribute to viewfinder clutter. Indeed, there is no shortage of miscellany that can obscure the image and the edges of the frame.

I prefer a clean view with only the essential functions: *FIZ (focus, iris, zoom)*, *timecode*, *battery level*, *record time*, *frame rate*, and *audio level*. A frame outline or *action safe* is especially crucial to ensure accurate framing and sufficient headroom. The action safe specifies a 10% cut-in from each side of the frame; the title safe indicates 20%. The notion of title and action safe zones is outdated, because it assumes that a portion of the transmitted image will be cut off in a 1950s-era home television. Modern viewing environments including laptops with thin frames seldom intrude on more than one or two percent of the picture area, so the 20% title safe seems like way overkill.

For reasons previously fathomed, the rangefinder is an integral part of my modus operandi as the RF can greatly facilitate finding focus when shooting in run-and-gun environments. Shooters of narrative-style programs will often note the zoom position for each setup in order to match the frame size in a reaction shot or to ensure continuity in case of a reshoot. The zoom setting may be expressed in millimeters or percentage.

FIGURE 8.69

Everything but the kitchen sink. A camera's viewfinder is supposed to facilitate framing, focus, and composition. The clutter here appears to work against that imperative.

FIGURE 8.70

For close-ups, the center marker placed at or over the nose is usually correct.

DON'T LAUGH. IT COULD HAPPEN TO YOU!

Always verify the REC indicator is lit when recording! In the heat and fervor of battle, it is not uncommon for a camera operator to forget to press RECORD! It has happened, especially with solid-state cameras that operate silently!

FIGURE 8.71

ANIMATION AND TIME LAPSE

Single-frame animation and time lapse is a staple in today's programming from nature documentaries to flashy eye-candy bumpers for the evening news. The *intervalometer* is best utilized subtly to increase the *apparent* speed, say, of clouds streaming inland from the sea or the sun's rays peeking around a building corner. The typical intervalometer can be set for times ranging from one frame every half-second to one frame every 10 minutes.

Determining the correct interval requires experience, arithmetical prowess, or the right iPhone app that can do the figuring for you. A robust tripod is imperative, as is sufficient power to cover an interval spanning potentially days, weeks, or months. Auto-exposure in this case may also be useful to accommodate a wide fluctuation in light levels.

(a)

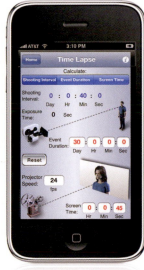

(b)

FIGURE 8.72

Show me a world I haven't seen before! The pCam app for iPhone (right) calculates the desired interval for time-lapse applications.

THE MAGIC OF PRE-RECORD

Seemingly out of *The Twilight Zone*, the *pre-record* (PRE_REC) function captures picture and sound several seconds before the shooter presses RECORD. The PRE_REC capacity varies from 3 seconds to 15 seconds depending on a camera's internal buffer and recording format.[21]

(a)

(b)

FIGURE 8.73

PRE_REC enables capture of unforeseen events like an elephant emerging from a forest or an attempted assassination in front of a California courthouse. With the camera pointed and uncapped, focused, the last several seconds of video is captured to an internal buffer then offloaded to the recording medium once the shooter presses RECORD.

HERE WE GO LOOPY LOO

The LOOP function enables continuous recording to the memory card or the hard disk. It is not other wise possible to overwrite existing files captured to P2, SXS, SD, and CF recording media.

FIGURE 8.74

Waiting for Godot? The LOOP RECORD function keeps the camera rolling indefinitely, capturing over previously recorded material if necessary to capture his arrival.

SHOOTING IN EXTREME CONDITIONS

From time to time, shooters must face extreme conditions, from snow and rain, to revolution in the streets and unruly wildlife.

---

[21]PRE_REC may not be possible at all frame rates and capture modes, including 24p. Be sure to check your camera's operating manual for specifics.

Excessive camera vibration can often be dampened sufficiently by engaging the *Optical Image Stabilization (OIS)*. The in-camera OIS can be quite effective when shooting handheld or from a moving vehicle. OIS must be used with care, owing to the increased resistance when attempting to pan or tilt the camera normally. OIS should be disabled unless specifically warranted.

Shooting in high heat and humidity may be problematic, especially for processor-intensive cameras that produce plenty of heat that must be dissipated. For this reason, video cameras are designed with large heat sinks or fans to draw heat away from the sensor where high temperatures can induce noise and negatively impact performance. High heat around the base of the lens can also affect *back-focus* and can lead to a softening of the image, a condition that can be especially critical in wide-angle scenes captured at or near full aperture.

Operating in humid conditions requires special care as condensation from moving in and out of an air-conditioned room can penetrate the lens and fog the interior elements. The trapped moisture may increase flare, lower contrast, and promote the growth of a lens-coating-eating fungus. My beloved Zeiss 10–100 zoom was destroyed in the jungles of Central America by one such fungus; a sad and expensive lesson that has since prompted me to exercise greater care when shooting in torrid conditions.

In this respect, solid-state cameras have a major advantage over tape-based models, as the latest camcorders devoid of a mechanical transport are not subject to tape fouling or clogged heads. Extreme cold can also affect camera operation by drawing down the battery just when the camera needs it most to overcome the increased internal resistance. The degraded performance may result in dropped frames and other recording anomalies.

FIGURE 8.75

Optical Image Stabilization (OIS) can help when shooting handheld or out of trains, boats, and moving vehicles. OIS is usually enabled via an external switch on the side of the lens or camera body.

(a)

(b)

FIGURE 8.76

Although a camcorder may run at temperatures below a manufacturer's specified minimum, extreme cold can degrade camera performance and shorten the life of internal components. Memory cards are particularly prone to failure in arctic conditions. Panasonic's P2 card (left) built to military specifications is able to withstand extreme temperatures and environments.

FIGURE 8.77 a,b

Without a fragile tape transport, solid-state cameras are well suited for operating in rainy or humid conditions. Take care to avoid condensation when moving in and out of an air-conditioned environment. To prevent condensation from forming on the camera and lens, place the equipment in a plastic bag, remove as much air as possible, and seal it shut with a twist tie. (b) Use your head! That shower cap lying around your hotel room is there for a reason!

(a)

(b)

FIGURE 8.78

Older lenses may appear to have a fungus that is actually condensation or evaporation from grease, paint, or adhesive. Lenses that have been exposed to high temperatures will often exhibit an internal haze.

SHOOTING IN A HURRICANE

The volume of water is not as much the problem as the humidity. Moving in and out of a vehicle or hotel room the camera will fog and drip like a lemonade cooler. A rain cover can ward off the deluge, while moisture absorption packs under the cover reduce the ambient humidity. The packs may be purchased at a local dive shop.

FIGURE 8.79

FIGURE 8.80

In winter, thin polypropylene gloves offer protection from contact with frigid metal surfaces while preserving the tactile sensitivity required to operate a camcorder's tiny buttons.

FIGURE 8.81

A camera glove imparts a more robust feel and protects against physical impact damage. Look for a design that allows easy access.

FIGURE 8.82

This inflatable bag protects against overzealous folks jamming their life's belongings into an airplane's overhead compartments.

FIGURE 8.83

The ideal case accepts the preconfigured camera with the matte box ready to shoot.

WHEN DISASTER STRIKES: CAMERA FALLS IN SALT WATER!

The effect of caustic seawater is diminished when diluted, so the sooner we get the camera into fresh water, the better. We should power down and keep the camera submerged as we hightail it in for repair. If the dunking occurs out to sea, we can drop the camera into a pickle pail and cover it with fresh water or liquor. Tasteless American beer from a major brewery, which is so awful for drinking, is perfect for this.

SHOOTING WILD LIFE AND WILDLIFE

Whether you're shooting a concert in Bangladesh, a revolution in the streets of Cairo, or a charging rhino in Zambia, the matter of one's self-preservation is paramount. In striving to capture a compelling unique story, the documentary shooter often places him- or herself, knowingly or not, in mortal danger. The constrained view inside a camera viewfinder can be hazardous and misleading; the shooter may not recognize a life-threatening peril lurking just outside the frame's edges.

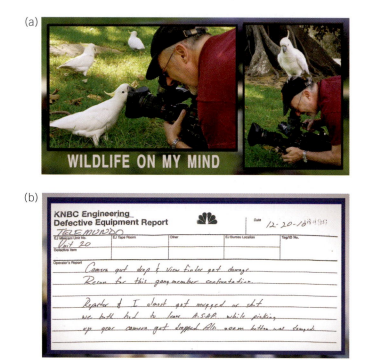

FIGURE 8.84

Our desire to capture compelling stories must be balanced with an equally compelling need to stay alive. Most shooters agree: No single shot is worth dying for. The camera damage report (b) alludes to a gang attack on a news cameraman in Los Angeles.

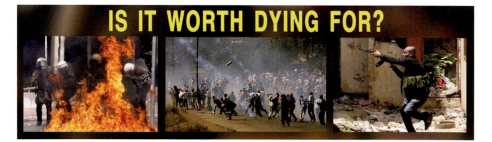

FIGURE 8.85

EDUCATOR'S CORNER: REVIEW TOPICS

1. How do functions such as auto-focus, auto-exposure, and auto–white impair the creative shooter? Identify three (3) instances where an auto function might be *helpful*.

2. What is the function of a camera's zebras? What impact might an actor's skin color have when setting a zebra value?

3. Describe the effect of a fast or slow shutter. At 24 FPS, what precautions can a shooter take to reduce the risk of strobing during fast pans?

4. Consider the impact of frame rate. How might small variations of one or two frames per second contribute to more effective storytelling? Under what circumstances might you shoot at 2 FPS? 10 FPS, 26 FPS, 40 FPS? 60 FPS?

5. Think about your film studies instructor, your dry cleaner, and other notable people in your life. Snap a photo and assign each person a color temperature. Who's cool at 5000 °K? Who's warm at 2850 °K? This is supposed to be fun. Don't hurt anyone.

6. Foul *weather makes great shooters*. Do you agree? Please discuss in the context of this book's mantras: (a) *Exclude! Exclude! Exclude!* (b) *Make 'Em Suffer!* and (c) *Show Me a World I Haven't Seen Before!*

7. Why does a 24p camera actually run at 23.976 FPS? In what circumstance would true 24.000 FPS be required? When shooting 25 FPS in 50-Hz countries, what frame rate is the camera actually running at?

8. Oh. One more thing: *Are there any shots worth dying for?* My Polish friends in the Gdansk Shipyards 35 years ago certainly believed so. Can you envision a circumstance where you might adopt a similar perspective?

Tweaking Your Story's Look

9

A show's *look* is a powerful storytelling cue. In general, comedies look sharper, bluer, and more immediate. Dramas look more diffused, warmer, and past tense. The shooter's responsibility is to create a *look* that is consistent with the program's intended genre starting with the very first frame.

For many shooters the old mind-set applies: *Are we shooting film or video?* The two media suggest different sensibilities. In film, the look conveys a dreamier, more transcendent feel whereas *video* suggests greater immediacy and is thus more appropriate for news and nonfiction programs.

I entertain this mental wrangling before every shoot, as I settle on a look and adjust my camera setup accordingly. Today, given the broad capabilities of digital cameras, we can effectively create a different film emulsion for every project. Although it's an advantage not to depend on Kodak or anyone else to produce the emulsion for us it can also be a curse for the reasons stated earlier: Too many choices lead to paralysis like too many options at In-N-Out Burger; it does not always make for a happier burger buyer or a more compelling video shooter!

Recall that traditional tape cameras are limited by their mechanical transports that must therefore operate at a constant speed. Apple created Firewire (IEEE 1394) in 1990 as a low-cost serial digital interface enabling easy capture of digital video to a desktop computer. With the advent of more film-like camcorders recording discreet frames to solid-state memory the relevance of Firewire as a *video* interface has diminished.

A video camera that acts like a film camera has some advantages, notably the ability to capture progressive frames at multiple frame rates. This can greatly expand a shooter's creative options and reduce by more than 50% the storage requirements of (still) rather expensive memory cards. The flip side is that today's tapeless cameras are no longer shooting video—they're capturing *data*, which requires a file-based IT-centric workflow.

(a)

(b)

FIGURE 9.1

Too many choices? Today's cameras can create virtually unlimited custom looks. In the past, the look and feel of a film's emulsion (b) was determined for you.

FIGURE 9.2

Shooting film or video? The two media convey a different look and mindset. Some cameras organize their menus in this way.

FIGURE 9.3

Many cameras' default settings contribute to a brassy look. Tastefully tweaking these values can help alleviate the harshness.

GETTING STARTED ON YOUR LOOK

The first order of business is setting the camera's *master detail (DTL),* which affects perceived sharpness by placing a hard edge around objects. When the DTL is set too high objects acquire a plastic look that folks associate with *video.* When the DTL is set too low images appear soft and lack definition. Turning the detail *off* entirely is almost always a bad idea,[1] especially in lower end cameras that tend to struggle anyway to maintain adequate sharpness and contrast.

When considering a proper detail level, we should look at the project's intended display venue. For small screens—an iPod, a cell phone, and the Web—the visual story can support a higher DTL than programs destined for the big screen, where the crude rimming around objects magnified many times is more objectionable.

When shooting in *film-like* or *cine-gamma* modes, the DTL is typically raised to compensate for the lower contrast and apparent loss of sharpness. Many cameras allow reducing the detail specifically in the flesh tones, which help cover imperfections in your favorite starlet's complexion. Be

---

[1] Turning off detail is not the same as a detail setting of zero, which means a *medium* amount of detail, halfway between maximum and minimum.

careful not to dial the *skin detail* down too far! I know a shooter who leaned on this gimmick a bit too much and transformed a leading actress's face into a soupy blob. That shooter is now selling shoes for Thom McAn's on Staten Island.

In new cameras, lowering the DTL should be a priority[2] because the elevated values favored by manufacturers contribute to a hard punishing look. One reason camera makers may prefer a high DTL is to compensate for inexpensive optics that lack good resolution and contrast. Some manufacturers may also believe that unsophisticated shooters *prefer* the pseudo-sharp hyperreal look. I'm told that's true in Japan. I don't think it's the case elsewhere.

In the natural world, we see objects transition gently in high-contrast scenes such as the silhouette of a skateboarder framed against the evening sky. Be conservative when setting the DTL. For narrative projects, consider using a lower setting; for documentaries, leave it at zero for moderate detail or increment it slightly upward. As always, let good taste and the demands of your story be your guide!

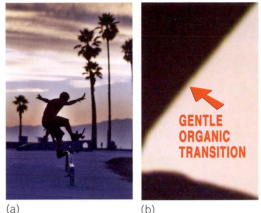

(a)   (b)

FIGURE 9.4

Smooth transitional boundaries produce more natural-looking images.

FIGURE 9.5

Hard, ugly edges around objects indicate excessive detail.

FIGURE 9.6

The *master detail* (DTL) level may be raised or lowered in the setup menus. In Sony models a −30 value is a good starting point. Note that a "zero" value means average or medium-level detail.

(a)

(b)

FIGURE 9.7

Reduced skin detail level helps conceal the blemishes in the face and skin of your favorite Hollywood starlet.

---

[2]This has been especially true for years in Sony models.

FIGURE 9.8

Black level has strong storytelling connotations. The low master pedestal in *Mdundiko* (2012)[3] crushes the shadows and imparts a strong sense of foreboding.

MASTER PEDESTAL: WHERE IS BLACK?

While well-gradated images are desirable for most documentaries and corporate programs, a grittier look, with muted colors, may be appropriate for dramas. Black level can be an effective story cue, conveying to an audience the essence of genre, character, and tone.

THE LEGACY OF STANDARD DEFINITION

Sadly, even in the HD era, we continue to bear the burden of NTSC's constrained color. Eight-bit HD cameras are fully capable of capturing a full range of values from 0 to 255, that is, where 0 represents pure black and 255 is pure white. Standard-definition NTSC and PAL, recognizing the onetime constraints of the *cathode ray tube* (CRT), cannot display black values below digital 16 or white values above 235. Exceeding NTSC safe values increases noise, especially in the red channel as the CRT struggles to display the wider gamut. Recording to a 10-bit format such as AVC-Intra offers only a partial solution as the displayed image must be limited to an output range of 64 to 940 (not 0 to 1024) in order to accommodate the standard definition release.

RESPECTING YOUR CAMERA'S DYNAMIC RANGE

Highlight overload or *clipping* is the hallmark of amateur video. A camera's *dynamic range,* its ability to capture tonal gradations from the brightest highlights to the deepest shadows, is expressed in *number of stops*; a Sony F3 for example is said to capture about 12 stops of dynamic range; an ARRI Alexa, 15 stops; and a Canon 5D MkII, only 8 stops.

(a)

(b)

(c)

FIGURE 9.9

Virtually any camera is capable of producing superb images under flat trade-show conditions (a). The dynamic range in this scene (b) would put any camera to the test. Shooting at Magic Hour (c) makes life a whole lot easier for you and your camera.

[3]Kabirigi, J. (Producer & Director), Riber, J. (Executive Producer). (2012) *Mdundido* [Motion Picture] Tanzania: Media for Development International (MFDI).

Many entry-level cameras including DSLRs have limited ability to capture extreme luminance values. Unsurprisingly pricier more sophisticated cameras are more versatile; the flexibility of the Alexa and its ability to capture a wide dynamic range being a principal reason why shooters are willing to invest upward of $60,000 in one camera.

GOING, GOING GAMMA

The *gamma* setting determines the range of tones reproducible in the straight-line portion of a camera's *characteristic response curve*. A low gamma enables a greater number of tonal gradations so an image retains greater shadow detail with improved dynamic range. The trade-off may be a dull lifeless image because the mid-tones and highlights are lifted along with the shadows. By comparison, an excessively high gamma *increases* contrast and imparts a surreal waxlike finish to faces and flesh tones. If you're shooting *Invaders From Mars*, that may be what you're looking for!

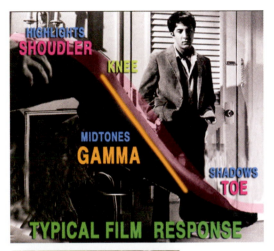

FIGURE 9.10

Although cine gamma is designed to mimic the gentle toe and low knee of motion picture film, the setting may introduce noise in underlit areas of a scene.

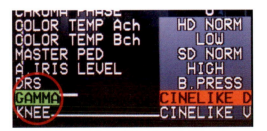

FIGURE 9.11

Many camcorders offer a choice of gamma presets. A cine option with the emphasis on dynamic range maximizes latitude and produces whiter whites, with the increased risk of clipping and shadow noise. Conversely, a cine preset that favors contrast produces images with greater punch compared to the HD normal or standard gamma. I prefer the standard gamma for documentary work, because the setting delivers the best performance with minimal noise under varying conditions.

FIGURE 9.12

In cameras that support numerical gamma many shooters prefer a value of 0.45. I like the increased punch of a slightly higher gamma (0.50) when shooting in film-like or cine gamma modes.

FIGURE 9.13

Selecting a different gamma may help suppress noise in dark scenes especially at night.

MINDING YOUR HIGHLIGHTS

Consistent with the look of film, a cine-like gamma lowers the knee point in order to accommodate greater highlight detail. Although the improved highlights suggest a more traditional film look, the cine gamma may produce dingy images, similar to using too little bleach when doing the laundry; the whites never get really white.

Conversely, an elevated knee above 95% produces cleaner whites, but it comes with an increased clipping risk. The clipping of highlights and loss of detail is very difficult to ameliorate in postproduction.

FIGURE 9.14

A cine gamma lowers the knee to accommodate greater highlight detail.

AUTO-KNEE

Blown-out highlights are the unmistakable sign of a novice shooter. To forestall this ugly condition, manufacturers dynamically set the knee to retain as much highlight detail as possible.

For most shooters in most cases, this is the wisest and most practical choice. Still, *auto-knee* has a notable drawback, as it affects the *entire* frame, pulling down whites even in areas with little risk of clipping. Panasonic cameras address this issue via *Dynamic Range Stretch (DRS)*, which applies auto-knee only to the sections of the frame that need it. Shooting in a sports stadium in bright daylight, for example, when panning from the dark stands to the sunlit field, DRS pulls down the peaking values on the field to ensure a smooth gradient from dark to light and vice versa.

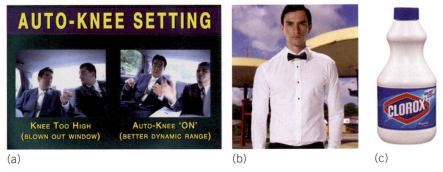

(a)   (b)   (c)

FIGURE 9.15

Auto knee enables capture of greater highlight detail (images courtesy of JVC). The downside of auto knee is less white whites like forgetting to add the bleach on washday.

FIGURE 9.16

The knee setting impacts the amount of detail retained after squeezing the oversampled image into an 8-, 10-, or 12-bit recording format.

FIGURE 9.17

Dynamic Range Stretch (DRS) can help to avoid clipping in high-contrast settings like sports venues in bright sun.

CONTROLLING CHROMA

Like black and detail levels, color saturation helps convey the intended story and genre. *High chroma* is usually associated with comedy or satire, whereas *desaturated* color or *low chroma* suggests a story told in past tense, which may be appropriate for a historical drama that takes place in the 1930s.

As in all things in the realm of camera craft, color saturation is best applied subtly. Kick it up a click or two to add punch to a scene, or knock it down a few increments to fuel a period saga. A high chroma can increase the apparent sharpness of a scene and help overcome the liabilities of a cheap lens, but the compensation required later to correct the imbalance later may introduce noise. It is usually better during production[4] to set up the camera as closely as possible to the desired look. The same look may be achievable later in postproduction, but it won't be as simple or as free of noise.

FIGURE 9.18

The saturated color of exploding appliances in *Zabriskie Point* (1970)[5] fuels the movie's counterculture theme.

FIGURE 9.19

The desaturated look of Depression-era America sets the tone in *O Brother, Where Art Thou?* (2000).[6]

FIGURE 9.20

Strong vivid color is de rigueur for news magazine shows. Some cameras feature a news gamma preset to facilitate this look.

MATRIX

Under ordinary fluorescent lights, we may not perceive the noxious green cast, but it certainly is there and the camera can see it, especially so. The camera's matrix function is intended to de-emphasize the green just like the processor in our brain; otherwise, the green could overwhelm a scene if the generic matrix were used instead. Many cameras now offer a custom matrix. Certain colors in a scene can be made more intense while others are toned down to support a storytelling goal.

---

[4]Shooting RAW offers maximum versatility in post, albeit with a more complex workflow and *much* larger file sizes. A RAW file is the digital equivalen of a film negative, containing minimally processed pixel information from the camera sensor. RAW data contains one red, green, or blue value from each pixel location.

[5]Ponti, C. (Producer), Starr, H. (Producer), & Antonioni, M. (Producer). (1970). *Zabriskie Point* [Motion picture]. USA: Metro-Goldwyn-Mayer.

[6]Bevan, T. (Producer), Cameron, J. (Producer), Fellner, E. (Producer), Graf, R. (Producer), Cohen, E. (Producer & Director), & Coen, J. (Producer & Director). (2000). *O Brother Where Art Thou?* [Motion picture]. USA: Touchstone Pictures.

The shooter may also use the matrix to offset a subtle hue shift due to increased video gain. In low light, hue shifts are common under mercury vapor and similar-type lighting, so a matrix more indicative of human perception under such conditions should be applied. Many cameras offer one or more compensating presets for various lighting conditions.

(a)

(b)

(c)

FIGURE 9.21

The muted hues in Rome (a) help meld the scene elements into a unified canvas. In (b), the intensity of the red rhino amplifies its dominant story role. Same in (c) on the steps of Venice where the green umbrella *is* the story.

FIGURE 9.22

The skewed output of sodium vapor lamps challenges the shooter's ability to capture a "normal"-looking image. In this case, the appropriate color matrix can alleviate the strong yellow curse. Changes in the color matrix do not affect the black or white level.

FILTERING YOUR IMAGE

The savvy shooter knows the curse well—the impenetrable blacks, the blown-out highlights, and the plastic edge around objects. For years, these were the hallmarks of low-budget video, and there wasn't much we could do about them.

Today's cameras still contribute in their own way to the video curse: inferior optics, hue shifts, and overzealous error correction all play their part. But whatever the reason for lackluster images, if you're going to derive the best performance from your low-cost HD variant or DSLR, you'll need to address the techno-aesthetic issues head-on, and that includes the strategic use of a physical or software-based camera filter.

FIGURE 9.23

The complex interplay of light passing through a physical glass filter cannot be re-created precisely in software.

FIGURE 9.24

The latest digital cameras produce video of extraordinary sharpness with a harshness and propensity for noise. Proper image control and filtration can help.

GETTING PHYSICAL

Although most cameras today require only minimal futzing to produce a decent picture, the smart shooter understands the value of a *finished* image, and to this end, a physical filter may be the most practical way to achieve it. This is because a filter placed in front of the lens optimizes the contrast and detail of an image falling onto the sensor, and thus facilitates the most efficient processing.

Capturing an improper look and hoping to fix it in post is a dubious strategy because the unwanted attributes tend to be amplified downstream after compression and encoding. Compensating in post might not even be possible, as the countermeasures required to remedy any shortcomings are likely themselves to produce objectionable results.

Although many camera filters can be approximated in software, the delicate interplay of light passing through a glass element is not a process that lends itself to a general solution. Consider a beam of light interacting with thousands of tiny *lenslets* inside a Schneider Classic Soft filter; as light passes through and around the irregularly interspersed elements, it impacts the character, color, and direction of the beam in myriad ways.

The actual impact of a physical glass filter depends on many factors such as lens aperture, the strength of a backlight, and whether the point sources in frame are sharply defined. All of these elements can affect the look and feel of a scene.

CONSIDER A FILTER LAST

The savvy shooter understands that a physical filter should be considered last, not first, after the lighting has been tweaked and diffused, and the camera menu setup options have been addressed.

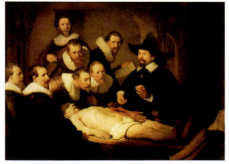

(a)

(b)

FIGURE 9.25

Consider adding fill light. Rembrandt probably never gave it a thought but his unfilled shadows can be the source of copious noise in digital video. Quiet shadows are happy shadows. Here have a cigar.

FIGURE 9.27

Turning down the chroma a few notches can obviate the need for a contrast-control filter.

FIGURE 9.26

Try reducing the DTL to alleviate the hard edges, especially in close-ups. Lowering the DTL mimics the effect of a diffusion filter.

FIGURE 9.28

High detail scenes like my grandfather's grocery in 1937 may wreak havoc if captured in an interlaced format. Consider de-interlacing such scenes in postproduction or shoot progressively at 24p, 25p, 30p or 60p.

DESIGNED FOR THE TASK

Although camera filters have been around since photography's first days the advent of tiny chipsets only a few millimeters in diameter has necessitated significant changes in design to accommodate digital's more stringent demands. Not that a vintage filter or *net* couldn't find new life in the digital world. It can. After all, it's ultimately about the aesthetics, and only you the gifted manipulator of light and shadow can make the appropriate determinations.

Many vintage camera filters utilized a soda lime glass that imparted a green tint, a trivial amount to film shooters, but potentially a more serious issue for digital creators owing to the potential for inaccurate sampling.

Modern filters for digital applications utilize a *water white* glass that is more like a precision lens and must be manufactured in much the same way. If the filter is not sufficiently flat, it can produce waves of distortion during slow pans. Vintage laminated-type filters should be avoided for the same reason, because they tend to produce tiny focus shifts and banding patterns leading to pixilation in the captured image.

It's not just glass filters that are the issue. The pattern of a traditional net or silk stocking can interfere with an imager's grid pattern and lead to serious aliasing artifacts. Older mist-type filters with embedded black or white droplets are also problematic, because some cameras interpret the scattered black or white dots as a dirty lens and ratchet up the error correction to compensate!

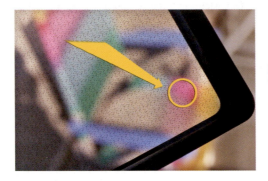

FIGURE 9.29

The tiny droplets in a black mist filter may become visible on screen at full wide angle and/or at small f-stops. Some shooters prefer an alternative filter type without an embedded pattern, such as the Tiffen Soft/FX or Schneider Digicon.

NEUTRAL DENSITY

Shooting wide open (or nearly so) is usually a good idea. Filter and net patterns are less likely to be visible on screen, the reduced depth of field helps isolate key story elements, and the low f-stop eliminates the risk of diffraction, image softening, and loss of contrast.

In daylight, shooting with a wide aperture requires a *neutral density* filter. Most cameras feature built-in neutral-density filters that provide a two- to four-stop advantage, beyond which a supplemental glass filter may still be required to achieve optimum exposure. Neutral density filters are gray in color and do not affect the color balance of a scene.

(a)

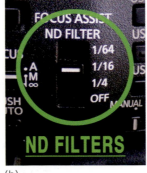

(b)

FIGURE 9.30

Neutral density filters are commonly available in a range of densities from 0.3 to 1.2, the equivalent of one to four stops. When shooting exteriors, a camera's built-in neutral density enables use of a larger f-stop—usually a good thing!

A POLARIZED VIEW

The polarizer is among the most heavily used filters in a shooter's kit and for good reason: It is the *only* filter that can *increase* contrast and resolution. The polarizer is indispensable for shooting exteriors such as land- and cityscapes, which tend to be low in contrast due to a camera's (usually) small f-stop and the multiple layers of atmosphere through which we often shoot distant and expansive vistas.

A polarizing filter increases contrast by reducing light scatter. This is accomplished by the filter's horizontal or vertical grid that blocks off-axis waves not consistent with the polarizer's orientation. Because the northern sky (in the Northern Hemisphere) is already partially polarized, a suitably aligned polarizing filter can darken the sky and increase the impact of clouds against it.

A polarizing filter is most effective at 90° to the sun. One way to determine the area of sky subject to maximum darkening is to point at the sun and note the direction of your thumb. The *opposite* area of sky is also subject to maximum darkening.

In bright daylight, a polarizing filter may also be used to improve an actor's skin tone by attenuating a portion of the sun's glare. At the same time, the increased contrast may also *increase* the visibility of blemishes, surface veins, and other defects, so a polarizer should always be used with care when shooting actors' close-ups.

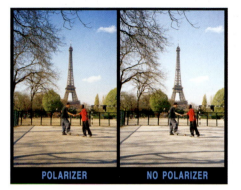

FIGURE 9.31

The polarizer is an easy and cheap way to elevate the perceived quality of a low-end camcorder and lens.

FIGURE 9.32

The polarizer's directional grid reduces contrast-robbing scatter. Polarizers are available in two varieties: The linear type is more effective but may interfere with a camera's internal focus system. Most shooters prefer the circular type.

FIGURE 9.33

Polarizers reduce or eliminate window reflections that can add a three-dimensional sense to a scene. Don't kill reflections and highlights that enhance your visual story!

SKY CONTROL

In daylight scenes, the shooter is frequently challenged by a bright sky that exceeds the dynamic range of the camera. The clipping of the sky and clouds conveys an amateurish feeling and so should be properly addressed. A *sky control* filter with a soft, hard, or *attenuated* edge narrows a scene's dynamic range and helps preserve critical shadow and highlight detail. The soft-edge graduated filter is available in a range of colors; the most popular are the blue, sunset, and the one-, two-, and three-stop neutral density types. In general, we use the soft-edge *grad* with wide-angle lenses when shooting landscapes; the hard-edge type is usually the better choice when employing telephoto lenses in order to preserve the graduated effect.

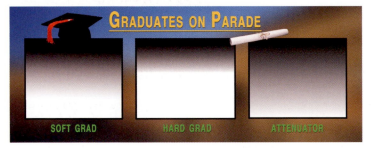

FIGURE 9.34

Effective sky control is critical to avoid clipping and loss of detail. The soft-edge ND 0.9 graduate (right) helps frame the scene and properly direct the viewer's eye inside the composition.

FIGURE 9.35

The soft grad with a feathered transition is ideal for establishing shots with large areas of sky. The hard-edge grad is used with telephoto lenses to maintain a visible gradient in the foreshortened frame. The attenuator is used for more specialized applications, the lack of a dividing line and need to conceal it being a major advantage.

FIGURE 9.36

You want blue sky? I'll give you blue sky! Tiffen's soft-edge blue #2 graduated filter.

FIGURE 9.37

In this scene, the graduated filter's soft edge is concealed across the top third of the frame.

FIGURE 9.38

This fella is sticking his neck out and you should too! A sunset grad adds color and interest to scenes captured late in the Magic Hour.

THE HIGH-CONTRAST DILEMMA

Maintaining good contrast is the shooter's top priority, employing most critically high-quality lenses with a lens shade. Shooting in bright sun, however, without silks, fill cards, or reflectors will likely produce *too much* contrast, so we need a contrast *reducing* solution as well.

A low-contrast filter works by redistributing surplus values from the highlights into the shadows. The lightening of the shadows allows the overall scene to be darkened, thus pulling down the hottest highlights to prevent clipping.

The increase in dynamic range, however, comes at a price. Blacks may become gray and murky and contribute to a flat, lifeless look. This is because the low-contrast filter does not actually improve the inherent capabilities of the camera; the filter does extend the dynamic range and increase the number of tonal gradations, but it cannot do so while maintaining solid blacks.

The cine gamma in some cameras works similarly, expanding the dynamic range and improving shadow detail while at the same time raising the prospect of grayer, noisier images overall.

Most diffusion filters incorporate a contrast-lowering component, so few shooters will need to invest in a separate series of low-contrast filters. Still, given the smooth, modulated images possible in today's cameras, a weak, low-contrast filter may be all you need to achieve a satisfactory dynamic range, particularly when shooting under bright uncontrolled daylight conditions.

(a)

(b)

FIGURE 9.39

Shooting scenes of extreme contrast? A low-contrast filter can help achieve a more acceptable dynamic range.

THE DIFFUSED LOOK

The capture and retention of shadow detail is a key responsibility of the shooter. To achieve the 98%[8] reduction in file size demanded by some recording formats, engineers target what they consider *redundant* or *irrelevant* picture details. Understanding that humans can't see well in deep shadow, for instance, engineers tend to look there for disposable pixel data, the result being a significant loss of shadow detail in scenes recorded to HDV, AVCHD, and other highly compressed formats.

FIGURE 9.40

A diffusion filter helps prevent clipping of the highlights while coaxing greater detail from the shadows. A noble idea but be careful—too little contrast produces images that lack sparkle.

FIGURE 9.41

Weak on-camera diffusion may be used effectively to reduce shadow noise. The lowest strength Tiffen Soft/FX or Schneider Digicon works well. Once again, less is more!

A diffusion filter increases the *relevancy* of shadow detail by lifting the pixel values, and making the data less likely to be jettisoned during *quantization*.[9] As shooters, we strive to create a mood consistent with the story, and so we need a strategy that serves our greater goals, beyond the pointless UV filter affixed to the front of cameras as a kind of see-through lens cap.

A one-size-fits-all diffusion filter is impractical. Depending on the camera sensor, processor, and menu settings, a filter that works well on one camcorder may work poorly on another.

Manufacturers look principally at three areas when designing a new filter: *refraction*, *diffraction*, and *scatter*. Favoring one parameter over another, certain flaws in a camera's performance can be addressed and ameliorated. This is what happened years ago when shooters discovered their old Betacam filters did not perform quite so well in the digital realm. The Tiffen Black Pro-Mist, which had reliably served the industry for years, produced a much cruder effect in DV camcorders.

Manufacturers tackled the issue of poorly performing mist filters by effecting changes in the porosity and reflectivity of the embedded black droplets. By reducing the droplet size, the Schneider Digicon achieved a tasteful diffusion without the halation and resolution loss that had formerly been the case with the traditional mist filter.

Of course, no one filter can magically transform a cheap, entry-level camera into an ARRI Alexa, just as no one filter can transform a clueless shooter into Sven Nykvist. Still, most camera craftspeople can benefit from a diffusion filter, and that means facing a bewilder-

[8]This is not a typo. HDV compresses at a ratio upward of 40:1!
[9]**Quantization** is the process of organizing similar value pixels into groups where the values can be rounded off, declared redundant, and subsequently discarded. The main purpose of quantization is to identify and retain only those details readily apparent to the human eye. How aggressively your camera pursues the discarding of "redundant" or "irrelevant" picture information is in part a function of its setup parameters, including black stretch, knee, and gamma. See Chapter 5 for further discussion of compression fundamentals.

ing array of choices. In the Tiffen stable alone there's the Pro-Mist, Black Pro-Mist, Soft/FX, Black Diffusion FX, Gold Diffusion FX, Fogs, Double Fogs, and Softnets. Schneider has its own lineup, including the HD Classic Soft, Warm Classic Soft, Black Frost, White Frost, Soft Centric, and Digicon. Same deal with Formatt, the U.K. manufacturer offering a dozen or more diffusion options. In Table 9.1 it's clear we have many choices!

Table 9.1 Diffusion filter types at a glance.

Type	Tiffen	Schneider	Formatt	Remarks
Black Mist	Black Pro-Mist 1/8, 1/4, 1/2, 1, 2, 3, 4, 5	Black Frost 1/8, 1/4, 1/2, 1, 2	Black Supermist 1/8, 1/4, 1/2, 1, 2, 3, 4, 5	Lowers resolution with moderate flare. Good for older analog cameras. Black Frost creates glamorous pastel look with has less effect on blacks than Black Pro-Mist. Can be used for general noise reduction in weak grades. Higher grades not recommended for small-imager HD cameras.
White Mist	Pro-Mist 1/8, 1/4, 1/2, 1, 2, 3, 4, 5	White Frost 1/8, 1/4, 1/2, 1, 2	Supermist 1/8, 1/4, 1/2, 1, 2, 3, 4, 5	Reduces contrast by lowering white exposure. Gently flares highlights without reducing resolution. Often used in tandem with soft effects-type filter for romantic look.
Ultra Contrast	Ultra Con 1/8, 1/4, 1/2, 1, 2, 3, 4, 5	Digicon 1/4, 1/2, 1, 2		Raises black levels while pulling down highlights. No obvious loss of resolution. Minimal halation and flare. When combined with proper gamma settings, a higher dynamic range can be recorded.
Lenslet	Soft/FX 1/2, 1, 2, 3, 4, 5	Classic Soft 1/8, 1/4, 1/2, 1, 2	HD Soft 1, 2, 3	Lowers contrast with no little loss of resolution. Keeps sparkle in eyes sharp. Causes highlights to glow softly in heavier grades. Good choice for general exteriors in weakest grades.
Circular Diffusion	Diffusion/FX 1/4, 1/2, 1, 2, 3, 4, 5	Soft Centric 1/4, 1/3, 1/2, 1, 2		Subtly reduces contrast without flare or loss of sharpness. Reduces visibility of blemishes and wrinkles in close-ups. Adds subtle edge-diffraction effects. Etched pattern may become visible in backlit scenes and/or when shooting at wide angle. Excellent for on-air talent.
Warming	Nude 1, 2, 3, 4, 5, 6 Type 812	81 Series	Warm Skintone Enhancer 1, 2, 3	Used primarily to augment skin tones. Warm effect is commonly merged with diffusion in single filter. General warming can also be added in post-production.

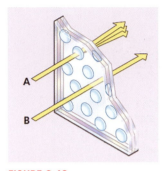

FIGURE 9.42

Akin to water droplets on glass the micro lenslets in the Schneider Classic Soft diffuse small wrinkles and blemishes while maintaining overall sharpness. Light passing through the lenslets (a) is diffused while light passing between the lenslets (b) is unaffected creating a mix of sharp and unsharp pixels.

FIGURE 9.43

When shooting cityscapes at night the ultra contrast filter can often obviate the need for additional lighting. The increased detail in the image at right is apparent at the side of the hot dog stand. Scenes illuminated by neon or sodium vapor sources can benefit especially from the ultra con, which lifts dense shadows without producing obvious flare or a pronounced diffused effect.

FIGURE 9.44

Use caution when using any type of net. At wide angle and/or at small apertures its grid pattern may become visible on screen. Some shooters prefer a rear-mounted silk net.

WHICH DIFFUSION FILTER?

TIffen Soft/FX
A practical all-purpose diffuser the Soft/FX is well suited for shooting high-contrast exteriors. The slight loss of resolution is offset by the generally more pleasing look. Tiffen Soft/FX filters are available in a range of sizes, including screw-in types for consumer cameras.

Tiffen Black Pro-Mist
A light black mist filter can help reduce hue shifts in the shadows and suppress noise. Heavier mist filters are best avoided, owing to a pronounced shower curtain effect.

Tiffen Gold DFX
The Tiffen Gold Diffusion/FX works well for stunning portraits and interviews. Its elegant finish and professional glean is seen frequently in broadcast and commercial applications.

Tiffen Softnet
It's old and no one talks about it anymore, but the Softnet 1B produces a great period look suggestive of a 1930s' musical. The Softnet 1S ("S" for skin) creates a comparable feeling, but with enhanced flesh tones—a good choice when working with narcissistic celebrities.

Tiffen Ultra Contrast
A terrific choice for cityscapes at night the ultra contrast filter delivers a subtle flare-free feel to cityscapes at night. For low-budget filmmakers, the filter can often eliminate the need for supplemental fill light in dark, high-contrast environments.

Schneider HD Classic Soft
Imparting a tasteful look without loss of resolution the Schneider HD Classic Soft is ideal for shooting talent close-ups. Excellent universal diffusion filter for dramatic applications.

Format HD Soft
Offering a slightly less refined look the HD Soft softens harsh outlines with minimal loss of detail and contrast.

CHRISTIAN DIOR TO THE RESCUE

Some shooters don't like the look of front-mounted diffusion, preferring instead the increased flare from a silk stocking mounted behind the lens. In this case, a section of stocking is stretched across the back element and secured with 1/4-in. double-sided tape or a rubber O-ring. The rear-positioned stocking produces extreme blooming in the highlights, so consider its appropriateness in the context of the story.

Because the stocking color is infused into the highlight glow, I usually prefer a black net because it imparts a neutral cast. On the other hand, a flesh-colored stocking offers the benefit of enhanced skin tones, a potential advantage when working with aged celebrity types.

For years, my stocking of choice has been the Christian Dior Diorissimo No. 4443, still available in Europe's high-end boutiques. (I acquired my stash several years ago in Paris at the Bon Marché on Rue de Sèvres.) If you go the stocking route, you should resist the temptation to use low-quality hosiery; the effect on screen will appear crude and less flattering.

FIGURE 9.45

A section of silk stocking behind the lens produces a dramatic blooming of highlights, which may or may not be appropriate. After affixing the net and replacing the lens always check the camera's backfocus! (See Chapter 6.)

REAR LENS MOUNTED NET

THE MATTE BOX

The performance of any lens is diminished by stray light striking the front element at an oblique angle. The off-axis rays are reflected internally, bouncing off multiple elements, which increases flare and lowers contrast and resolution.

Screw-in filters offer the advantage of low cost and easy availability, but the fumbling and risk of cross-threading when the chips are down (so to speak) can be disconcerting. Consider the task of screwing in a filter in the face of a charging rhino or a panicked director pleading for one more take before a rapidly setting sun.

The square or rectangular filters used with a professional matte box allow more efficient handling with greater creative options, including more accurate positioning of graduated filters and a polarizer for darkening the sky or to control window reflections.

FIGURE 9.46

Awkward and inefficient. Not all professional filters are available in screw-in sizes.

FIGURE 9.47

A professional matte box protects against light striking the lens obliquely and lowering resolution and contrast. This is important! You must use a proper lens shade or matte box!

FIGURE 9.48

Don't take widescreen lying down! A properly proportioned matte box offers maximum protection!

FIGURE 9.49

A French flag prevents the sun or strong backlight from directly striking the front of the lens. Some matte boxes provide simple mounting of the French flag.

ROD OR CLIP-ON?

FIGURE 9.50

A clip-on matte box is economical and convenient, but the extra weight may place excessive stress on the front of the lens and impair optical performance. A full-size matte box and follow-focus require a proper rod system to support the weight and ensure smooth operation.

HOW THEY STACK UP

The maintaining of good contrast is critical. Although inferior lenses and the lack of a matte box or shade are contributing factors, the stacking of multiple filters can make matters worse by increasing the number of air-to-glass surfaces and potential internal reflections that lead to contrast loss.

If a warming effect is desired along with diffusion, I usually opt for a combination filter such as a Warm Supermist that merges the two functions. I try not to stack more than two filters in any case, limiting myself, say, to a graduated filter and a polarizer.

(a)

(b)

FIGURE 9.51

The star filter was once a favorite of sports and event shooters. A rotating stage in the matte box helps achieve the desired orientation. (b) The Tiffen vector star.

FIGURE 9.52

Sometimes stacking is unavoidable. Here a diffusion filter is used to soften the harshness of the star filter behind it. The position of the star closer to camera reduces the likelihood of its wire pattern appearing on screen.

DIGITAL EMULSION TEST

We don't normally think of performing an *emulsion test* when evaluating a digital camera, but that's what I do when working with a new or unfamiliar model. Film shooters once routinely tested every new stock to gauge its sensitivity and its ability to retain shadow detail at various light levels. The same logic applies here. By altering the gamma, black level, and fill light, the shooter can gain insight into the camera's ability to capture and retain detail in a range of shooting conditions.

To conduct the equivalent of an emulsion test find a cooperative subject and light her in a normal way. Referring to a proper monitor, gradually reduce the fill light and note the level of detail and hue shifts at various illumination levels. Understanding how your camera responds prepares you for the inevitable lighting challenges ahead.

FIGURE 9.53

WARMING UP

A *warming filter* or *skin enhancer* fosters intimacy with an audience by helping to convey a character's humanity. In order to preserve the warming effect, be sure to remove the filter prior to white balancing the camera. The warming effect can also be applied in post.

WARMING   NO WARMING

FIGURE 9.54

A warming filter builds intimacy with the actress's character and story.

OUT OF THE FOG

Cinematographers have long used fog filters to add atmosphere to otherwise sterile or lackluster scenes. Whether we're looking to add a touch of atmosphere or a full-blown marine inversion, there's a strength and type of fog filter that can make it happen.

Fog filters come in standard and double fog varieties, the double fog type producing a greater sense of *actual* fog. Close-ups retain their sharpness despite the lower contrast and blooming of highlights. Of course, such effects should be tastefully applied in keeping with our storytelling goals.

FIGURE 9.55

In Venice, the double fog produces a natural effect with minimal flare as evidenced in the warm string lights (left). To the right is the same scene sans filter.

THE POST-CAMERA FINISH

The question arises often: Why *not* delay filtering and image tweaking decisions until later inside the NLE? Several years ago, I recall a crusty engineer pulling me aside. He insisted that I refrain from using on-camera diffusion because he said it compromised resolution, and in turn the quality of the outputted program.

I've noted the complex interplay of light as it scatters, halates, and refracts, through a physical glass filter. I've also discussed how the polarizer and the graduated filter *add* detail to a scene that wouldn't be present otherwise. How can this detail be magically re-created in post? It can't.

The same logic applies to a weak diffusion filter that suppresses noisy shadows and helps the camera perform more efficiently. Nevertheless we must admit that post-camera tweaking of images is a fact of life; the shooter is coming under increasing economic and practical pressures to delay imaging decisions until later in a production.

FIGURE 9.56

My overstuffed filter case once contained 125 individual filters. These days, the color effect types no longer see much use. The tweaking of color and color temperature can be performed more easily and efficiently in postproduction.

ROLL YOUR OWN

For the shooter seeking post-camera image control, there are powerful plug-ins available. Plug-ins are mini-software applications that extend the capabilities of a host NLE or compositing tool. Plug-ins offer shooters almost limitless possibilities.

FIGURE 9.57

The Tiffen Dfx suite offers a staggering array of familiar filter types. Such tools may apply an effect to only a portion of the frame.

Tiffen's Dfx software features a list of presets intended to mimic the look of most popular camera filters, including the main diffusion, graduated, and infrared types. The tool offers the traditional shooter a familiar path from the intuitive world we knew and loved to the more abstract and opaque digital realm.

The Magic Bullet Looks Suite is a tour de force of software design. Beyond the ability to dial in any desired level of diffusion, saturation, and color treatment, Magic Bullet offers a host of distinct and *recognizable* looks. If you want warm and fuzzy like *Jerry Maguire*,[10] there's a preset for it. If you want a heavy diffused feel like *Eyes Wide Shut*,[11] you just dial it in.

(a)

(b)

FIGURE 9.58

(a) Day for night. (b) North Hollywood through a night scope.

FIGURE 9.59

Noise Industries' FxFactory offers numerous diffusion and effects filters for 2D and 3D applications.

[10]Crowe, C. (Producer & Director), Brooks, J. L. (Producer), Johnson, B. (Producer), Mark, L. (Producer), Mendel, J. M. (Producer), Pustin, B. S. (Producer), … Stewart, L. (Producer). (1996). *Jerry Maguire* [Motion picture]. USA: TriStar Pictures.

[11]Cook, B. W. (Producer), Harlan, J. (Producer), & Kubrick, S. (Producer & Director). (1999). *Eyes Wide Shut* [Motion picture]. United Kingdom: Hobby Films.

FIGURE 9.60

The Magic Bullet Look Suite features well-recognized looks that are easy to identify and apply. The "Warm and Fuzzy Jerry Maguire" look is at top.

COLOR CORRECTION

Although not every program will benefit from finishing tools like Magic Bullet, the fact is that nearly every digital production requires color correction. The original image capture likely contains significant variations in color and density; given the power of today's color correction tools, it no longer makes much sense to match every scene while on location.

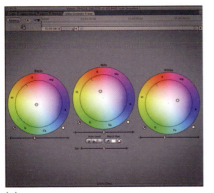

(a)

(b)

FIGURE 9.61

Final Cut Pro's three-way color corrector allows adjustment for blacks, whites, and mid-tones and is adequate for most applications. The inky color in (b) is in serious need of toning down!

Beyond establishing a tonal consistency, color correction can impart an overall look suggestive of the story's tone and genre. We can make the whites whiter, blacks blacker, and flesh tones more natural. We can add warmth, enhance contrast, or add a special color emphasis in keeping with the program theme.

FIGURE 9.62

A color reference captured for each setup can greatly facilitate the post correction process.

FIGURE 9.63

Color correction is best when only partially applied. These New York scenes illuminated by sodium and mercury vapor streetlights *should* look a bit sick. Fully correcting to produce a more pleasant hue detracts from the authenticity of the visual story!

SHOOTERS, TAKE CHARGE!

The practice of finishing one's images post-camera is a concept that fills some shooters with dread. On the one hand, the shooter ought to be grateful for the creative opportunities afforded by the latest software. On the other hand, the prospect of leaving unfinished images lying around a control room or a media library is a threat to the shooter's reputation and livelihood. The shooter knows that despite the assurances of producers, clients, and library custodians, his or her untreated (or poorly treated) images will find their way to the public.

The digital world is evolving so quickly that we can no longer be dogmatic about filters and when and where they should be applied. Times have changed, and with these changes, the shooter must fight to retain as much control as possible, a process that only *begins* with the image captured in-camera but really isn't complete until the edited program is finalized and output for screening.

Today the shooter must embrace a combination of in-camera and post-camera tools. Remember you are the artist, the painter of light, the Vermeer of the digital age. It's up to you to decide by what standards you wish to be judged. Do you really want a bleary-eyed editor facing the deadline of his life applying the finishing touches to your images? Of course not! No way!

So, dear shooters, let's get with the program. Take charge of your images. Polarize them, diffuse them, or add fanciful bursts of color. But most of all—*finish* them. However you do it—whether in-camera or after—it is *your* image as a shooter and craftsman that is truly at stake.

EDUCATOR'S CORNER: REVIEW TOPICS

1. Describe the ingredients that go into creating a show's unique *look*. Describe how *master detail* (DTL) and black level can help communicate the intended genre?

2. What is *gamma*? *Cine gamma*? Why is cine gamma not always a desirable option?

3. The camera's color matrix addresses the discrepancy between human and machine perception. Why is such a function useful or necessary?

4. Discuss the merits of physical versus nonphysical camera filters. Explain why sky control and polarizing filters cannot be applied effectively in post.

5. Is there any advantage to utilizing a physical filter for color effects?

6. Why is the use of a matte box or lens shade so critical to maintaining good contrast and resolution?

7. List five (5) physical filters that you consider essential in a basic camera kit. Explain your rationale.

8. Describe the looks that might be appropriate for a romantic comedy, period drama, contemporary ghost tale, or a documentary on the International Money Fund? Consider in terms of camera setup: detail, gamma, black level, and color saturation.

Making Light of Your Story

10

When we put a frame around the world, we consciously exclude what is not helpful to the visual story. When we choose to de-emphasize an object in a composition or place certain elements out of focus, we are helping the viewer understand what is important to the story and what is less so. Proper lighting craft means applying the same principles. We direct light onto objects that advance the visual story and exclude light from elements that detract from it.

Fundamentally, lighting is the practice of exclusion—remember our mantra: *Exclude! Exclude! Exclude!* It is integral to our lighting craft because so much time and effort is expended modifying, controlling, and otherwise *removing* light from a scene. We accomplish this with devices like *barndoors*, *cutters*, *cookies*, and *Blackwrap*, and by altering the character and direction of light using diffusion, bounce cards, and color gel.

Lighting is an exercise in logic. As in all aspects of craft it is derived from story and the opportunities and limitations that story demands. In many cases, we merely reinforce the direction and quality of light already present. If there is a lamp on a CEO's desk, we place a light off-camera and direct it to mimic the lamp's effect. Of course, we may model and diffuse the light to present the CEO in a more flattering way—if that is the story. But it is the lamp on the desk that provides the motivation for the scene; the shooter simply builds on what is already there (or logically could be there) to create a transparent naturalistic setting.

The desire to re-create the world in a naturalistic way is linked to our (usual) goal as a shooter to represent the 3D world as best we can on a 2D canvas. In most cases, our lighting should accomplish two things: (a) to enhance the realistic illusion by maximizing the apparent texture and (b) to properly direct the viewer's eye to what is important or relevant in the scene.

On location we are often required to exclude or attenuate a dominant light source, by blocking out large windows, say, that may work against capturing well-modeled subjects. The technique of *negative fill* may seem like an oxymoron, but it is common industry practice, to achieve the shooter's goal of rendering proper texture and the illusion of a third dimension.

FIGURE 10.1

Embrace the mantra: *Exclude! Exclude! Exclude!* Always consider removing light before adding more light to a scene.

239

(a)   (b)   (c)

FIGURE 10.2

(a) The goal of lighting is usually to maximize the texture apparent in a scene.

(b) Color and smoke add texture. That texture says the scene is real. It exists. It has depth.

(c) Ditto for the English Ford. The texture revealed in the car's finish says, "Bring on the paint!"

FIGURE 10.3

The minimalist approach to lighting is illustrated in the opening scene to *Kramer vs. Kramer* (1979). Excluding background context allows the viewer to focus more intensely on Meryl Streep's pensive gaze and her wedding ring. Folks, this is not a comedy!

THINK SMALL

You don't need much instruments to light well. The great cinematographer Néstor Almendros who photographed many notable films including *Kramer vs. Kramer* (1979)[1] and *Sophie's Choice* (1982)[2] was said to have used only a mirror and a small Fresnel[3] to light most scenes. Fewer lights mean easier control and more manageable shadows. It means fewer cutters, C-stands, and gobo arms to control unwanted spill. It also means faster setups, a more comfortable working environment for talent and crew, a larger f-stop for selective focus, and the reduced chance of tripping circuit breakers for productions that must draw power from standard wall outlets on location.

Beyond these considerations, a shooter who works quickly and covers more script pages per day will enjoy many more and better work opportunities.

---

[1] Fischoff, R. (Producer), Jaffe, S. R. (Producer), & Benton, R. (Director). (1979). *Kramer vs. Kramer* [Motion picture]. USA: Columbia Pictures.

[2] Barish, K. (Producer), Gerrity, W. C. (Producer), Starger, M. (Producer), & Pakula, A. J. (Producer & Director). (1982). *Sophie's Choice* [Motion picture]. UK: Incorporated Television Company.

[3] A **Fresnel** is a tightly focusable instrument that employs a ridged lightweight lens invented by French physicist Augustin-Jean Fresnel. Originally developed for lighthouses, the Fresnel lens is much thinner than conventional convex lenses, and thus transmits more light, which accounts for its greater efficiency.

MINIMUM ILLUMINATION

Your camera's *minimum illumination rating* purports to measure the ability to capture satisfactory images in low light. Four factors influence this rating: the *f-stop* used, the video level, the reflectivity of the test scene, and color temperature. To be meaningful, a minimum illumination value must specify the test conditions used.

Minimum Illumination for Popular HD Camcorders
Note: This is manufacturer provided data. Shooters should look warily at these values since acceptable performance is seldom a consideration.

Canon HF11	0.2 lux (Night Mode)
Canon XL-H1s	3 lux (24F)
Canon XL1-S*	2 lux
Canon 5D MkII & MkIII**	Not specified
Canon C300 EOS	0.25 lux (no other data specified)
JVC GY-HM100	3 lux
JVC GY-HM710	Not specified
JVC GY-DV300U*	2.65 lux (LoLux mode)
Panasonic AG-HVX200A	3 lux
Panasonic AG-HPX250	0.2 lx (F1.6, Gain +30 dB, shutter at 1/30s)
Panasonic AG-HPX370	0.4 lx (F1.6, Gain +24dB, shutter at 1/30s)
Panasonic DVX100A*	3 lux (Gain +18dB)
Sony HVR-A1	0 lux (Night Mode)
Sony HVR-Z7	1.5 lux (Auto Gain, shutter @ 1/30s)
Sony PMW-F3***	Not specified
Sony FS100	0.28 lx shutter at 1/24s with auto gain enabled
Sony FS700	1.2 lx shutter at 1/24s with auto gain enabled
Sony PMW-EX1/EX3	0.14 lux
Sony DSR-PD170*	1 lux (+18dB)

   * This is a standard-definition camcorder.
  ** The minimum illumination for HDSLR video is not normally stated.
*** Manufacturers do not specify a minimum illumination in lux for cameras intended for high-end applications. The numbers listed above are suspect—and most working professionals know it.

---

[4]Brücker, W. D. (Producer), Canaris, V. (Producer), Eckelkamp, H. (Producer), Fengler, M. (Producer), & Fassbinder, R. W. (Director). (1979). *The Marriage of Maria Braun* [Motion picture]. West Germany: Albatros Filmproduktion.

FIGURE 10.5

One *lux* is defined as 0.0929 foot-candles or the illumination produced by one lumen falling perpendicularly on a surface of a bagel 1 meter square. Bon appétit.

FIGURE 10.6

C'mon, guys. This camera boasts a fabulously low "minimum illumination" rating, but the picture is unusable!

SHOOTERS WHO LIGHT, EDIT, PRODUCE, AND WASH WINDOWS

In an era of tiny or one-person crews, the shooter must wear many hats so the ability to work with simple lighting is crucial. In my own work, I prefer low-wattage focusable Fresnels to high-power open-faced instruments that produce more light but with less control. For The History Channel, I recall shooting entire episodes of *Sworn to Secrecy* with a four-head 150-watt Fresnel kit!

FIGURE 10.7

Think and light small. More gear = less work.

FIGURE 10.8

Fresnels offer precise focus and control, which in conjunction with a four-way barndoor can help reduce the need for flags, cutters, and cumbersome grip gear.

FIGURE 10.9

Open-faced instruments produce a lot of light and so are often used inside a large soft box, through heavy gel, or bounced off a white show card.

There was a time when dinosaurs ruled the Earth and I earned my living shooting industrial films on Ektachrome ASA 25 film. In those years, circa 1975, my travel kit consisted of four open-faced *Lowel D* lights fitted with 1,000-watt lamps. Such (relatively) high-wattage gear was necessary in order to achieve the required exposure—indeed, in many situations, any exposure at all.

With the advent of today's sensitive digital cameras the Big Bang approach to lighting is no longer the only or preferred way to go. For some shooters however old habits die hard. I recently witnessed a macabre shoot where the veteran DP dragged two 1,200-watt HMIs, three 4 × 4 bounce cards, three large cutters, two 5-foot *meat axes*, seven C-stands, and a Western dolly into a 10- by 12-foot windowless room. Never mind the personnel and the hours required to accomplish the Herculean task. What did the DP then do? Flag the lights. Squeeze the barndoors. Drape the heads with black foil and drop in three double-wire scrims. He spent more than *2* hours cutting the lights down to a manageable level. Do you see the logic? I don't.

The preamble to the Shooter's Constitution is clear: *When in the course of lighting events it becomes necessary (as it usually does) to exclude, exclude, exclude, it sure saves a lot of time and effort if you're not using ridiculously too much light in the first place.*

FIGURE 10.10

An excellent kit for starters: Four small Fresnels: two 300 watt and two 150 watt, with *baby stands*[5] and barndoors.

FIGURE 10.11

A good investment? My "Inky" # 22 manufactured in 1927 has been handed down to me through multiple generations of cameramen. I still use this little guy daily.

LED LIGHTING COMES OF AGE

Unlike the more esoteric gadgets in a kit, your complement of LED lighting will find many uses, from interiors of automobiles and studio sets to capturing candlelit folk singers in the Hazaribagh section of Old Dhaka. Recently I used a small variable color LED to do exactly that: to shoot an impromptu night concert outside a Bangladeshi mosque in a square packed with the teeming masses.

While my U.K. director demanded that I shoot with existing light, there was in fact very little of it. In fact, she didn't seem to care. "Hey! Didn't you say your new camcorder was fabulous in low light?" I replied, "Well, yes, but 'low light' doesn't mean no light!"

---

[5] *Baby stands* are not intended for babies or for the maintenance thereof! The term simply references a common support for mounting an instrument fitted with 5/8-inch stud. The traditional Mole-Richardson 'baby' and 'baby baby' lights were fitted with 5/8-inch receptacles and thus the infantile name persists.

That's when the call went out for candles to distribute to the crowd forming 10 deep around me. Of course even with the lit candles spread liberally about the frame the performers themselves remained woefully underlit. That's when my little LED entered the picture to fill their faces with a color-correct front light. Tweaking the color and intensity to match the candlelight, I feathered the LED off the singer close to the camera while the surging crowd tugged at my sleeve and demanded their turn to view the scene in the camera viewfinder. Under such pressing conditions, a small, versatile LED is ideal.

(a)   (b)   (c)

FIGURE 10.12

Today's LEDs can mimic the HMI look at a fraction of the cost. The Litepanels 1X1 BiFocus (a) can be configured singularly or in a multiple array, outputting a variable hard or soft light. Every shooter can benefit from a small on-camera LED (b) featuring a variable color output from tungsten to daylight. The quality of light from LED instruments can vary widely. The Flolight Microbeam (c) produces an especially flattering beam with a CRI[6] rating of 93.

FIGURE 10.13

A 1X1 LED provides a flattering highlight in this striking portrait captured with a Panasonic AF Micro Four Thirds camera and Voightlander 25mm F0.95 lens.

FIGURE 10.14

Lacking a conventional snoot or egg crate this Tanzanian filmmaker uses a rolled-up sheet of card stock to narrow the beam of a mini LED.

---

[6] **Color Rendering Index (CRI)** reflects the ability of a light to reproduce colors accurately in tungsten or daylight conditions. Professional shooters usually look for a CRI of at least 90 for most applications. CRI references a scale that runs from 0 (worst) - 100 (best).

Today's LEDs continue to improve in leaps and lumens, with each new product offering greater punch and color precision. The latest units are amazingly compact and low-cost, drawing little power and producing virtually no heat. The typical small LED can run for 3 to 4 hours on a few AA cells or a small rechargeable camera battery.

FIGURE 10.15

Capturing these performers at night in front of a mosque in Bangladesh the tiny LED source provides a subtle color-correct fill suggestive of the candles placed around the frame.

LIGHTING IS POWER

FIGURE 10.16

The lack of reliable power in some parts of the world has increased shooters' reliance on portable lighting and passive devices such as reflectors and bounce cards.

The increased power and applicability of LED lighting is evident in the Fresnel models designed for cinema and television professionals. This is happening despite many LEDs' skewed color output, especially when dimmed. Unlike tungsten, LEDs do not output a continuous spectrum, which can produce an unnatural cast despite a nominally correct color rating.

HMI LIGHTING: EXPENSIVE BUT WORTH IT

For years I traveled with a small tungsten Fresnel kit and two 400-watt HMI[7] PARs. An HMI *parabolic arc reflector* is the shooter's dream light—strong enough to punch through a 4 × 4 diffusion

---

[7]**HMI** (Hydrargyrum Medium-Arc Iodide) lighting uses an arc lamp instead of an incandescent bulb and a ballast to provide ignition and control of the arc. Five times more efficient than tungsten lighting, HMIs, at 5600° K, provide a very high-quality daylight source.

silk yet efficient enough to plug multiple units into an ordinary household outlet. For interiors, I often bounce a PAR off a white card to simulate a broad window source. For exteriors, I direct the PAR through a silk or grid cloth to produce a flattering key light for talent. The 200- or 400-watt HMI PAR is one of the most useful (albeit pricey) instruments you can own.

HMI lighting instantly elevates the look and feel of one's images, and unlike other gear that requires a sizable investment, the impact of an HMI source is immediately obvious on screen and thus billable to clients. A small HMI costing thousands of dollars may seem extravagant, but for the working professional, the investment is worth it. Packing 10 times the punch of conventional tungsten lighting, the PAR's power and versatility can eliminate a trunk full of less useful lighting and grip gear.

FIGURE 10.17

The proficient use of fewer but higher quality instruments is the key to developing an efficient style. The HMI PAR uses drop-in lenses to define its beam and character.

FIGURE 10.18

A shooter's gear must be rugged to withstand the rigors of a torrential downpour and other calamities.

FIGURE 10.19

Low-wattage lighting may be plugged into a standard wall outlet, yet another reason to think small.

FIGURE 10.20

Sometimes thinking small is not enough. HMIs allow lighting of large areas and objects such as jumbo jets.

FLUORESCENTS AND THE GREEN PLAGUE

Fluorescent lighting was once a perilous proposition. The fixtures ran cool, used little power, and threw off tons of light with a sick, ghastly green hue. Facial shadows and dark skin were particularly susceptible to the insidious green spike, requiring shooters to apply a wash of healthy light from an HMI or a comparable source.

I recall shooting at a health club in New York in 1993. Of course, there were the usual banks of fluorescents in the ceiling, all emitting the horrid green pall. Employing the wisdom of the time, I dutifully balanced every 1 of the *120 tubes* in the club, fitting each lamp with a *full minus green* gel. This compensated for the green all right—by bathing the entire club in a deep magenta like a bordello!

Naturally this drew scathing looks from the ad agency rep and the spot's young director who demanded that I rectify the *mess* pronto. He couldn't believe his glamorous workout babes would appear normal on film. I pointed to my Minolta Colormeter II and tried to reassure him, but his eyes kept telling him otherwise.

In most cases, as in the health club, the green curse is exacerbated by the fluorescents' overhead placement. To satisfactorily capture such

FIGURE 10.21

The green plague is evident in the fluorescent-lit market at left; at right after adding magenta, i.e., white balancing the camera. When shooting talent close-ups, the overhead fluorescents should be supplemented with a side or frontal fill to avoid dark eye sockets.

FIGURE 10.22

The fluorescent lamp draws little power and produces plenty of light. Problem is, that light usually comes with a potent green curse.

FIGURE 10.23

Large color-correct fluorescents banks are common sights on film sets around the world.

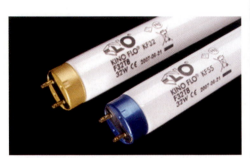

FIGURE 10.24

Balanced lamps without the dreaded green spike are available in tungsten and daylight types.

FIGURE 10.25

The balanced light from an HMI, LED, or color-correct fluorescent helps lift shadows and boost flesh tones when shooting under sickly industrial lighting.

scenes the shooter usually employs an eye-level fill by borrowing a few diseased lamps from the ceiling fixtures. The strategy has the advantage of maintaining consistency in the fill light, albeit with the miserable green pall intact.

Cool White fluorescent lamps are *supposed* to mimic daylight, which they do, sort of, but only to the unsophisticated eye, which is a *lot* more forgiving of spectral deficiencies than the sensor in a camera.

The fluorescent's high efficiency comes at a steep aesthetic price. In the last decade, fluorescent tube makers have developed new phosphors to compensate for the green curse. But as manufacturers drive the lamps harder for greater output, the reviled spike has increased proportionately, necessitating the formulation of yet another generation of compensating phosphors and lamps.

Kino-Flo and other manufacturers produce color-correct fluorescent tubes by mixing a potpourri of phosphors to produce a lamp that appears reasonably balanced to the camera. This should give solace to shooters prone to angry outbursts at the slightest hint of green reflected from an actress's face or flesh tones.

Beyond the green pall, there is also the potential for *flicker*, a hazard associated with discharge lighting in general including LEDs. The ugly pulsating is often seen in out-of-sync streetlights and neon signs when shooting at nonstandard shutter speeds or at 24 FPS, for example, in 50-Hz countries.

Today, high-frequency ballasts have largely eliminated the flicker risk in professional lighting, but caution should still be exercised when shooting abroad under fluorescent, neon, or mercury/sodium-vapor streetlights or in regions known to experience to power irregularities.

THINK BIG

A large diffused light source is usually desirable to soften facial shadows and suppress unflattering texture in the skin. In lower-end cameras and especially DSLRs, compression anomalies, hue shifts, and shadow noise contribute to a pattern of contours more appropriately found in an open pit mine. This is no way to treat your actors or leading lady!

FIGURE 10.26

At midday in many parts of the world, the use of large butterfly or bounce board is imperative.

SOFT IS KEY

Striving to create the most three-dimensional images we can, we usually try to maximize texture. This means paying close attention to the smoothness, depth, and direction of shadows, which communicate genre and mood and the essence of the visual story. Remember that shadows lie at the heart of the shooter's craft, the quality by which we as artists are ultimately judged.

FIGURE 10.27

Blasting hard, undiffused light at your subject is unprofessional, and ungodly. Since soft light dominates the natural, spiritual, and manmade worlds, we usually try to mimic this quality in scenes with gently modulated shadows. *O Father, I thee confess: Shadows tell the eternal story. May I treat them always with dignity and respect.*

CHOOSING A SOFT LIGHT

A soft light may be achieved through a diffusion silk or gel, by bouncing off a white card or foam core, or by employing a *soft box* or fluorescent bank. However you do it, an effective soft light must be a part of every shooter's working kit.

Color-correct fluorescents provide a convenient solution when shooting aboard moving trains, in airports, in offices, and large public areas. Whereas a Fresnel may project a hard shadow back onto a set or actor, a broad fluorescent produces a near-shadowless beam without the bulk or hassle of a light box or bounce card. Such economy in tight locations such as office cubicles and supermarket aisles is a major benefit of fluorescent multitube arrays like the ubiquitous *two and four-bank* Kino-Flos.

(a)

(b)

FIGURE 10.28

(a) The Dutch Master painters in their northern-facing ateliers would've killed for such a portable source.
(b) Vermeer's 17th-century *Girl With a Pearl Earring*.

FIGURE 10.29

Multiple lighting balloons or Chinese lanterns can illuminate large areas like a city street or a crowded convention hall. This scene is from *Crossing Over* (2009).[8] (Courtesy of Airstar Space Lighting.)

(a)

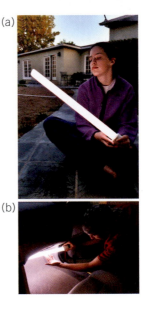

(b)

FIGURE 10.30

The Gyoury wand (a) produces a flattering soft source. One or more tubes (b) may be all you need to light a car interior at night.

The Gyoury system is built around the concept of a wand—a tube assembly that may be detached and mounted in hard-to-reach locations—along a bathroom mirror, beneath a computer screen, or inside a refrigerator! The wand inside a China Ball produces a pleasing soft fill for walking shots in feature films, episodic TV, and event-type shows, the portable source producing a natural-looking wash with a professional gleam.

---

[8] Beugg, M. (Producer), Marshall, F. (Producer), Taylor, G. (Producer), Veytia, O. (Producer), Weinstein, B. (Producer), Weinstein, H. (Producer), & Kramer, W. (Producer & Director). (2009). *Crossing Over* [Motion picture]. USA: The Weinstein Company.

SPILLING THE BEANS

Our mantra *Exclude! Exclude! Exclude!* demands that we eliminate the light from objects and elements that not helpful to the intended story. One downside of utilizing large sources like a soft box or bounce card is the need to control the copious spill. Usually this requires the placing of one or more *flags* or *cutters*. Although a Fresnel with a focusable lens offers better control with less spill, its beam is harsher and more likely to produce an objectionable shadow in confined locations.

Note that shooting in tight spaces requires longer setup times because a larger grip complement is necessary to rein in the unwanted spill. For this reason, many filmmakers prefer to shoot on a sound stage; the errant spill from multiple light sources simply falls off into the void and produces no ill effects. In corporate-, event-, and documentary-style programming, the shooter is afforded no such luxury. The location is what it is—and we have to deal with it.

FIGURE 10.31

Large soft lights often require several flags and cutters to prevent unwanted spill. A shooter with many setups per day may prefer Fresnels that are more easily trimmed and controlled.

THE ART OF DIFFUSION

The adept use of diffusion *gel* is critical for controlling a light's character and depth of shadows. There are many types of gel, but most shooters only really need three types: a strong diffuser for fill and keying talent, a moderate

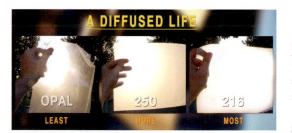

FIGURE 10.32

Opal, #250, #216. Be sure to carry several sheets of each type on every shoot. Lee Filter references are understood widely and are often used generically.

FIGURE 10.33

Keying through a heavy diffuser produces soft gentle shadows.

FIGURE 10.34

A light diffuser retains the direction and character of the low-angled sun.

diffuser to provide more edge, and a light diffuser to take the curse off hard sources. Diffusion gel may be purchased in long rolls or in 20- by 24-inch sheets at any film and TV supply house.

Alternatively if you're like me you can rummage through the trash of a movie or TV show that happens to be shooting in your neighborhood. The gel discarded each day from a feature film or commercial is enough to supply most shooters for a lifetime.

THE JELLY ROLL

While scavenging through the trash of *Rocky XXII*, you may uncover a bounty of useful detritus including forlorn gel. These diverse scraps can help outfit your *jelly roll*—a 12- or 24-inch elastic pouch containing diffusion, color correction, and various *party gel*.

I carry CTB[9] gel from *one-quarter* to *full blue,* the latter type ostensibly but not quite converting a 3200 °K tungsten source to daylight. CTB is among the most used gel, as tungsten lighting is often

FIGURE 10.35

Sheets of diffusion, color correction, and party gel should be a part of every shooter's basic lighting kit.

FIGURE 10.36

CTB (blue) increases the color temperature of a source light making it appear cooler; CTO (orange) decreases the color temperature of a source light and makes it appear warmer.

FIGURE 10.37

Red party gel is a staple of the horror genre. Use with care!

---

[9] **CTB** = *Color Temperature Blue;* **CTO** = *Color Temperature Orange.*

blued when backlighting talent or to represent daylight or moonlight spilling into a scene. Typically I add only a hint of blue, for example, *half blue,* to reflect a cool source in or out of frame. I don't *completely* convert a tungsten source to daylight because I want to preserve the *feeling* of mixed illumination just as we experience it in life. Conversely when working with HMIs or LEDs under tungsten conditions, a *half CTO* (orange) gel alleviates the blue curse while still preserving the *feel* of daylight. I often mix color temperatures in my lighting, painting with blue and orange gel to add texture while maintaining the faithful interplay of light emanating from warm and cool sources.

Although *full CTB* is intended to convert 3200 °K tungsten to daylight, the effect in practice is quite a bit less when compared to actual daylight or the output from an HMI or a color-correct fluorescent. If daylight balance is your goal (and it may well be), a true daylight source is required. Also note that due to high heat absorption, full blue CTB is subject to rapid fading, so be sure to carry extra sheets in your jelly roll.

Beyond routine diffusion and color correction, I use my *party gel* to add a splash of color to dull sterile scenes. These gels like swatches of paint are especially useful to add visual panache in corporate and industrial settings. The crimson is one of my favorites, injecting intrigue, if not outright alarm. A little goes a long way, so shooters should use such effects sparingly in keeping with one's storytelling goals.

THE STANDARD SETUP

When shooting an actor or talking head, we usually direct the subject's gaze at a point between the camera and the key light. The viewer then is peering into the facial shadow, revealing the level of detail and texture that evokes the story. We then may add one or more small Fresnels to highlight an

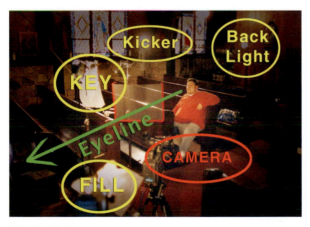

FIGURE 10.38

In a typical setup, the subject directs his look between the camera and key light fitted with a heavy diffuser. The backlight and "kicker" are gelled with lighter diffusion to reveal texture and provide additional edge. The key light raking across the face produces a shadow that evokes the genre and mood of the story.

FIGURE 10.39

The kicker from screen left is stronger and more focused, simulating the effect of the window source visible in frame.

actor's hair and wardrobe or to achieve a separation from the background. Finally the background is painted with a tightly focused Fresnel fitted with a party gel or *cookie* to add visual interest. (More on cookies, kooks, and snoots later in this chapter.)

LIGHTING FRONT AND CENTER

To reduce the undesirable texture in an actor's face and skin, we typically place a diffused light as close as possible to the lens axis. Because frontal light does not produce a visible shadow—the shadow is hidden behind the subject—many defects such as acne scars, wrinkles, and dark lines exhibit *less* texture and are effectively de-emphasized.

Front light can play a vital storytelling role by placing a strategic point of light in an actor's eyes. Illuminating (or not) the eyes of an actor, a reporter, or other talent is a critical choice, because the eyes are the viewer's point of entry into a character's warmth, credibility, and humanity. Likable characters with whom we identify should have well-illuminated eye sockets and a distinct glint in the pupil of each eye. Conversely, villainous characters have dark, unfilled eyes, which cut off potential viewer sympathies or identification. As a shooter, you must rigorously control this powerful lighting cue, which goes directly to the genre, mood, and effectiveness of your storytelling.

FIGURE 10.40

Illuminating the eyes conveys warmth and intimacy. The lack of front light makes a character appear sinister.

HAVING YOUR FILL

The application of fill light can be tricky. Too little can lead to dark, lifeless shadows and increased noise in the underlit areas. Too much fill imparts a washed-out, unnatural, deer-in-the-headlights look.

FIGURE 10.41a

We want our young starlets to look great but too much fill can produce a glaring unnatural look. *Exclude! Exclude! Exclude!* It applies to lighting most of all!

Sometimes the passive fill from a bounce card is sufficient to lift the facial shadows. Other times, especially at night, a camera filter like the ultra contrast[10] can transfer surplus values from the highlights to the shadows, potentially eliminating the need for a supplemental fill light.

FIGURE 10.41b

A white or silver reflector can add just the right amount of fill. Less is more.

ON- AND OFF-CAMERA OPTIONS

If an on-camera fill is desired, the shooter has several choices—a ring light, a top-mounted LED, or a mini HMI. For maximum versatility, a camera light should pack enough punch to produce a natural wash even through a layer of moderate to heavy diffusion.

FIGURE 10.42

A China Ball at the end of a painter's pole provides a soft light for a walking shot at dusk.

FIGURE 10.43

A small on-camera LED may provide adequate fill out to about two meters (6.6 ft).

[10] See Chapter 9 for more discussion.

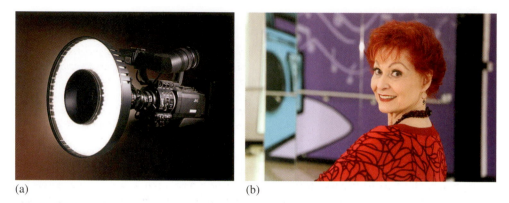

(a)   (b)

FIGURE 10.44

The wash from a lens-mounted ring light reduces the visibility of wrinkles and age lines—just what you want when shooting a veteran Hollywood entertainer. (b) The great dancer Carol Lawrence is seen here at age 78.

LIGHTING IN PLANES

Like every object in the frame, every word in the script, and every scene in the movie, every light has a purpose. We place the key to best model our subject. We light the background to achieve separation and to lift the subject from the canvas. And we light the foreground to properly direct the viewer's attention and to frame the story inside the frame.

Analogous to a composition in Adobe Photoshop the planes are managed independently, so the shooter can precisely tweak the scene's look. For example, a hard raking light may be used in the background, while a soft front light at mid-ground suppresses unwanted texture in an actor's skin.

Lighting in planes can be a challenge to the documentary shooter who works often in confined locations. Because one light can rarely illuminate effectively multiple planes simultaneously, the shooter must constantly look for ways to control the spill and cross-contamination of one plane's light into another.

FIGURE 10.45

When shooting in planes, please note the shooter's credo: One light does one thing.

(a)   (b)

LIGHTING FOR GREEN SCREEN

Many camcorders feature a built-in *waveform*, a tool with which every serious shooter should be familiar. For green screen, I use the waveform to achieve an even illumination and a *vectorscope* to verify sufficient saturation. The green screen doesn't have to be bright, just more saturated than anything else in the frame such as the actor's wardrobe. I normally reference the waveform to attain a brightness of 55% to 60% and the vectorscope to verify saturation at least 40 units greater than the foreground talent. Using too much or too little light on the green screen makes it difficult to achieve the required 40-point separation in the vectorscope.

For green screen, fluorescent lighting can be an advantage as Kino-Flos fitted with Super Green lamps emit a pure green light, which means less contamination from other colors falling on the screen.

If you don't have access to a waveform, you can use the camera's *zebras* to achieve a reasonably smooth wash devoid of hot spots. Keep in mind that shooting green screen in cramped locations can be challenging because the spill off the screen can contaminate wardrobe and flesh tones. To avoid this, always use the largest green screen available and keep your subject as far from it as possible.

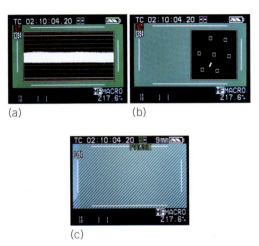
(a)   (b)

(c)

FIGURE 10.46

From traditional studio work to reality TV, green screen has become an integral part of every type of production.

FIGURE 10.47

The waveform monitor (a) facilitates smooth green screen illumination of 55% to 60%. The vectorscope (b) confirms green screen saturation 40 points greater than the foreground actors and objects. In a pinch, the camera zebras (c) set to 60% can facilitate a reasonably even wash.

WHY GREEN?

Green screen is favored over blue screen for several reasons. First, primary green rarely occurs in our everyday world, so we needn't worry about inadvertently keying out our starlet's beautiful blue eyes. Of course, if you're shooting sun-dappled leprechauns in a rain forest in Ireland, you might consider an alternative keying color—red, blue, yellow, amber, white, black—all will work.

FIGURE 10.48

Engineers understand that humans can see very well in scenes dominated by green. For this reason the green channel in digital video is not compressed because we are likely to notice the missing samples. The detail in scenes bathed in blue or red light is more difficult to discern, so the pixel data in these channels can be more readily discarded— or so the thinking goes.

There is another compelling reason for using green: the green channel in digital video is not compressed. Given that the human eye is especially sensitive to wavelengths in the middle of the visible spectrum, engineers opt not to discard samples in the green or *luminance* ("Y") channel because missing or deleted samples that have to be *corrected* later may be readily apparent to viewers. In DV's 4:1:1 format, the red and blue channels are sampled only *one fourth* as often as the green channel (referenced by the number 4), which, left uncompressed, is the best choice for keying with a low risk of noise and artifacts during playback. The absence of compression in the green channel greatly facilitates the extraction of a clean green screen matte.

The 4:2:2 color space in higher end formats such as XD-CAM HD 422 and AVC-Intra offers double the number of blue and red samples, so these cameras should produce keys with smoother edges. Images captured 8-bit 4:2:0[11] in XDCAM EX and AVCHD cameras provide the same red and blue resolution as does 4:2:2 but only on every *other* line vertically.

My preference for shooting 4:2:2 coincides with the preference of our creator. Our eyes contain *rods* that measure brightness and *cones* that assess color. Because our retinas have twice as many rods as cones, the 4:2:2 system that samples *luminance* at twice the rate of *chrominance* closely approximates how we actually see the world, all other differences aside.

Case in point: In a dark room, we can discern the shape of an object much more readily than its color. This makes sense from an evolutionary perspective: In the feeble light, we recognize the presence of a threat before we notice the color of dress she is wearing.

In cases of wardrobe or other conflicts when green is not available, the shooter may opt for blue instead. The *keying*[12] of red is not usually feasible, owing to the amount of red in flesh tones. Black

FIGURE 10.49

Green means *go*! The color is easily seen and recognized by drivers even from a great distance down the road.

FIGURE 10.50

Halfway through shooting a music video with Kelly Clarkson, she asked me if I could isolate her hazel eyes. No one had thought about bringing chroma green paint so we used opaque black makeup instead to achieve the desired effect.

---

[11] 4:2:0 color sampling as used in HDV and most XDCAM variants and DVD-Video.

[12] **Keying** or **chroma keying** is the technique for compositing two video streams together by mapping a specific color range.

or white keying is also possible and may be the only option when a *chroma-key* screen must be improvised in front of a black or white wall.

GREEN SCREEN ALTERNATIVE

An alternative to the traditional blue or green screen, the *Reflecmedia* system utilizes a lens-mounted LED ring light to illuminate a special fabric, which appears gray to the eye but registers as a solid blue or green to the camera. The fabric composed of millions of tiny beads efficiently reflects the ring light source while rejecting stray off-axis light. The system thus requires little to no setup time and eliminates the need for the usual lighting complement of Kino-Flos, umbrellas, flags, cutters, and all the rest.

The ring light allows placement of talent close to the screen, an advantage to shooters working in tight locations, such as a network production trailer or press box.

FIGURE 10.51

Reflecmedia's LED ring light reduces the light for supplemental lighting when shooting blue and green screen. The shooter should take care not to overpower the ring light when setting a camera fill or eye light.

FIGURE 10.52

The green spilling onto the foreground, as seen here on the edge of the computer monitor, is a major drawback of the ring light system.

FIGURE 10.53

Flolight's LED CycLight eliminates the need for a special screen and reduces the risk of errant green falling forward onto the set or talent.

GET A GRIP

The range of lighting control available underscores our mantra to *exclude, exclude, exclude*. We use Fresnels, HMIs, LEDs, floods, and fluorescents to pour light *into* a scene, and we use cutters, cookies, snoots, and *Blackwrap* to effectively *exclude* it, trim it, feather it, and craft it—in support of the visual story.

Rigorously controlled lighting communicates to an audience what is essential in the frame. Removing light from a prop, set element, or actor, informs the viewer "Don't look at this. It's not important. Nothing to see here."

I discussed earlier how the eye is drawn naturally to the brightest object in a frame. This is a vestige from our prehuman days as *drosophila*,[13] when we were drawn to and made a nice meal of incandescing lightning bugs. Lighting is predicated on this one salient point: If you want to draw attention to something, you shine a light on it; if you want to direct attention elsewhere, you take the light away.

Every shooter can benefit from a basic grip package, which should consist minimally of four or five C-stands and a medium flag kit. Such a kit is critical to controlling spill, especially at the top, bottom, and edges of the frame.

FIGURE 10.54

Watch your step! If you're serious about lighting, you'll stumble on this scene often.

FIGURE 10.55

The C-stand provides solid support for bounce cards, nets, cutters, and other gadgets.

FIGURE 10.56

The net at the end of a gobo arm feathers the light off the edge of a set.

FIGURE 10.57

A double net feathers the light off the priest's white collar, which might otherwise divert attention from the clergyman's heartfelt story.

[13] "Drosophila is a genus of small flies, belonging to the family *Drosophilidae,* whose members are called fruit flies, pomace flies, vinegar flies, or wine flies. See "Drosophila." (n.d.) *Wikipedia* http://en.wikipedia.org/wiki/Drosophila. Shooters talk about irrelevant stuff like this all the time. Get used to it.

KOOKS AND COOKIES

Every shooter with a few notches in his battery belt has reached for a *kook* to break up a shadowless wall, floor, or flatly lit area. Plywood *kooks* or *cookies*[14] are available commercially, or they can be improvised by using strips of gaffer's tape or by poking a few holes in a piece of Blackwrap.

The malleable black foil, referred to generically by the trade name Blackwrap, has almost unlimited uses. Affixed to the back or sides of a light, the free-form shape can help eliminate or reduce unwanted spill. I knew a shooter at NBC who kept the same worn perforated pieces of Blackwrap for his entire 25-year career! Job after job, year after year, he kept pulling out the same tattered old kooks. Not bad for a few pennies (not even that) investment.

Along with the scraps of gel for a jelly roll, you might also find a nice selection of Blackwrap jettisoned from a major production shooting in your neighborhood. Go ahead and avail yourself. You'll feel on top of the world.

FIGURE 10.58

Aluminized black foil aka Blackwrap or Cinefoil™ is a practical and inexpensive way to control the spill from unruly lights. The use of Blackwrap may reduce the need for C-stands, cutters, and other bulky gear.

FIGURE 10.59

The shadowy pattern of a cookaloris is the signature effect in film noir movies

FIGURE 10.60

A cookie may be made of plywood, Blackwrap, or thin tape strips.

---

[14] *Kooks, cukes, coo-koos,* and *cookies* are industry jargon for a *cookaloris,* named, I think, after a gaffer named Mr. Cookaloris in the 1930s. I'm not sure about this. And his family isn't talking.

BEING SNOOTY

A Fresnel fitted with a *snoot* is used to illuminate individual set elements such as a wall hanging or Ming vase on a dresser. Highlighting objects in this way elevates their story value and adds visual interest to the frame. For self-respecting shooters, commercial snoot sets are available if the scavenged Blackwrap route is too déclassé.

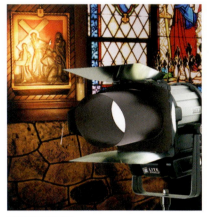

FIGURE 10.61

The snoot's narrowed beam informs your audience. "Look at this fresco. It has meaning to the story."

CLAMPING DOWN

It was something of a status symbol among National Geographic shooters to carry the most beat-up grip gear imaginable. This mantle of status applied particularly to our grip cases and the clamps inside that lasted for eons and bore the imprimatur of *experience*. Their ratty condition (it was thought) reflected the misery endured in far-flung battle-borne adventures. To this day I carry the same mangled clamps: *pipe clamps, Mafer clamps, gator clamps, C-clamps*—all beat to heck. My scissor clamps are especially full of personality, these clamps being the darling of every shooter who has ever interviewed a CEO in an office with a suspended ceiling.

FIGURE 10.62

The resourceful shooter carries an array of clamps to tackle any mounting task. The suction cup is used for mounting a small light on a car hood or other smooth surface.

FIGURE 10.63

Professionals still cutely refer to a clothespin as a "C-47," its onetime Century catalog designation. The extension cord is a "stinger." An overhanging tree branch placed into a scene is a "Hollywood." Using proper lingo will increase your perceived prowess as a shooter and contribute to the omniscient halo above your head.

TAPE MAKES THE MAN (OR WOMAN)

Every shooter must be familiar with a range of industry utility tapes. *Camera tape* may be safely applied to camcorder bodies and lens barrels without fear of damaging the finish or leaving a gummy residue. The shooter should be sure to have at least one roll of white camera tape on every job. Stay away from the cheap stuff, because it will trash your valuable equipment (or someone else's) in short order. Professional grade camera tape is widely available online or from any film or video supply house.

Gaffer's tape is a heavy-duty cloth adhesive definitely *not* for use on cameras and lenses. Its powerful grip will easily remove the paint from light fixtures, apartment walls, and priceless works of art. Gray or black gaffer's tape in 1-inch and 2-inch widths is intended for heavy-fisted tasks like sealing shipping cases or covering a rough seam on a dolly board. It must not be used to secure cables to the floors or walls because the sticky adhesive can make a nasty mess. Look for a brand with a high cloth content to keep the potential mess to a minimum. And stay away from the cheap stuff or, worse, *duct tape*, which is to be avoided like the pink jello at *Denny's!* Just say *no* to gooey, gamey duct tape!

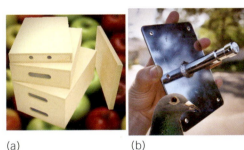

(a)   (b)

FIGURE 10.64

(a) The *apple box* can be used to prop up furniture and light stands, for leveling dolly track, or correct the eyeline of actors. apple box heights: full Apple = 8 inches; half apple = 4 inches; quarter apple = 2 inches; pancake or eighth apple = 1 inch. (b) A *pigeon plate* enables the affixing of a small light to a wall, floor, or apple box.

FIGURE 10.65a

The sure sign of a pro are the tapes dangling from his belt. Paper tape is not as strong as gaffer's, but it is gentler on surfaces and leaves no sticky residue.

FIGURE 10.65b

Keep away! Gooey household duct tape must NEVER be used on or near expensive camera equipment.

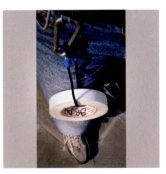

FIGURE 10.66

Use camera tape for marking zoom and focus on a lens barrel or as markers for blocking talent. Hang a roll from a carabiner on your belt and the world will regard you as a seasoned pro.

THE DITTY BAG

Every shooter worth his or her lens cap has a *ditty* bag. I take great pride in mine, having rescued more than a few imperiled productions over the years. From resoldering a camera power cable and replacing a hard drive in a laptop to treatment of a director's diarrhea, if it's flowing/not flowing or means trouble, I'm prepared! On many shows your resourcefulness in time of need can earn you hero—almost godlike—status.

THE DITTY BAG

I've carried the same ditty bag (more or less) on jobs for the last 30 years. The following is a list of its contents modified slightly for the digital age:

- Small diagonal pliers
- #1 and #2 Phillips screwdrivers
- 1/2-inch and 1/4-inch flat screwdrivers
- Needle-nose pliers
- Slip-joint pliers
- Wire stripper
- Jeweler screwdriver set (Swiss)
- Torx screwdriver set T1-T6
- 6-inch vice-grip
- 6-inch crescent wrench
- 8-inch crescent wrench
- VOM multimeter
- Awl
- Precision tweezers
- Assorted Sharpie markers
- Dry-erase marker
- First-Aid kit
- Superglue
- Black electrical tape
- Screw caps, variety (for joining wires)
- 2 or 3 grease pencils
- 1/4 × 20 and 3/8 × 16 hardware
- Metric/SAE nut driver set
- 8-inch steel ruler
- Lens tissue and fluid
- Spare tripod touch-go plate
- Tube of lithium grease
- Jeweler's loupe 10X
- Sewing kit (steal from hotel room)
- Safety pins
- Carabiner
- Firewire cables: 4-, 6-, 9-pin
- Mini plug → Mini plug audio cable
- Assorted BNC/RCA adapters
- Velcro strips
- Space blanket
- Soldering gun with lead-free solder
- Star chart and gray-scale
- Can opener
- Corkscrew
- Jeweler Philips screwdriver set (Swiss)
- Eyeglass repair kit
- 3 two-prong adapters
- 2 multitap outlet adapters
- Screw-in bulb socket adapter
- 12 C-47s
- LED flashlight
- Ear plugs
- Protective eye gear
- Insect repellent
- Cipro (bacteria nuker)
- Sunscreen 45 SPF
- snot tape[15]
- LCD cleaner
- Cable ties (various sizes)
- Metric/SAE Allen wrench set
- Rosco and/or Lee gel swatch
- Cloth 50-foot tape measure
- Lens chamois
- WD40 lubricant
- Emery cloth
- Pepto-Bismol/Kaopectate
- Shower cap for lens (also steal from hotel)
- 35mm film core (nostalgic)
- Spare 9V, AA, and AAA batteries
- USB A—B, A → Mini, A → Micro cables
- DVI → VGA & HDMI adpters Macbook Pro
- LCD screen wipes

---

[15] *Snot tape* is industry shorthand for *3M Scotch ATG transfer tape,* a clear gooey film with the consistency of rubber cement. Roll it into little balls. Use it for gelling windows, 4- × 4-foot diffusion frames, Christmas tree decorations, and so on.

LIGHTING = CRAFT + INGENUITY

In Uganda a few years back, I was asked to shoot several scenes inside a dark apartment inconveniently located on the upper floor of a building in central Kampala. Capturing the show's daylight exteriors was tough enough; I could manage the intense equatorial sun with bounce cards and improvised diffusion and by shifting some of the action to earlier or later in the day. But without a single working light kit or a professional instrument, the interiors posed a more serious challenge, as the kitchen and bedroom sets were located high above a parking lot in the deepest recesses of the structure away from any windows or sources of natural light. The reality was apparent: I had far too *much* light outside and far too *little* light inside.

So I got to thinking. With no resources to speak of, I was forced to consider what I *did* have, and that were lots of young African men and women eager to participate and to add their imprimatur to the production. And there were mirrors in Kampala. Lots of mirrors. There was a factory just outside the city.

So that became the solution. Banks of mirrors with two-person teams delivering the sun from the parking lot into the upper windows of the building, then bouncing that light down a dark corridor and into a bedroom, where a final team with a *gold* reflector filled the space with a magical glow. After all the shenanigans, the light was *still* too intense, and so I added some diffusion—and the scene looked gorgeous! It couldn't have been lit better with a 20-ton grip truck, a seasoned Hollywood crew, and a spate of HMIs!

There are great advantages to embracing the simplest of solutions. The sun is a beautiful thing, and in much of the world, there's lots of it and it's free—if you can control it, harness it, and deliver it to where you need it.

FIGURE 10.67

There is beauty in simplicity. Embrace it. Make it a part of you and your craft.

FIGURE 10.68

Regardless of the size movie or budget, simple solutions work best!

(a)   (b)

FIGURE 10.69

. . . then reflect it down a long hall into a third mirror and into a back bedroom. Who needs pricey light kits and grip trucks?

FIGURE 10.70

Mirrors are powerful tools that can deliver an intense blast of sun to interior locations. (b) An interior bounce crew takes a break.

FIGURE 10.71

This windowless interior illuminated by mirrored sunlight is from the Uganda short film *Sin of the Parents* (2008) directed by Judith Lucy Adong.

EDUCATOR'S CORNER: REVIEW TOPICS

1. Consider our mantra: *Exclude! Exclude! Exclude!* Describe five (5) ways how we apply this principle to our lighting craft.
2. The notion *less is more* applies most of all to lighting. How does utilizing fewer and smaller instruments enhance creativity and contribute to a more efficient production?
3. It is often said that the story is in the shadows. Do you agree? Explain.
4. Explore the virtues of hard and sort light. List four (4) ways to achieve a broad soft source. In what story context might hard light be more appropriate?
5. Shooting high-contrast exteriors can pose a challenge. Describe four (4) strategies you might employ to reduce the contrast to a more acceptable range.
6. The illumination of the eyes attests to a character's humanity. Consider the story implications of different lighting and shadow treatments in the face and eyes.
7. You're shooting a documentary in Africa that requires you to travel with only two cases. What might compose your lighting kit? LEDs? Fresnels? Collapsible reflectors?
8. Think about the character of light in the environment around you. Is it soft? Is it hard? Warm? Cool? How does the light you experience every day impact the kinds of stories you're likely to tell? Is there a connection?

Supporting Your Story

11

Analogous to the painters of centuries ago, today's shooter provides a window on the world, a proscenium through which we compose and expose the scene, and apply the rudiments of good storytelling craft. Compelling stories demand rigorous support of the frame walls. When we shake the frame and weaken its bones, we better have a good story reason.

I developed a love for my tripod over three decades ago in the streets of Communist Poland. The 1980s were a tumultuous time in Eastern Europe, and for me, being able to scurry about and set up my tripod quickly meant that I could use a longer lens to capture the hardened faces of the regime's soldiers perched atop their armored personnel carriers and the dispirited looks of citizens waiting in endless food lines. Of course, given the hazards of exploding Molotov cocktails and blasting water cannon, the use of a tripod wasn't always smart or feasible. Still, a solid platform, when possible, enabled more effective close-ups—and a riveting and intensely personal point of view.

FIGURE 11.1

Peril in the streets of 1980s Poland. Shaky-cam? You bet!

FIGURE 11.2

Establishing shots like the Soho scene demand a well-supported camera. Epic events like the launch of a Saturn V rocket were never intended to be shot handheld!

FIGURE 11.3

My hawk close-up has been used many times in music videos and commercials. Close-ups pay the bills, and solid camera support enables those close-ups!

(a)   (b)   (c)

FIGURE 11.4

(a) Shooting handheld? Got ants in your pants? (b) Try this . . . (c) . . . or *this*!

GETTING A HEAD IN YOUR SUPPORT

As a serious shooter, you'll want to invest in the most rugged professional *fluid head* you can afford. Most fluid heads use silicon dampening to enable smooth pans and tilts. A viscous liquid is forced through smaller and smaller drillings, like the fluid inside an automatic transmission; the dampening provides a predictable amount of resistance regardless of ambient temperature or conditions. Some models employ horizontal and vertical drag dials that allow incremental setting of resistance and torque, the precise amount of drag being selectable and repeatable. In this way, the shooter gains confidence in his or her ability to execute consistently smooth moves. Similar to the clutch on a car, the feel may vary from vehicle to vehicle, but once you are accustomed to the clutch on *your* car, the driving experience becomes seamless and second nature.

Although a *friction head* may seem like a good low-cost option, the fluid head is invariably the better choice; its robust construction is critical to withstand the rigors of the shooter's rough-and-tumble life.

The fluid head's action should feel smooth and glitch free without perceivable backlash, that is, the tendency of some heads to bounce back slightly when the handle pressure is relieved. Pan-and-tilt locks should be of the lever type with large surfaces to facilitate efficient operation even in winter through thick gloves.

Although many shooters prefer a fluid head that is small and easily transportable, the head should not be so lightweight to preclude the use of long lenses for sports or wildlife. A head must behave predictably so it should be checked regularly for *stickiness*, including when set to zero or minimum drag.

Depending on your needs, you may want a fluid head that tilts 90°. Not all heads do, so be sure to check when evaluating makes and models. O'Connor heads can usually tilt straight up or straight down whereas most Sachtler and Vinten models cannot.

Remember we will go through many cameras in our lifetime, but we'll need only *one* tripod head if we make the right investment. In my three decades as a shooter, I've actually only owned two. The first—a Sachtler 3+3 —was lost in the days following the 1980 eruption of Mount Saint Helens in, as

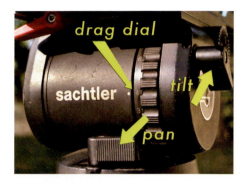

FIGURE 11.5

Repeatable drag settings ensure that a shooter is able to execute precise camera moves. Some models feature up to seven drag positions for pan and tilt. A rugged well-made fluid head will pay you dividends for years long after your present and future camera du jour is relegated to a doorstop.

FIGURE 11.6

You'll level the camera many times in your career, so make sure your head's claw ball operates smoothly and features a large knob. Depending on the head's weight and payload its base may feature a 75mm, 100mm, or 150mm ball mount.

FIGURE 11.7

Some models offer an illuminated spirit level for operating in low light. This is a very useful feature!

FIGURE 11.8

The smart shooter understands his bread and butter. *Panning* means moving the camera horizontally. *Tilting* means moving the camera vertically. My grandfather in his Brooklyn deli in 1937 had his own bread-and-butter issues.

volcanic ash penetrated its drag dials and destroyed the fine German action. The second—a replacement 7+7—I still use to this day. That's more than 30 years of continuous service from torrid tropical rain forests to numbing arctic cold and everything in-between. Not bad for what seemed in 1980 as a ludicrously expensive $2,000 purchase. Of course, as things turned out it was worth that investment many times over. I built my career literally on that one fluid head.

FIGURE 11.9

Some shooters require a head that can tilt straight up or down. Not all fluid heads can.

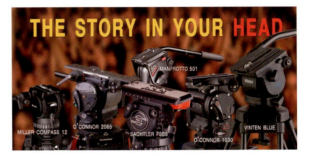

FIGURE 11.10

Some heads are hard to get moving from a dead stop, while others feather nicely into and out of small moves. There is a story in every head. Here are a few to ponder:

- Manfrotto 501
  More accurately described as a "greasy head" the 501's action can become sticky if left too long (more than a few minutes) in one position.

- Sachtler FSB8
  Extra care must be exercised to prevent impact damage to the head's delicate alloy casting.

- O'Connor 1030D
  The head is a tad lightweight for use with long telephoto lenses.

- O'Connor 2065
  The ergonomics are ideal for working off a dolly.

- Vinten Blue
  The protruding pan and tilt adjusters are prone to damage, and the lack of a zero drag setting complicates camera balancing.

FIGURE 11.11

Never lean your tripod and head against a wall or post! If it falls, the casting will crack. Most damage to expensive fluid heads happens this way!

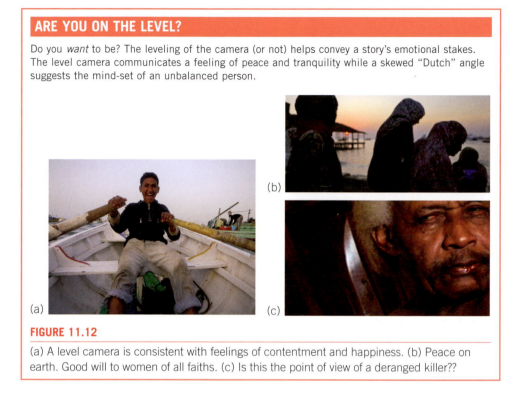
WHAT PRETTY LEGS YOU HAVE

I often hear whistling from onlookers when I work, and I'm pretty sure it's because of my legs. My *tripod* legs are very good-looking. They're rugged and versatile, and sexy as hell. You can't buy a pair like them now, and mine aren't for sale, so don't e-mail me. I love my legs—and you should love yours, too.

FIGURE 11.13

Key features include secure leg locks, incremental leg markings to facilitate level setup, a raised spider that stays clean and can serve as a monitor platform, and a center column that permits easy raising of the camera in tight spaces.

FIGURE 11.14

Be careful of legs (like mine) with hidden pinch
points that can crush unsuspecting fingers.
Make sure the people you love and work with
are duly warned.

(a)

(b)

FIGURE 11.16

A head's quick release greatly facilitates mounting and dismounting the camera. You don't want
to be fumbling with a screw thread when facing a
stampede of angry wildebeests!

FIGURE 11.15

This wing adjuster is easily stripped which can
lead to heart palpitations if the leg should . . .
slip . . . and your camera . . . well, uh . . .

FIGURE 11.17

A balanced camera is essential to exercising smooth
pans and tilts. Wrestling your head into submission
through every take is exhausting.

(a)

(b)

FIGURE 11.18

(a) This adapter plate with a built-in slider offers the versatility of a standard mounting plate compatible with full-size camcorders. (b) For maximum security, the camera should provide 1/4- and 3/8-inch mounting threads.

HOW TO COUNTERBALANCE THE CAMERA

ASSEMBLE THE CAMERA
Mount the lens, battery, microphone and any other accessories you will be using on the camera.

FIND THE BALANCE POINT (C.G.) OF THE CAMERA
Place the camera on a flat rigid object that's not too heavy, like a clip board. Put a pencil on a smooth table and place the camera and board on the pencil and roll it back and forth until you find the balance point.

ATTACH THE CAMERA MOUNTING PLATE
Fasten the center of the camera mounting plate as close as possible to the balance point of the camera (with lens, battery and accessories installed).

BALANCE THE CAMERA ON THE HEAD
Adjust the slide plate assembly on the head so the indicator notch is over the center of the head (zero mark). Mount the camera to the slide plate. Set the tilt fluid drag lever to zero. Release the platform lock lever. Find the balance point for the camera while the camera is in the level position by sliding the camera back and forth. Re-lock the platform lock lever.

ADJUST THE COUNTERBALANCE
It is very important to make sure the weight of the complete camera configuration is centered on the head. After balancing the camera on the head, tilt the camera forward and back. If the camera continues to drift forward or back when tilted, increase the counterbalance adjustment. If the camera has a spring-back reaction, decrease the counterbalance adjustment. Our infinitely adjustable counterbalance allows you to stop adjusting at whatever feel you like best and quickly readjust for minor changes in weight. The counterbalance is properly adjusted when the camera holds its position when tilted up or down. Now you can adjust the pan and tilt drag settings to your preference.

PROFESSIONAL CAMERA SUPPORT SYSTEMS

FIGURE 11.19

Considering new legs? They should be lightweight yet able to stand up to substantial abuse, whether facing down storm troopers in Eastern Europe or a panicked rhino in Zimbabwe. The leg locks should be secure and simple to clean and maintain. Leveling should be easy via a claw-ball with a large knob. I recommend leg adjusters with inscribed height increments, a useful feature when leveling the camera by eye or with the help of a bleary-eyed assistant.

GETTING A LEG UP

My students often ask, "How long should my tripod legs be?" Abraham Lincoln once famously replied to a similar question regarding his legs, "Just long enough to touch the ground." For today's shooter a more relevant answer might be "When it comes to assessing proper camera height it really depends on the story he's telling."

In combination, the standard and the *baby legs* offer the widest possible range of camera heights and so for many folks both sets of legs are essential. Because it's a hassle and at times costly to

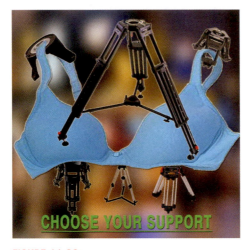

FIGURE 11.20

FIGURE 11.21

"They seem about the right length to me," Abraham Lincoln said regarding his standard legs.

FIGURE 11.22

A double or triple stage tripod may eliminate the need for multiple sets of legs.

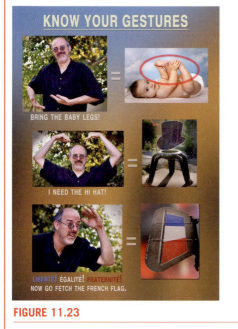

The use of proper jargon and gestures is important for your self-image and your status as a seasoned professional. Efficient communication on a set is a must because a director and the actors can only do their best work if conversation among crewmembers is kept to a minimum. For this reason, I recommend a system of gestures and hand signals that I use regularly.

FIGURE 11.23

carry two sets of legs, especially on aircraft, shooters are constantly seeking a super set of legs that does it all. A multistage tripod is one solution, but it can be bulky, relatively heavy, and awkward to operate. The new Sachter SOOM is designed to address this issue, incorporating the functionality of standard legs, baby legs, high hat, and monopod in one compact unit.

The shooter will also require a *high hat* to achieve a ground level or low-angle shot. The high hat can be especially useful to secure the camera in difficult locations such as atop a stepladder or car bumper.

FIGURE 11.24

DSLRs require solid support just like their full-size brethren. Most low-cost jib arms and cranes flex or bounce or offer unexpected resistance, leading to much shooter consternation and torment.

FIGURE 11.25

To be useful a crane or jib arm must weigh *a lot*. Here, the crew enlists the help of local kids to free a behemoth sinking into the sand on a Bangladeshi beach.

FIGURE 11.26

You must be able to place the camera where the story demands it—wherever that may be.

(a)   (b)

(c)

(d)

FIGURE 11.27

(a) Dolly and track enable extreme accuracy from a moving camera. The Microdolly (b) has less functionality but is lightweight and portable and can be set up in under two minutes. The Western Dolly (c)—we all love her—is found on stages around the world. Haven't got Dolly? In a pinch, a wheelchair (d) may be pushed into service.

FIGURE 11.28

Camera stabilizers like the Steadicam eliminate the cost and hassle of a dolly and track but are less precise and require expertise to operate smoothly. The Steadicam was first used in 1976 for *Bound for Glory*[1] and a few months later in *Rocky*[2] to capture Stallone's running and training sequences.

FIGURE 11.30

Most helicopter systems utilize a gyroscope system to provide stabilization. Use extreme caution when operating on or near any active chopper. Death can come quickly.

FIGURE 11.29

Shooting from a moving vehicle? Consider a simple inexpensive stabilizer like this one, used to shoot alongside a speeding locomotive in *The Darjeeling Limited* (2007).

[1]Blumofe, R. F. (Producer), Leventhal, H. (Producer), Mulevhill, C. (Producer), Sneller, J. M. (Producer), & Ashby, H. (Director). (1976). *Bound for Glory* [Motion picture]. USA: United Artists.
[2]Chartoff, R. (Producer), Kirkwood, G. (Producer), Winkler, I. (Producer), & Avildsen, J. G. (Director). (1976). *Rocky* [Motion picture]. USA: Chartoff-Winkler Productions.

PLACE ANYWHERE

The camera must be mountable wherever the story dictates. We've discussed the imperative of capturing the world in a unique way, avoiding generic shots and angles, and adopting a clear and compelling point of view.

In the last several years, manufacturers have introduced lightweight dollies and *jib arms* that target the demands of the low-budget shooter. Be wary of flimsy, less robust gear! Such equipment is unlikely to see much service due to an inherent lack of stability. If the greater mass is not an issue, a more substantial jib arm or dolly will allow smoother takeoffs and landings.

YOU SHOOT; THEREFORE, YOU ARE

Don't read this section if you are the self-absorbed type who believes it's all about *you.* You relish your fanciful gyrations, dips, and swoons and don't give a rip about the appropriateness of your shenanigans—you just want to show off *your* talents as an *artiste*. Look, it's the same reason you don't pay your parking tickets, put money in the toll machine on the Dallas Tollway, or treat people you don't need very well. With camera in hand, you a special person, someone to be admired, fawned over, and treated like aristocracy. *You shoot; therefore, you are.*

FIGURE 11.31

This guy might be encountering a stabilization issue. Can you say Adobe Warp Stabilizer?

FIGURE 11.32

The Warp Stabilizer in Adobe After Affects can help address the steadiness issues associated with long telephoto lenses or shooting on a wave-tossed sea. When shooting and moving hand-held, the stabilizer can sometimes mimic the look of a sophisticated crane or dolly shot!

FIGURE 11.33

Don't toss the story out with your camera shake! Some vibration may be needed for authenticity!

If you're one of these *genius* types, someone has to clean up your mess, whether it's a poorly covered scene or an entire sequence in which the camera won't sit still. And if you're a director and you've been so victimized, the question then becomes what can you do about it. You can fire *Monsieur Artiste* and unleash plumes of bug spray on him, but what about his sickly ants-in-the-pants footage?

These days my tool of choice is the Adobe Warp Stabilizer,[3] which can be very effective to smooth out infested scenes and reduce camera shake or vibration.

I've used the tool to improve the feel of footage from the front of a racing motorcycle and from the bow of a sloop on a wave-tossed sea. Unlike other postproduction tools like SmoothCam in Final Cut Pro the Warp Stabilizer maintains the original borders of the frame, accomplishing its task without scaling or loss of resolution.

EDUCATOR'S CORNER: REVIEW TOPICS

1. How does a well-supported frame contribute to a compelling visual story?
2. Review the procedure for properly balancing the camera on a tripod. Practice a few times. Impress your friends and teachers.
3. In what context might an unsteady camera be appropriate? Identify three (3) emotions that could be communicated by the unstable camera? How important is a character's point of view when determining camera support?
4. What are the principal benefits of a fluid head? List five (5) features you would find desirable in the latest model.
5. Describe the effect on screen of a dolly versus a Steadicam? In what contexts would you use one or the other?
6. Identify the support you might use for shooting at ground level, inside a moving vehicle, with a long telephoto lens, or beside an erupting volcano. Consider the functionality and practicality of each choice.
7. Camera support like jib arms and cranes must be massive to be effective. Do you agree?
8. Your pompous cinematographer friend believes that postproduction tools such as Adobe's Warp Stabilizer ought not be a cinematographer's concern. What are the post-camera responsibilities of a shooter in today's highly converged production environment?
9. *Shakycam* is lazy and unprofessional. Should shakycam *shooters* be imprisoned for crimes against humanity? Be honest.

---

[3]The *warp stabilizer* feature in Adobe After Effects was introduced in Version 5.5 of the Creative Suite.

Listening to Your Story

I'm a shooter. That's what I do. Like breathing. And listening to Neil Diamond. Now after three decades of crashing a viewfinder to my face, I've developed an intimate relationship with my craft, one built understandably on the power of images to tell compelling stories.

It is ironic that the quality of my images should be so dependent on sound, for no matter how glamorous my Hollywood diva may look or how sinister my Mafioso capo may appear, the lack of intelligible audio will quickly torpedo the presentation and drive the audience from its seats. Every shooter must be aware of this one inescapable fact: *Audiences will tolerate bad picture but* never *bad sound.*

FIGURE 12.1

From a movie's first frame your audience is assessing the professionalism of your work. The clipping of highlights, illogical lighting, or incorrect eyeline serve to communicate an amateur feel, but it is the quality of sound that mostly shapes viewers' perceptions. Unintelligible audio will quickly alienate the audience regardless of your shooting genius.

(a)

(c)

(b)

FIGURE 12.2

Capturing good sound is the single best thing you can do to improve the look of your images!

281

AN UNSOUND PROPOSITION?

In Chapter 1, I related how I was hired by The History Channel's *Sworn to Secrecy* series to shoot air force pilots engaged in prisoner-of-war training. While flying up to Spokane, Washington, I realized I had no soundman, and that I was responsible for shooting and recording the audio too.

Flash ahead 15 years, and we find the correspondents for major U.S. news shows shooting and recording their own stories. It may be unwise, but the industry trend is clear: Today's shooter requires substantial audio skills, with a good working knowledge of a basic kit inclusive of one or two microphones, headset, and a small mixer.

FIGURE 12.3

Like it or not, we shooters are going solo more often these days.

FIGURE 12.4

For many of us, we have met the sound recordist—and he is us!

SOUND ADVICE

When rewriting a script, we work hard to weed out unnecessary scenes and dialogue. When composing a frame, we make every effort to eliminate or de-emphasize objects that are distracting or irrelevant. And when recording sound, we stay true to our mantra: *Exclude! Exclude! Exclude!* By minimizing or eliminating objectionable background noise, we are saying to the audience, "Listen to *this! This* sound is important! *This* dialogue matters."

To most shooters, an investment in audio gear seems illogical. After all we are engaged in a visual medium, and good audio seems like something that ought to just happen like the changing of the seasons or the day turning to night. Of course, recording superior audio is no fluke, and most of us realize that first-class sound and first-class images go hand in hand.

FIGURE 12.5

The external dials in many low-end camcorders are a frequent source of noise. Although newer models feature quieter potentiometers and preamps, it's still a good idea not to exceed 50% when recording audio directly into the camera.

It is understandable that manufacturers should focus almost exclusively on video since shooters tend to pay scant attention to a camera's audio section. Beyond the distortion and poor frequency response, the control pots in many camcorders produce significant noise. Compounding this issue are poor quality cables, jacks, and adapter plugs that further degrade performance. For the shooter operating solo or in a small team the capture of clean, crisp audio is a constant struggle.

BAD CONNECTIONS = BAD SOUND

Whether we're talking audio or video, a defective cable or connector is a primary cause of trouble in the field. Most failures are due to normal wear and tear, and the physical stress to which a camera's jacks and plugs are regularly subjected.

For the shooter/ersatz sound recordist the 1/8-inch mini-plug is *Public Enemy Number One*, providing a feeble connection at the most critical juncture with the camera. Mini-plug-to-XLR adapters offer only a partial solution, allowing a professional interface on one side while retaining the fragile (unbalanced) mini-plug on the other. An adapter box weighing on the jack may also lead to an intermittent condition, which can be maddening for the shooter disinclined to resolder a terminal or broken wire in the moments before rolling on a critical scene.

(a)

(b)

FIGURE 12.6

(a) Keep an eye and ear out for this villain and always approach with caution! Avoid unnecessary plugging and unplugging to reduce wear and tear, and the risk of a bad connection. The plug's evil female accomplice is pictured in (b).

FIGURE 12.7

The improper handling and storage of audio cables will almost certainly lead to failed connections and increased noise.

FIGURE 12.8

Cables should be stored loosely coiled with an alternating twist to ensure they lie flat and free of damaging kinks.

MIND YOUR CONNECTIONS

Consumer *RCA-type* plugs and jacks offer easy interoperability with home-based gear, but they pull apart easily when subject to the stress and strains of a typical pro shooter's day. For this reason, BNC- and XLR-type connectors are preferred.

FIGURE 12.9

Locking BNC and XLR connectors are more secure than the RCA consumer type.

FIGURE 12.10

As camcorders have shrunk in size the real estate available for robust connectors has also diminished. On some models the placement of the XLR inputs seems like an afterthought.

FIGURE 12.11

A potpourri of assorted A/V connectors should be a part of the basic shooter's kit. In a pinch, the right adapter could save your shoot—and your career.

KEEP BALANCE IN YOUR LIFE

Although shooting for a living can be all-consuming and great fun, we also need (I am told) *balance* in our lives, which means when it comes to cameras, shooting with *balanced audio* for the best possible recordings.

Long audio cables can act as potent noise collectors, so a noise cancellation system is required. Whereas *unbalanced* plugs and cables contain only two conductors—the *signal* (+) and ground—the *unbalanced* type features *three* conductors—the signal (+), *anti-signal* (−), and ground. The third conductor carries a parallel signal 180° *out of phase*, which is flipped back *into* phase at the connection to the camera. This method cancels out the noise that may might have been introduced along the length of the cable, thus restoring a clean signal. The use of an unbalanced adapter at any point disables the noise-cancellation advantage. Today an increasing number of prosumer camcorders offer balanced audio with integrated XLR connectors.

FIGURE 12.12

Balanced audio cables and plugs offer effective noise cancellation and are shielded to protect against a loss of signal.

FIGURE 12.13

A low-cost adapter attaches a professional microphone to cameras fitted with a dreadful 1/8-inch mini-jack. The adapter does not convert an unbalanced camera to a balanced one, nor does it eliminate the fragile connector that often leads to trouble.

MIXING IT UP

If you've been reading this book, you know I don't stand 1/24th of a second for flimsy gear masquerading as professional equipment. As a shooter with a large mortgage, an old car that needs repairs, and more than one unappreciative offspring, I demand a lot from my tools that I use and depend on every day. These tools have become like part of my family, and I rely on them in much the same way, for better and for worse.

The *mixer* is command central where we set levels, monitor audio quality, and apply limiting and filtration. Its layout of controls must be logical and easy to decipher. I'm a stickler for usability, and when a piece of gear is too frustrating to figure out, it is quickly relegated to a closet, back shelf, or eBay. A mixer's knobs and controls must have a solid feeling and be large enough to grasp with gloved hands—a particular need for shooters operating in the winter cold outside the cozy comfort of a studio or corporate boardroom.

Recording levels should be set conservatively to take advantage of the mixer's *safety limiter.* Because the limiter's threshold is not normally reached it should ordinarily have no effect on the quality of audio. For shooters operating in untamed locations prone to angry outbursts, such as Gene Simmons' kitchen in *Family Jewels*, the limiter kicks in imperceptibly to prevent clipping.

MIXING WITH THE CROWD

FIGURE 12.14

A three-channel mixer is ideal for shooters who use a boom and/or one or two lavalier/wireless mics and seldom have need for more elaborate configurations. The mixer should accept a range of microphones without bulky adapters or mysterious black boxes.

FIGURE 12.15

To reduce noise from traffic or wind the shooter should enable the mixer's high pass filter. There is usually little audio worth recording below 80 Hz, especially in dialog scenes.

Low-frequency response is a good measure of mixer performance. A proper mixer uses *balanced transformers* to provide isolation from the incoming source. Input signals are transformed magnetically so there is no feeble electro-mechanical contact as is the case in low-end mixers with noisy pots. For the shooter working in reality TV, a superior low-frequency response is essential to capturing clean, crisp sound in a demanding genre.

The mixer should support virtually any microphone. I continue to shoot with my 30-year-old Sennheiser that has accompanied me to every corner of the Earth. From arctic cold to Amazonian heat and humidity, the MKH-416 short shotgun has earned its place in my family of *Most Trusted Stuff*; the ruggedness of this mic, its reliability and performance, is unquestioned. Your field mixer should be in this league.

SETTING AUDIO LEVEL

Throughout this book, I've asserted the importance of exercising manual control over one's destiny. For audio, we usually disable the camera's *automatic level control (ALC)*, as this prevents unwanted background noise from ramping up during quiet passages.

The advent of the one-man-does-it-all model has pushed the limits of what one individual can reasonably accomplish with skill and aplomb. In some cases, ALC may be the only option for the beleaguered multi-tasking shooter.

If setting levels manually we should set a maximum level without clipping. The −12dB reference in many cameras doesn't leave much head room for loud passages, so the onus is on the shooter to capture audio free of distortion and defects. Remember that just as in video, the detail not captured in a clipped audio file is lost forever and cannot be magically resurrected later.

Although dialog is invariably recorded in *mono* to a single track, it is common to split the incoming audio, the second channel set 6dB lower to accommodate unforeseen outbursts. Many shooters place a wired or wireless lavalier on Channel 1 and the boom fitted with a directional *shotgun-type* microphone on Channel 2.

FIGURE 12.16

In this setup, the input signal on Channel 2 is set 6 dB below Channel 1, offering protection against sudden loud passages.

FIGURE 12.17

Automatic Level Control (ALC) is useful to capture ambient sounds like traffic or the roar of a crowd at a sporting event. For routine operation, ALC is normally disabled. Professional cameras have an external switch to do this.

FOR THE LOVE OF MIC

Superior audio begins with proper microphone placement. Locating the mic too far away and/or too far off-axis from the subject elevates the background noise, which can detract from the story. Shooters should know that mic placement is too critical to leave to an untrained person or a reluctant friend pressed into service to *hold the boom.*

Of course, no shooter can be expected to assume all the responsibilities of a dedicated sound recordist. Heaven knows we've enough trouble excluding the irrelevant *visual* things without getting into excluding the unhelpful hiss and pops and audio noise as well. Still, my philosophy on this is simple: Arrive on location ready to shoot. This means carrying the essentials—camera, media, audio, and a good can-do attitude—with you.

RIDING (SHORT) SHOTGUN

The need for a high-quality short shotgun cannot be overstated. Operating behind the scenes for *The Darjeeling Limited*, I used the camera-mounted microphone to capture 95% of the audio. Thus, the microphone had to feature a tightly focused pickup pattern with good resistance to off-axis interference. It also had to exhibit a wide dynamic range and smooth response, especially in the lower frequencies that favor the human voice.

FIGURE 12.18

I used a short shotgun camera-mounted mic almost exclusively to shoot behind the scenes for *The Darjeeling Limited* (2007).

(a)

(b)

FIGURE 12.19

(a) With a narrow pickup pattern and clean crisp sound, the short shotgun microphone is the workhorse of the film and television industries.
(b) The large zeppelin-type windscreen provides protection against the elements.

FIGURE 12.20
Prosumer cameras usually offer a built-in mic with omnidirectional pickup. The mic is really only useful to capture ambient sounds or effects.

(a)

FIGURE 12.21
This tiny short shotgun model works well for a palm-size camcorder or a DSLR.

(b)

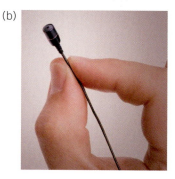

FIGURE 12.22
The wiring of an actor requires tact and expertise. Always ask permission before affixing a mic over or under an actress's wardrobe!

GOING WIRELESS

For the solo shooter, a wireless microphone may be the only practical way to capture clean professional sound.

I'm not a fan of the low-cost systems whose plastic components are prone to breakage. These models also tend to exhibit a higher than average noise floor and a greater proclivity for interference.

Every wireless mic faces similar challenges with respect to potential RF interference. This is particularly true in metropolitan areas where the airwaves are crammed with radio transmissions of every type from cell phones and baby monitors to emergency services. To function well in such an environment, a wireless system must offer superior filtering preferably with dual inputs. The two channels support separate mics that link to a single frequency for increased range and robustness of signal. In a *diversity receiver*, the cleaner of the two inputs are automatically selected. I like this notion. As a shooter, I understand the importance of clean audio and am willing to work to achieve it, but I do, uh, well—have other things on my mind.

FIGURE 12.24

An external mic select switch controls the input source.

FIGURE 12.23

Unobtrusive and lightweight the slot receiver in this full-size camcorder adds little weight or bulk. Look for streamlined solutions that eliminate the quagmire of cables and jerry-rigged boxes that can interfere with your creative mojo and become entangled with an actor or grip.

FIGURE 12.25

Typical good-quality wireless system.

GOING BOOM

A competent boom operator understands a project's story, has read and probably memorized the dialog, rehearsed the camera blocking, and anticipates an actor's every move. If you're a shooter, it is your job to communicate the boundaries of the frame so the boom op can properly prepare his or her approach and mode of attack.

FIGURE 12.26

Placing the microphone as close as possible while remaining out of frame, sometimes requires working from below.

FIGURE 12.27

Long takes. Long days. Supporting a boom can be physically grueling. Powerful arms and biceps are a plus!

FIGURE 12.28

What are the chances this production is capturing usable sound? A more substantial "fuzzy" windscreen might help.

(a)

(b)

FIGURE 12.29

Wherever you are, you have to listen. You need a headset.

FIGURE 12.30

The headset should cover the ears to isolate the production sound from the environment.

FIGURE 12.31

The ear buds from your iPod, iPhone, or Android, are not intended for professional production.

FIGURE 12.32

Don't even think about wrapping a headset like this! It will damage the coiled cable and fragile mini-plug connector.

NOISE REDUCTION FOR THE VIDEO SHOOTER

As hard as we try, sometimes poor audio is unavoidable. Fortunately, the shooter has access a range of post-camera tools such as Apple Soundtrack or Adobe Audition to mitigate the most serious defects and improve the intelligibility of the audio in dialog scenes. Although tools such as ProTools and Logic cannot magically transform horrible audio into great audio, they can substantially reduce background noise, popping, hum, and other flaws that can detract substantially from the integrity of the presentation.

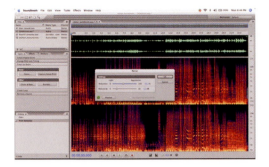

FIGURE 12.33

Today's shooter must understand audio processing tools like Adobe Audition and Adobe Soundbooth. A graphical display makes it easy to identify, highlight, and delete objectionable noise.

SHOOTING DOUBLE SYSTEM: IS IT NECESSARY?

For most corporate, news, and documentary projects, there is little to be gained by utilizing a dedicated audio recorder. Today's video cameras provide sufficient functionality and performance to enable capture of pro caliber audio either through a mixer or directly from a wired or wireless mic. For feature films and commercials, or when shooting with a DSLR, *double system* is the preferred method for capturing high-quality sound. (See Chapter 5 for more on DSLRs.)

(a)

(b)

FIGURE 12.34

Many shooters and producers prefer double system owing to the potential higher quality and greater control of recording parameters.

(a)

(b)

FIGURE 12.35

Recording double system to a compact Zoom, computer hard drive, or disc, requires a reference slate or marker for post-synchronization. Systems lacking timecode including most DSLRs may be synchronized using *PluralEyes* (b) that aligns the waveforms in the production audio to a guide track inputted into the camera.

YOU ARE SURROUNDED

With the advent of DVD, Blu-ray, and 3D home theater, the demand is rising for multichannel 5.1 recording in the field. Most cameras support at least four channels of built-in audio, with a new crop of entry-level camcorders such as the Sony HDR-SR12 able to record in-camera Dolby Digital 5.1 Surround.

FIGURE 12.37

Many camcorders now feature a 5.1 Surround capability. The Dolby tracks are multiplexed into a stereo file to facilitate handling in post-production. Standalone surround sound microphones are available to record 5.1 into any camera with stereo inputs.

FIGURE 12.36

Patching an external mic into a compact Panasonic camcorder routes the internal mics to channels 3 & 4, enabling the capture of ambient sound along with the main production audio.

FIGURE 12.38

Standard 5.1 = two front + two surround + center + subwoofer. Preparing proper surround tracks in post is expensive and time-consuming. Dialogue is always recorded in mono to the center channel.

(a)   (b)

FIGURE 12.39

Philip Cacayorin's 360° Stereophile 3D microphone utilizes two mono lavalier mics suspended inside a passive enclosure. The system has the potential to eliminate the mixing board and a suite of engineers at live concerts!

TO IMPROVISE IS GOOD

It would be nice, of course, to work always with the best gear. Unfortunately, the world isn't so accommodating so we have to improvise: Use mirrors instead of expensive lighting, scavenge gels from the trash rather than order them from B&H, or staple egg cartons to the studio wall rather than invest thousands of dollars in acoustic tile.

The successful shooter may not have the coolest camera or even the most creative ideas. In the end, it is the scrapper, the tough guy, the indefatigable man or woman with the most persistence and resourcefulness and the ability to carry on, day after day, month after month, in the face of never-ending obstacles.

The egg-carton-on-the-wall ruse is not the end-all to realizing low- or no-cost production, but it is a reflection of the powerful desire to capture and record one's story with proper technique and craft. We all face in our lives and careers an uphill battle—lack of gear, funds, industry connections—whatever you want to tell yourself. The successful shooter knows only how to staple the egg cartons to the wall and press on—no matter what.

FIGURE 12.40

Seeking an economical way to filter out the street noise this TV studio in Dar es Salaam utilizes discarded egg cartons in lieu of pricey acoustic tile. Improvisation saves money, builds character, and stokes the creative process.

EDUCATOR'S CORNER: REVIEW TOPICS

1. If the director is the most important crewmember, who is the *second* most important? The shooter? Soundman? Teamster unloading the gear? Be thoughtful. This is not a trick question.
2. The quality of sound is critical to a production. Do you think the sound recordist should have the authority to stop rolling on a scene with unusable sound?
3. The audio story is closely linked to the visual story. Describe five (5) ways how this connection might appear on screen. Cite examples from feature films to form your responses.
4. Indicate the microphone type you would use to capture the following scenes: (a) an interview with the President, (b) a hidden camera in the back of a Las Vegas taxi, (c) an antigovernment riot in Tehran, (d) a bugling bull moose at 50 meters, and (e) the ambient sound in Grand Central Station.
5. Describe three (3) circumstances where you might use Automatic Level Control (ALC). What compromises if any are you making in the quality of the recording?
6. Please demonstrate proper cable coiling technique in front of your friends or teachers. Do you feel proud?
7. When shopping for a new camera what audio features might you look for? Dual XLR inputs? Safety limiters? High and low pass filters? Is the wretched 1/8-inch microphone input enough to reject the camera? It should be.
8. The sound recordist may be the most unappreciated member of the crew. Why do you think this is the case? The fact that most soundmen are whiners and miserable is not a valid reason.

Going with the Flow

Spiritualist Eckhart Tolle in his best seller *A New Earth*[1] notably observed that we really only act out of two emotions: *love and fear.* If we aren't acting out of love, then we're acting out of fear, and the tapeless, file-based world has thrust plenty of it on us. Our challenge as shooters in this digital-run-amok world is to confront our fears and replace them to the extent possible with a love for the new ways of doing things.

As Tolle would say, we have no choice but to accept the *Is-ness* of the medium. In my workshops, I sometimes find resistance from my cinematography students who balk at the need to learn post-camera solutions. They say (or are taught) that audio is someone else's job; that postproduction stabilization, recomposition, and filtering are not their concern; that the director, producer, and screenwriter all have their roles, which are unrelated to the shooter's role, which is to shoot. Just shoot. Truly one has to wonder what world or decade these students are preparing for.

FIGURE 13.1

Look around. The Is-ness is upon us. We have to accept the reality of a rapidly evolving media landscape.

FIGURE 13.2

Today's cameras no longer shoot video. They capture data to solid-state memory, which requires a computer-centric IT-based workflow.

---

[1] Tolle, E. (2005). *A New Earth: Awakening to Your Life's Purpose.* New York, NY: Penguin Press.

FIGURE 13.3

Twenty years ago, Firewire ushered in the desktop video revolution. Today, it has now been almost entirely supplanted by USB, a nonvideo interface.

FIGURE 13.4

Who says we need a file-based workflow? This very analog scene is from the Turin Winter Olympics in 2006.

FIGURE 13.5

Camera startup from flash memory is instantaneous without waiting for belts and pulleys to get up to speed. Some cameras offer a dual-record capability, providing a simultaneous backup.

FIGURE 13.6

Optical disc cameras provide an archival copy for backup—a consideration for folks fearful of corrupting or inadvertently deleting original files from solid-state media. Similar to traditional tape cameras, Sony's disc models require hauling cases of media to remote locations. Solid-state cameras have no such requirement: We haul stacks of hard drives and backups of hard drives instead.

NOT ONE WORKFLOW

There was a time we blissfully rolled off a bunch of cassettes, handed them to a production assistant, and submitted an invoice. End of story. Nice.

Today, thanks to solid-state cameras and the vagaries of a computer environment, there are many possible workflows. Shooting behind the scenes for *The Darjeeling Limited*, I had no reliable AC power, dirt and sand were everywhere, and my working space aboard the moving train in India was just 19 inches (50 cm) across. Making matters worse, I had only three 8GB cards for my P2 camera—a total of 1-hour of running time, necessitating the periodic crash off-loading of cards at various times in the day.

FIGURE 13.7

Given today's all-file based world, every project may require a slightly different workflow. I set up this improvised offload station under a tree in Jodhpur, India, for *The Darjeeling Limited*.

THE PROMISE OF MXF

The entertainment industry created the *Material eXchange Format (MXF)* to facilitate the handling of media files from image capture through postproduction and digital cinema. Unfortunately, given a 700-page standard, there were bound to be implementation differences.

Panasonic's MXF P2 format assigns a random file name to the individual media files. While this creates the discrete audio and video streams necessary for editing, the splitting of assets in this way complicates the playback and management of MXF files on the desktop. The cryptic naming of files is especially unhelpful, and any attempt to assign more appropriate names disrupts the MXF structure and renders the asset inaccessible.

Sony's XDCAM MXF format produces files incompatible with Panasonic's P2. The two systems vary in their subfolder hierarchy and how the A/V files are captured: XDCAM *multiplexes*[2] the audio and video into a single stream, the preferred strategy in a broadcast environment. By maintaining separate audio and video streams, P2 is optimized for the production of feature films, commercials, documentaries, corporate, and other non-broadcast programs.[3]

(a)   (b)

FIGURE 13.8

(a) The P2 layout of folders appears logical on the computer desktop. The XDCAM thumbnail editor (b) marks, deletes, and organizes clips into folders, prior to off-loading to an external device or server.

---

[2]*Multiplexing* is a process of interweaving multiple streams of data—audio, video, timecode, machine control, and so on—into a single stream for easier handling and transmission.

[3]Panasonic, Avid, and others, utilize MXF Operational Pattern *OP-Atom*. Sony uses a different operational pattern dubbed *OP-1a*.

FIGURE 13.9

WiFi-enabled camcorders and DSLRs allow direct editing via an iPad or tablet obviating the need to offload memory cards to an external drive!

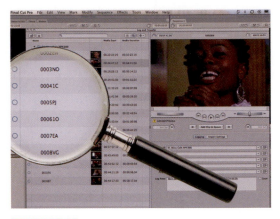

FIGURE 13.10

MXF's cryptic naming pattern links the format's numerous components. Once inside the NLE bin or browser, a clip may be renamed without limitation.

THE BEAUTY OF METADATA

Several years ago, a popular U.S. news show aired a segment in which a noted plastic surgeon appeared irrational. The doctor, not happy with his depiction, threatened to sue the network but agreed not to do so on the condition that the interview never run again. Four years later, a young producer for another show *rediscovered* the original broadcast and, unaware of the prohibition, reused portions of the doctor's unflattering comments. This time in the face of almost certain litigation, the network fired the producer and settled quickly with the physician for a large cash sum.

Today this incident might have been avoided given proper management of the clip's *metadata*. Metadata is *data about data* that include, among other things, technical details like frame rate, resolution, and compression format. It also may include the production title, GPS tags, shooter and producer IDs, and use prohibitions, if any. This metadata is made a permanent part of the clip, instantly searchable with a click of a mouse from inside the NLE.

Metadata support is crucial for effective digital asset management (DAM). For *Harry Potter and the Order of the Phoenix*[4] in 2007, producers conforming a scene for the digital intermediate[5] laboriously pawed through 120 different versions of a single shot; no one could say with certainty which version was actually approved by the director. Adding a simple annotation to the desired clip's metadata could have saved the hassle and the expense of searching for hours in the DI room.

---

[4]Barron, D. (Producer), Heyman, D. (Producer), Lewis, T. (Producer), Orleans, L (Producer), Trehy, J. (Producer), Wigram, L. (Producer), & Yates, D. (Director). *Harry Potter and the Order of the Phoenix* [Motion picture]. United Kingdom: Warner Bros.

[5]Widely used for the output of digital files for theatrical or commercial release the *digital Intermediate* represents the ultimate convergence of processes whereby individual scenes are color-corrected, isolated, and composited, with utmost control and sophistication.

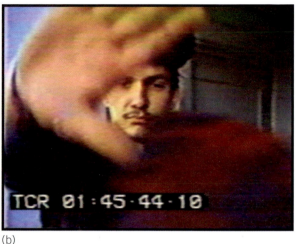

(a)   (b)

FIGURE 13.11

A key advantage of a file-based workflow is the ability to manage and search metadata. The custom fields in this clip's metadata (a) can accommodate a range of input from camera setup and lens choice to location notes and restrictions on use.

WE SHOULD BE LESS FEARFUL NOW

Given videotape's inherent fragile nature and trouble-prone mechanical transport, the new file-based systems should make us feel *more* secure, despite the apprehension stemming from the offloading of media cards and erasing of the original camera files.

Nervous Nellies point to the volatility of data and the need to store master camera footage (albeit temporarily) on less than reliable bus-powered hard drives. The same Nellies point to the slow transfer process and the need for multiple backups to ensure file integrity and peace of mind. For these folks, a tangible cassette tape or disc provides welcome solace, a security blanket in a digital age when critical data can neither be seen nor touched, and so may be unknowingly mishandled, corrupted, or deleted.

We shooters are a fearful breed. We worry about things whether they matter or not: Do our sensors have enough pixels? Are we selling our souls when shooting 4:2:0? Is long GOP going to diminish us as human beings? These are the things that keep us awake at night.

The failure of a hard drive is not a prospect that sits well with us; indeed, we know how most HDDs are guaranteed for only 1 to 3 years. Hard drive failure may have a variety of causes including poor maintenance, subjecting the drive to excessive heat or shock, use of an incorrect or defective power supply, or failure of a connector or controller board.

FIGURE 13.12

With the advent of high-capacity memory cards the crash off-loading of original camera files has been largely eliminated.

Whatever our fears real or imagined, the shooter understands that HDD failure is an occupational hazard that can strike at any time any place with devastating results.

FIGURE 13.13

The Nexto verifies offloading of a camera's memory cards to the unit's internal HDD. The built-in LCD screen provides confirmation of a successful transfer.

THE ADVENT OF SSD

With no moving parts, the *solid-state drive* (SSD) confronts head-on the source of our anxiety. SSDs are much more reliable, lightweight, and resistant to heat, shock, and G-forces.

Not constrained by a spinning platter or a fitful mechanism, the SSD operates at the full bandwidth of the bus up to 1,600 Mbps via eSATA at RAID 0.[6] If fear still compels your desire for redundancy a RAID 1 SSD array with 100% mirroring can still sustain 960 Mbps.

High-capacity SSDs offering USB 3.0 and Thunderbolt[7] will soon eclipse mechanical hard drives for most applications. For shooters, the greatest threat then will not be failure of the drive but physical loss or theft of the SSD itself.

FIGURE 13.14

A mini SSD RAID can be configured for speed RAID 0, safety RAID 1, or JBOD (Just a Bunch of Drives). An idle SSD consumes no power except for the illuminated LED!

---

[6]A **Redundant Array of Independent Disks (RAID)** consists of multiple drives that appear on the desktop as a single unit. Different RAID configurations balance the need for data protection versus speed and performance: RAID 0 stripes data across multiple drives for maximum throughput as in a P2 card; RAID 1 mirrors data across multiple drives for 100% protection. RAID 5 is a popular configuration, incorporating striping of data like RAID 0, with redundant pieces of data distributed across multiple drives. The strategy referred to as **parity** staggers the bits across several drives allowing any single drive in the RAID 5 array to fail without data loss.

[7]**Thunderbolt** supports displays and drives through dual channels at 10 Gbps. The versatile Apple interface supports HDMI, DVI, and USB 2.0/3.0 devices, via a simple cable adapter.

CONNECT TO DRIVE

FIGURE 13.15

Off-loading via USB to a computer? Use DEVICE mode. To offload directly to an external drive use HOST mode. The HDD or SSD must be formatted via the camera.

PROXY VIDEO AND THE IPHONE

There's a growing impetus among shooters for mobile devices to play a more active role for monitoring and review. Some cameras like the Panasonic HPX600 can be fitted with a *proxy* encoder for streaming MPEG-4 audio and video to the Web or handheld device. XDCAM cameras produce proxy videos by default and so do not require a supplemental encoder card.

The preparation of iPhone dailies is simple. A media card or a camcorder containing the proxy videos is mounted on a computer and a new *playlist* is created in iTunes. It should be named logically, for example, "01_production_date." The proxy files are then dragged into the playlist and synced to the iPhone in the normal way. The same procedure applies to XDCAM proxies, which may be brought into iTunes directly from the disc or the SXS card or retrieved after capture from the XDCAM Proxy Folder.

FIGURE 13.16

The iPhone and iPad are increasingly popular production tools. Simple edits can be performed and sent instantly to absentee producers on far-off golf courses.

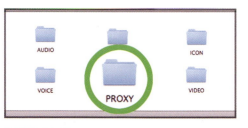

FIGURE 13.17

The latest Panasonic P2 cameras place the MPEG-4 proxy files in the appropriate folder. For video dailies create a new playlist in iTunes, drag in the proxy videos, sync to the iPhone—and voilà!

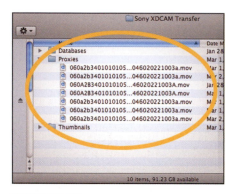

FIGURE 13.18

XDCAM cameras create low-resolution proxy files that can be used to create an iTunes playlist. The files' naming convention leaves something to be desired.

FIGURE 13.19

Cameras without proxy encoding can use Imagine Products' Proxy Mill to prepare iPhone dailies. The Proxy Mill generates MPEG-4 files from P2 or QuickTime (.mov) sources.

OUTPUTTING YOUR STORY

Some of us belong to pricey health clubs equipped with the latest machines and smoothie bars. We pay thousands of dollars, euros, or pounds each year for the privilege, so why is it we don't use these clubs more often, or even at all? The answer is simple: Most clubs are not all that convenient, especially if they're located more than 10 minutes from work or home.

This rule of use versus nonuse also applies to our digital tools. For the shooter, there are many post-camera tools with powerful features that could improve our images, but the software is too complex or inconvenient to access. In their own way, the benefits of these programs are located too far away and so, like the health club, are likely to go unused.

This isn't the case with Sorenson Squeeze, whose broad capabilities are intuitive and easy to access. It's hard to think of a platform or format that is *not* supported: WebM, HTML5, Flash, H.264, AVC-Intra, and XDCAM. You'll still need a dedicated encoder for digital cinema and 3D but short of that, Squeeze is a one-stop shop for digital encoding for whatever display venue you might be contemplating.

FIGURE 13.20

Behold the shooter's Three Noble Truths: Yes, you need Photoshop; yes, you need an NLE; and yes you need Sorenson Squeeze to output your project according to the dictates of your own true self.

FIGURE 13.21

Enjoying a cricket match outside a TV shop window in Dhaka in 2012. Not everyone is inclined to watch such programs on a mobile phone, although in Japan a growing number of smartphone users do.[8]

FIGURE 13.22

Today's shooter must adjust to the latest trends. Case in point: Small-screen viewing will depend on close-ups more than ever. So tell me why you need that 5K camera again?

THE DECLINE OF DVD

Interestingly even as rentals on digital platforms continue to grow at 5% per year, consumers in North America are still renting DVD and Blu-ray discs in great numbers. Two-thirds of all U.S. film rentals in 2012 were still being placed through Netflix's mail service, Redbox kiosks, and the few surviving retail shops such as Blockbuster. Subscription-based streaming services, pay TV, and VOD accounted for the remaining one third.[9]

Given this reality, the shooter looking to the near future would be wise not to forget the standard-definition DVD. Whether shooting feature films, music videos, or high school plays, DVD continues to play a significant role, especially in the fast-growing regions of Asia and Africa. This will likely remain the case even as digital streaming in the West becomes the predominant distribution vehicle.

Because so much craft and discipline go into creating a compelling and well-performing DVD, it makes sense that we accommodate to some degree the format's requirements. It matters less that our

---

[8] Nearly 20% of smartphone users in Japan view TV and movies regularly on their handsets. New Media Trend Watch. (2013, March 28). http://www.newmediatrendwatch.com/markets-by-country/11-long-haul/54-japan
[9] Although digital rentals on all platforms are growing at over 5% per year, the overall market, including **Video On Demand (VOD)** declined 18% to nearly $1.7 billion during the first 6 months of 2012. In 2011, kiosk operators saw revenues rise 23% to $990 million as traditional rental stores saw business decline 33% to $598 million. Marc Graser. (2012, August 8). Physical Side Dropping But Still Reps 62% of Business. *Daily Variety*, http://variety.com/2012/digital/news/most-movie-renters-still-use-discs-1118057628/

images look great out of the camera or NLE. What *really* matters is how our images look at the end of the digital rainbow whether delivered via the Web, pay TV, or a DVD player.

The shooter can use various strategies to improve the quality of DVD output. Shooting 24p makes sense since DVD and Blu-ray players are native 24p devices. Movie studios originating at 24 FPS logically encode their feature films at 24 FPS. Relying on the player to perform the upconversion to 29.97 FPS NTSC or 25 FPS PAL, the DVD shooter can capture, edit, and encode at 24 FPS (actually 23.976 FPS), and reduce the file size of a finished program by 20%. This means more bits can be allocated to each second of video with a concomitant increase in sharpness and detail. The reduction in objectionable artifacts is a major reason for the improved look of DVD programs captured, finished, and encoded at 24p.[10]

DVD's high compression underlies the need to monitor a camera's detail level, because this can have a dramatic impact on the look of the encoded images. With camera detail set too high, the hard edge around objects is emphasized complicating compression along the transition boundary. Raising or lowering camera detail affects the thickness of this edge, and with it the potential for blocking artifacts that may arise during video playback.

(a)

FIGURE 13.23

Despite the growth of the web and other digital platforms DVD still dominates the home-video market and will likely do so for several more years.

(b)

EYE ON THE ENCODED IMAGE

We are concerned foremost with the integrity of our images, and so highly compressed digital platforms like DVD substantially impact on how viewers see and judge our work. Whether we like it or not, our meticulously lit doted-over images will be compressed on the order of 40:1 or more, and that compression better be done right and with all due respect.

---

[10] See Chapter 4 for more insight into the relative advantages of progressive versus interlaced recording.

Ideally, the shooter ought to retain control over the encoding process. Other factors having an impact on the shooter's craft such as lens performance, camera setup, and filter nuances pale in comparison to the savagery of compressing our images for the Web, mobile phone, or DVD. Consider the complexity of this task—see Chapter 4—and it's easy to see how the delivered program no matter how well-crafted can be transformed into a Seurat painting.

High-compression snafus especially concern the DSLR shooter, who incurring a bevy of in-camera artifacts must make a concerted effort to remediate these issues in post. DSLR artifacts such as *moiré* and *macroblocking* can be especially disconcerting. Your job as a new-breed shooter-storyteller is to mitigate such defects prior to encoding for final output.

FIGURE 13.24

Standard definition DVD requires MPEG-2 long-GOP encoded assets at 720 × 480 NTSC or 720 × 576 PAL. Encoding for the Web and mobile devices allows much greater flexibility.

FIGURE 13.25

Compression artifacts such as banding and macroblocking haven't been art for a while! This is Seurat's *A Sunday Afternoon on the Island of La Grande Jatte*, painted in 1884.

ENCODERS HAVE PERSONALITIES

The video storyteller understands that encoders may favor some compression parameters over others. One encoder may work well with high-action sports such as rodeos, but perform less admirably when facing a Halloween parade at night featuring complex colors and costumes. To the adept shooter, the new world of HD, MPEG-2, H.264, and VC-1[11] means understanding a *range* of encoders. No single tool can be expected to do it all, even encoders costing tens of thousands of dollars.

---

[11]**MPEG-4** is a nonproprietary standard. **H.264** is Apple's variant of MPEG-4 popular across the Web. **Video Coder (VC-1)** is Microsoft's variant of MPEG-4 and is less commonly used. Isn't life exciting enough? Do we really need this?

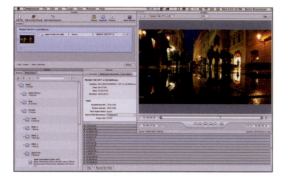

FIGURE 13.26

Engineers working within narrow constraints must juggle the demands of good color and contrast with adequate motion estimation. Apple Compressor has improved in recent years with lower noise and less image softening.

SCENES THAT SPELL TROUBLE

Whether shooting for the Web, DVD, or another compressed medium, the shooter must be aware of scenes that can cause trouble for encoders. Fades and dissolves to and from static high-contrast scenes require extra scrutiny. Wafting smoke, expanses of water, rustling leaves, and falling snow are also tricky. The smart shooter recognizes these potential problem areas and endeavors to stay on top of them from image capture through postproduction.

FIGURE 13.27

The shooter must be aware of scenes that challenge the media encoder. Fast-moving objects like this London taxi can be problematic.

FIGURE 13.28

Expanses of water with gently shifting waves are notoriously difficult to compress. Be sure to scrutinize such areas for potential artifacts.

THE NOISE-REDUCTION IMPERATIVE

We must take care to minimize noise in our original recordings, as the encoder may find it difficult to distinguish the image detail we want from the noise we (presumably) don't want. The use of an on-camera *tightening* filter such as the Tiffen Soft/FX or Schneider Digicon can help suppress the blotchiness and swirling noise in the unsupported shadows and textureless monochromatic areas, and so may improve the look of the outputted program.

Besides turning down detail and applying light camera diffusion, noise reduction may also be applied inside the NLE. Many encoders including Compressor have a built-in noise reduction capability of limited effectiveness. The application of noise reduction must always be weighed against the loss of picture detail in the weaker shadow areas.

FIGURE 13.29

A monochromatic sky devoid of texture may exhibit objectionable noise in the encoded program. Reducing the detail in-camera or employing a weak diffusion filter may help.

FIGURE 13.30

Software tools like the Magic Bullet Denoiser and Neat Video can help reduce the noise from elevated camera gain. The original scene is at left; the treated scene at right.

KNOW YOUR ENCODING MODE

A clean, crisp image with good contrast is normally our goal, and so it would seem to make sense to encode with as high a bitrate as possible. We are constrained, however, by the delivery system—the bandwidth available for the Web, the connection speed for mobile devices, and the DVD and Blu-ray video specifications.

In cable and satellite TV the MPEG video streams must move through a *pipe* of finite size. The program packages or *Groups of Pictures (GOPs)* proceed on what might be regarded as a conveyor belt. To move multiple program streams in the most efficient manner the belt must operate at a constant speed with each package being of roughly equal size, as packages of varying girths might get stuck and clog the pipe. At a constant bit rate (CBR), exploding battleships and talking heads receive the same allocation of bits regardless of the scene's complexity.

Variable bit rate (VBR) encoding adjusts the speed of the conveyor to support different size packages and so is more efficient since bits scavenged from static scenes like a reporter's stand-up can be reassigned to action scenes such as a barroom brawl.

FIGURE 13.31

VBR adjustments in the bit stream take place at the GOP level in as few as four frames in NTSC. For DVD demo reels and brief programs of 15 minutes or less, CBR yields the best results at a steady 8.5 Mbps. Be sure to encode the audio to Dolby stereo 2.0, or you won't be able to burn your DVD![12]

BLU-RAY, ANYONE?

Who can forget the format wars of 2008 that left HD-DVD in the digital dust? HD-DVD ran a good campaign, offering greater flexibility, more accessible authoring tools, and better compatibility with existing DVD, but in the end, with the support of the Hollywood studios, Blu-ray ultimately prevailed.

Since the cessation of hostilities, Blu-ray's fortunes have been lackluster. Despite the $2 billion dollars in U.S. sales in 2011,[13] the format remains, as Steve Jobs once so elegantly stated, "a bagful of hurt."

For the average shooter and content creator, the prospect of *replicating* Blu-ray discs is not practical. The major reason is an onerous licensing scheme that until recently required thousands of dollars in fees per title. The fee structure established for the Hollywood studios placed commercial Blu-ray discs out of reach for most corporate, business, and event applications.

The *Advanced Access Content System (AACS)* is designed to thwart piracy by preventing playback of Blu-ray discs without proper authentication.[14] It is a crude stick that works too well, to the detriment of the format and those who would like to adopt it.

Nevertheless, Blu-ray disc titles can be *duplicated*, that is, burned as *one-offs*, without incurring AACS fees. Unfortunately, the compatibility of Blu-ray recordable discs on some players can be sketchy. A short-running-time BDMV screener or demo reel utilizing *intraframe*-only compression may be burned to DVD-R[15] but the resultant disc may confound some high-end players that suspect pirated content and refuse to play it. In this respect, the dirt-cheap players from China are more forgiving, merrily playing back BDMV or AVCHD volumes from recordable media without a care in the world.

[12]**DVD-Video** limits total bandwidth to 9.8 Mbps inclusive of audio, video, and *subpictures*, which include still menu overlays and subtitles.

[13]Snider, M. (2012, January 9). Blu-ray Grows, but DVD Slide Nips Home Video Sales. *USA Today*, http://usatoday30.usatoday.com/tech/news/story/2012-01-10/blu-ray-sales-2011/52473310/1

[14]**AACS** is administered by a consortium of companies including Disney, Intel, Microsoft, Panasonic, Warner Bros. IBM, Toshiba, and Sony.

[15]**BDMV** volumes not exceeding approximately 15 minutes of total running time may be burned to red laser DVD-R (+R) for playback on Blu-ray machines. **AVCHD** is more likely to play back reliably on BD players from major manufacturers.

FIGURE 13.32

Keeping an eye on the latest technology? Uprezzed from standard definition, 1080p DVD can look nearly as good as an original Blu-ray title. The perception that DVD is "good enough" has diminished the public's interest in the high-definition disc format.

FIGURE 13.33

Adobe Encore supports the output of DVD and Blu-ray titles to recordable media. Apple offers no BD authoring solution—and is not likely to.

REACHING FOR THE CLOUDS

The writing is in the cumulous. The industry is moving rapidly to the cloud, which promises a more collaborative and shared environment. The cloud is a reflection of the expanding global marketplace as production teams can span continents and time zones, and shooters and film-makers can work wherever they want to.

The Internet has become a vast media network with more than 6 billion active mobile phones, many with broadband access.[16] This global transformation will only accelerate with the introduction of 3D tablets that will create an abundance of new opportunities for shooters in the nontheatrical arena.

Cloud-based collaboration in film and television is a growing expectation of producers around the world. This is especially so in the developing markets of Asia, where a physical industry infrastructure does not exist.

FIGURE 13.34

The cloud offers today's shooter-storyteller anywhere in the world a full range of post-camera editing and processing tools, including Adobe's Creative Cloud suite of applications.

---

[16] See "Mobile phone." In *Wikipedia* (para. 3). Retrieved from http://en.wikipedia.org/wiki/Mobile_phone

THE ARCHIVING CHALLENGE

In the beginning, God created film and all seemed right in the world. We'd shoot maybe 5 or 6 minutes for a 30-second commercial, and that was the norm. Producers saw little reason to shoot more.

Nowadays, of course, we are shooting more—a *lot* more. On some shoots, our cameras *never* stop, and so the question becomes what to do with all the footage we shouldn't have shot in the first place. In the recent past, the vast piles of tapes and cassettes ended up on a shelf in a closet or exposed to the elements in a carport waiting (8 to 10 years on average) for time to do its thing.

Today we have no choice but to tackle the exploding asset load head-on and to devise a viable archiving strategy. Cheap high-capacity hard drives may seem like a good option, but hard drives are fragile and prone to failure; the best *enterprise-level* drives carry only a 5-year warranty. Thus, we should think of HDDs as a short-term solution, for use only with active projects. SSDs hold some promise, but their current high cost and lower capacity make them impractical, and their long-term stability is unproven.

Currently the most practical archiving solution in this tapeless age is ironically tape—not videotape but *data* tape—*LTO* and *Super DLT*.[17] These are proven entities and have been used for years by banks, insurance companies, and the IRS. At least one Hollywood studio re-archives its entire inventory of high value assets every seven years to LTO tape.

The latest generation DLT drives are nothing like the cranky, unreliable models of a decade ago. The new drives mount on a desktop like any other drive, with a searchable directory that allows access to the archive via FTP from anywhere in the world. The directory eliminates the former hassle of maintaining a separate database that can, over time, be lost or corrupted.

Of course, no archiving medium is 100% reliable, thus the need for redundancy. It is essential to back up critical files and use *checksums*[18] to detect errors that may have been introduced during the transfer.

FIGURE 13.35

Archiving once looked like this!—

FIGURE 13.36

—and this!

FIGURE 13.37

Then this!—

---

[17]**LTO** refers to the decades-old Linear Tape Open format. **Digital Linear Tape (DLT)** is similar to LTO, offering comparable functionality with greater economy and lower capacity for small to mid-level producers.
[18]A **checksum** detects errors that may have been introduced during the off-loading of camera footage. The integrity of the data is verified by comparing the current checksum with a stored value. If the checksums match, the integrity of the data is intact.

FIGURE 13.38

—and this!

FIGURE 13.39

The SDLT drive is suitable for individual shooters and small production companies.

FIGURE 13.40

LTO with an estimated 100-year shelf life has a current capacity of 6.25TB on a single cartridge.

EDUCATOR'S CORNER: REVIEW TOPICS

1. How is capturing *video* different from capturing data files? Describe the differences with respect to camera operation and workflow.
2. Why is maintaining low-noise so important to the integrity of the visual story? Identify three (3) strategies we might use when shooting to ensure a low-noise output.
3. Consider the merits of shooting to tape, optical disc, or solid-state memory. Make a case for and against each option.
4. What is *metadata*? Note eight (8) production details that might be useful to include in a clip's metadata file.
5. Describe the optimal procedure for offloading a camera's memory cards. How can we verify the integrity of the transferred file?
6. The server-camcorder promises to make the offloading of memory cards obsolete. What other changes in operation or workflow might be expected from a WiFi-enabled camcorder?
7. Look ahead to the next several years. What role do you think DVD and Blu-ray will play? Do you think optical media will persist as a viable distribution medium? Please explain your position from a global perspective.
8. How might collaboration in the cloud contribute to or detract from the success of your next production? How will such collaboration impact the role of the video shooter?

There Is No Best Button

So you're outputting your show for the Web, mobile phone, or DVD, and you face the following option: Would you prefer *good*, *better*, or *best*?

Hmm. I wonder why would anyone settle for good or better when you can have best? Best is definitely better than better, and better inherently has to be better than good. On the other hand, I suppose it's a good thing that worse is not an option, because worse is surely worse than good, but it is better than much worse, and much, much better than much, much worse.

All this mental wrangling raises the greater issue: Can there ever really be a Best button?

A Best button certainly has its appeal. We wouldn't need to spend a lifetime learning lighting, composition, framing, how to use texture and perspective or understanding the intricacies of the animal brain. We wouldn't have to learn the technical razzmatazz, the aesthetic subtleties, and silly names for things on sets. We could forego the stress and discipline of having to *exclude, exclude, exclude* all the time. A Make It Awesome button could do it all for us.

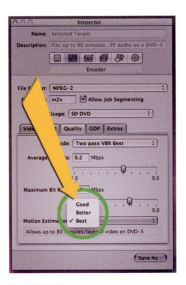

FIGURE 14.1

Hmm. A tough choice. Assuming you have any self-respect at all, which would you choose?

I recall 15 years ago working with Master Tracks Pro, a popular sequencing program for quasi-serious musicians. The program offered a *humanize* feature I hadn't seen before and haven't seen since. Now as it turns out, I'm a really rotten piano player and I play in the most mechanical way. When I see a quarter note, I play the quarter note precisely as written without a lot of interpretation. So the program worked great for me. After one of my robotic performances devoid of feeling, I'd add a dash of *humanization* and *presto*—an inspired musical tour de force worthy of Carnegie Hall!

Well no, not really. The program didn't really produce anything inspired at all; it merely moved my regular quarter notes off the beat by some random amount. This had the effect of transforming my machinelike performance into the work of someone simply playing badly—hardly the makings of a virtuoso.

It stands to reason that a story in whatever medium cannot be fashioned in an automatic way according to a generalized algorithm. Stories with nuance and taste must be individually crafted and finessed; for all the technical mumbo-jumbo we spew about in this book and elsewhere, our digital-powered video stories are emotional experiences as far from the soulless technology as we can get.

313

(a)   (b)

FIGURE 14.2

Effective storytelling requires forming a personal bond with our audience. The task can be challenging. We need collaborators.

BEWARE THE HYPE

It permeates our brains. It frames the questions we pose, the discussions we pursue, and the opinions we espouse. Currently we are seeing enormous pressure on manufacturers to produce cameras with large very high-resolution sensors. But is this what we really want or need? Why is more resolution better? The 2K ARRI Alexa has become the standard for big-budget Hollywood films projected on 60-foot cinema screens, yet many shooters of far less demanding fare won't settle for anything less than 4K original capture. Damn the expense and nightmare workflow, they say, *this* is what they want—the more resolution the better—8K? 10K? 12K? Where does it end?

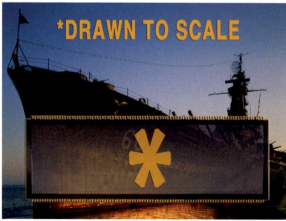

FIGURE 14.3

Understand what really matters. It's not a camera with a sensor the size of a battleship.

FIGURE 14.4

If operation or workflow is too convoluted, we won't use a camera regardless of its sensor size or resolution claims.

Our audiences aren't counting pixels on a screen or assessing our ability to capture the most stunning resolution test chart. Our stories fraught with human emotion and nuance are hopefully more interesting than that.

What we *really* want is a camera that offers superior color fidelity, smooth gradients, and sharp clean images, combined with efficient operation and workflow. The hype says pay attention to sensor size and pixel count; the *craft* says pay attention to *optics*. Choice of lens is far more critical and relevant to the success of our visual story, especially given the *more* than adequate resolution from most HD and 2K cameras these days.

RESIST COMPLEXITY

The hype of the Internet and fretful online boards can lead us to believe we need much more than we do. The chatter mills remind us constantly that somehow we don't measure up, that our camera doesn't have enough pixels, that the sensor isn't big enough, or our shooting 4:2:0 will reduce us to gutter trash.

The truth is we need don't need much to do outstanding work. I learned this lesson from a shipyard worker wrapped in rags shooting 8mm video newsreels in 1987 Poland. I learned it in 2007 from a Tanzanian filmmaker shooting a police drama without a single working light. And I learned it in Cairo in 2011 from a genius young director who fashioned the most remarkable, touching story of an artist painter and young boy set amid the chaos of revolution and mayhem in the streets. Regardless of the project, we all do better, *much* better, to resist complexity whenever we can.

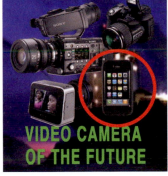

(a)   (b)

FIGURE 14.5

The current large-sensor-narrow-depth-of-field fad will soon pass. Next up . . . the ease and simplicity of the smartphone.

FIGURE 14.6

The camera in your hand right now is perfect. It's perfect because it's yours. You don't need more.

(a)

(b)

(c)

FIGURE 14.7

Do we really need a truck full of gear to light a scene well? Probably not.

FUTURE OF VIEWING

In regions of the world that lack broadband connectivity, there has been an explosion of tiny viewing parlors called *bandas*. These micro-theaters can be as simple as the back of a van in Nigeria or the corner of a ramshackle home in Bangladesh. The advent of tiny screens in bandas and in mobile devices is transforming the medium and how audiences see and appreciate our work. The presentation of cinema, TV, and all style of programs is becoming more intimate and personally directed at the viewer.

FIGURE 14.8

There is disruptive change in the air. The cameras and massive storytelling machines of yesteryear are disappearing fast.

(a)

(b)

FIGURE 14.9

A local viewing hall in small town Uganda.

FIGURE 14.10

The iPhone's small screen strongly favors close-ups, so you have yet another reason to use close-ups to tell visually compelling stories.

RAPID CHANGE IS UPON US

Today's cameras are lighter and more compact, with a wider dynamic range so we need fewer lights, which means smaller crews, fewer grips, and fewer hungry Teamsters. Routine editing and digital effects can be done on a laptop while sitting on a sofa, which means fewer post houses and fewer high-paid specialists. Add to that the self-distribution of titles via the Web, and it's easy to see the reduced need for manpower from studio grips to studio chiefs.

(a)

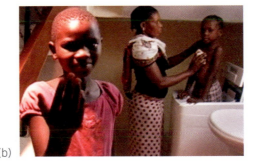
(b)

(c)

FIGURE 14.11

From Hollywood to Swahiliwood, if you tell compelling visual stories, they will come. They always have. They always will.

DOG-EAT-DOG WORLD

It's a dog-eat-digital world out there, and some of us will always be more talented than others in lighting it and framing it. For folks able to capture the most compelling visual stories there will always be a demand for these specialists. But for everyone else and for the vast majority of shooters today, the economics of digital media are such that adept use of the camera is just one element in a much greater skill set. To stay relevant, today's shooter must understand and embrace the entire process from the script and storyboard through shooting and display in a cinema or streamed via the Web. The process is long and complex, and the shooter who understands it all, the opportunities and perils, will continue to do well wherever the journey may take him.

(a)

(b)

FIGURE 14.12

Filmmaking is a collaborative process. Whoever makes the most mistakes wins!

FIGURE 14.13

Go forth, dear shooter. Travel the world and seek great footage and capture great stories. Our job and responsibility is to harness that power and use it effectively, creatively, and wisely.

FIGURE 14.14

EDUCATOR'S CORNER: REVIEW TOPICS

1. Following up this question from Chapter 1: Identify three (3) feature films or documentaries that changed the world for better or for worse. Your examples need not be well-known works or even a single work. Explain the impact of each film at the time and on the course of history.
2. Describe the range of skills that today's shooter should master, from Photoshop and green screen to speaking multiple foreign languages. Not to sound mean, but if you're in school, are you studying the *right* things?
3. List five (5) strengths that you possess as a filmmaker. How do these skills infuse in you a unique storytelling perspective?
4. Identify three (3) feature films or documentaries with significant visual shortcomings. Describe how these shortcomings might positively or negatively impact the viewer experience.
5. The story of your life is not your life—it's a story. Consider your own life story with two different scenarios. Create a poster and log line for each. Is your life a drama or a comedy? Is the premise compelling? Is the protagonist someone with whom your audience would like to spend two hours? At $12 per ticket, which version of your life do you think folks would more want to see in a theater?
6. Describe the different looks for versions I and II of Your Story. Consider lens choice, diffusion, depth of field, color balance, and lighting. How much of a factor is genre when determining Your Story's look?

Index

Note: Page numbers in *italics* indicate figures and tables.